Transforming the Culture of Schools

Yup'ik Eskimo Examples

Sociocultural, Political, and Historical Studies in Education

Joel Spring, Editor

Transforming
the Culture of Schools

Yup'ik Eskimo Examples

Jerry Lipka
University of Alaska, Fairbanks

with

Gerald V. Mohatt
University of Alaska, Fairbanks

and the Ciulistet Group

LEA LAWRENCE ERLBAUM ASSOCIATES, PUBLISHERS
1998   Mahwah, New Jersey   London

Lawrence Erlbaum Associates, Inc., Publishers
10 Industrial Avenue
Mahwah, NJ 07430

Cover design by Kathryn Houghtaling Lacey

Library of Congress Cataloging-in-Publication Data

Transforming the culture of schools : Yup'ik Eskimo examples / by Jerry Lipka with Gerald Mohatt and the Ciulistet group.
p.   cm. — (Sociocultural, political, and historical studies in education)
Includes bibliographical references and index.
ISBN 0-8058-2820-6 (cloth : alk. paper). — ISBN 0-8058-2821-4 (pbk. : alk. paper)
1. Yupik children—Education (Elementary)   2. Pacific Gulf Yupik language—Study and teaching (Elementary) 3. Yupik Eskimos—Social life and customs.   4. Educational innovations —Alaska—Bristol Bay. 5. Educational change —Alaska—Bristol Bay. 6. Elementary school teachers—Training of —Alaska—Bristol Bay. 7. Bristol Bay (Alaska)—Social life and customs. I. Lipka, Jerry. II. Mohatt, Gerald Vincent. III. Series
E99.E7T715   1998
372.9164'34—dc21   97-39258
                                                                            CIP

Books published by Lawrence Erlbaum Associates are printed on acid-free paper, and their bindings are chosen for strength and durability.

Printed in the United States of America
10 9 8 7 6 5 4 3

Contents

Foreword

This is the most interesting and instructive book I have read in a long time. It is interesting, indeed fascinating, because of the gripping way it reveals a culture derogated, dominated, and insensitively controlled by the larger society unaware that "Americanizing" that culture involves a process that not only cannot succeed, but will make matters worse for everyone. History, Voltaire said, is written by the victors. However, there comes a time when that history is exposed for what it is: a kind of double-entry bookkeeping of which the reader is told next to nothing. More correctly, the reader is told only what the prejudiced historian—who, of course, saw him or herself as unprejudiced, objective, and on the side of unassailable virtue—regarded as "real." There are many examples of this attitude in our national history, for example, toward slavery, native Americans, and scores of immigrant groups. This book, however, is not about the long past, but about present day Eskimo cultures struggling to maintain their identities and traditions and to adapt to changing circumstances in ways that will allow them to keep their self-respect. They are not asking the larger society to go away or to forget them, but rather to allow them to adapt in ways congenial to their outlooks and traditions. There is, after all, a difference between being forced to adapt and being willing to adapt. The Yup'ik Eskimos are willing to adapt but not at the price or in the ways asked of them. The fact is that they were not asked to adapt, they were told.

What is so instructive and inspiring about this book is the story of what happened when an unusual group of Eskimos and Whites from the University of Alaska, Fairbanks, spearheaded an effort to transform Yup'ik Eskimo schools from contexts of unproductive to contexts of productive learning. The model American classroom has features: It is organized and informed by a predetermined curriculum; learning does not start with, or take into account, the interests, curiosities, or questions of students; and parents and the larger community, for all practical purposes, play no role in school learning. Those features were true in spades in the Eskimo schools.

What this book describes in fascinating detail are the obstacles that were encountered and, to a significant degree, overcome by the writers of this book.

Make no mistake about it, this book has relevance far beyond Eskimo culture because it deals with issues of educational theory and practice that should be included in the literature on school change, but is often missing or glossed over. For more than 20 years I have written about the differences between contexts of productive and unproductive learning. In fact, beginning in 1965, I wrote that unless the culture of schools was transformed to make contexts of productive learning possible, the reform movement was doomed. In 1998, I have no reason to change that depressing prediction. One other observation that experience forced on me concerned teachers: Unless contexts of productive learning existed for teachers, they could not create and sustain those contexts for their students. This book confirms that observation. Transforming schools is not for the faint-hearted. Without a readily available network of collegial support, it is highly unlikely that one will even get to first base. I do not know Jerry Lipka (but I sure would like to). However, I do know Professor Mohatt and I am, therefore, in no way surprised that he played a key role in bringing and keeping together a group of courageous individuals who in this book have taught us a good deal, not only about changing Eskimo schools, but also about how we should be thinking about changing schools elsewhere in our country.

—Seymour B. Sarason, PhD
Yale University

Preface

"This is KDLG Dillingham, Alaska. It is now 10:25 am, October 5th, and time for our public service radio messages. Our first Bristol Bay Messenger goes to the land planner in Portage Creek: Alice will be out today. To my husband up river (trapping) on the Mulchatna, we have company—please come home. And our last message goes to the students in the Cross-Cultural Education Development Program of the University of Alaska. Jerry Lipka will be arriving this afternoon."

After rushing out to the airport to catch the Cessna 207 (a seven passenger plane), I waited an hour for it to take off. Lifting in a steep vertical climb, we leveled off, heading due north for the village. Snow could be seen on the low mountains and ice was forming in the rivers. We landed 30 minutes later. The houses were spread out along the riverbank and the smell of wood-burning stoves filled the air. A few months ago, wooden fish racks laden with salmon were drying for the winter. Now, folks were back to their winter routines, including schooling.

As the plane landed, the villagers greeted it and I was given a ride back down to the school. I entered a first-grade classroom; the bilingual aide was a student in our teacher education program and she was just beginning a lesson. She was demonstrating a way of preparing food and the students had moved their chairs close to the aide, forming a tight semicircle. Some students were seated while others were standing; all were in good view of the aide. The regular classroom teacher entered the room and immediately came over to the group of students and began rearranging them into rows, moving them away from the aide's demonstration. The bilingual aide objected and the teacher and aide argued. When the teacher left the room, the students moved their chairs back into a tight semicircle around her.

The aide explained afterward that she had wanted the students to gather close to her so that they could observe her demonstration. She objected to the teacher's intervention and "her Eurocentric ways." Incidents like this were unfortunately too common as the first Yup'ik aides became certified classroom teachers. These first Yup'ik teachers were themselves punished as students for speaking their Yup'ik language. Now, as these teachers are capable of transmitting their language in school, most of the children no longer speak Yup'ik. Our story does not stop at the frustrations and experiences of these teachers but begins with our perseverance as the Yup'ik language and culture, once devalued and scorned, is now becoming a part of schooling. This book is a story of transforming the circumstances surrounding schooling, which now enables the wisdom of the elders and their cultural knowledge to become a basis for developing curriculum and pedagogy. Because we persevered, what was once "hidden" and considered irrelevant has now found acceptance. Our story of working together—elders, Yup'ik teachers, university consultants, and now school district personnel—shows how, through human understanding, possibilities that once were virtually nonexistent can become reality.

This book presents a series of rather remarkable personal narratives of Yup'ik Eskimo teachers. These stories not only tell a story of struggle, perseverence, and hope, but they also tell a story about transforming the culture of schooling. These teachers, in collaboration with university consultants and elders, created a group that, through study and research, revealed that Yup'ik ways of teaching supported a more conversational classroom interactional routine that differed substantially from the typical classroom discourse routine of elicitation, response, and evaluation. By working in a collaborative, community-based model for more than 15 years, the group began to connect ancient Yup'ik wisdom to the teaching of core academic content. Through these processes and by increasing community involvement, this group began to change the culture of schooling.

This book is organized into four distinct parts and a conclusion. The first part of the book establishes both a personal and theoretical framework, first presenting a personal narrative that highlights the major issues that this book addresses and then grounding its theoretical perspective in relation to the narrative. The second part of the book presents three personal narratives of Yup'ik teachers. Here, the teachers describe the barriers and obstacles they faced in their efforts to be considered full-fledged members of the school community and how they accommodated themselves to situations. The narratives are followed by commentary and analysis by a university "outsider" with whom each teacher has a long-standing professional relationship. The third part of the book describes how the Yup'ik culture and language can become a reality within schooling. Here, the book examines Yup'ik pedagogical approaches to teaching and ways of documenting ancient Yup'ik wisdom, and making that wisdom accessible to schooling. The fourth part of the book includes an appendix that describes the methodological approaches used during this long-term collaborative relationship.

This book is primarily designed for undergraduate and graduate classes in education. It is particularly useful for the preparation of teachers who will teach in multicultural, ethnic minority, and linguistic minority communities. It is also useful for teachers and administrators in such settings. For both teacher educators and administrators, this book provides concrete examples of how to include minority cultures and languages in the processes of schooling based on the experiences of these Yup'ik teachers. Although the personal experiences of the Yup'ik teachers will reverberate with other indigenous teachers, educational leaders particularly interested in transforming schooling will find the book provocative. Those in the fields of anthropology and education can use this book as a source of examples of the role that long-term community-based and ethnographic research can play in transforming schooling. Oftentimes, the fields of anthropology and education are criticized for inattention to the actual processes of schooling (including the relationship between school and community). This book stands as a counterpoint to that criticism.

The book can be used as a text or to supplement texts in courses on teacher education, anthropology, and education. It will be useful to those concerned about school change in a multicultural society. The book can also be read from the standpoint of bicultural and bilingual education, because much of what drives this book concerns Yup'ik language and cultural practices and how they might be included within the core of schooling. In this vein, the book also applies to the current debates raging about the place of minority cultures in schooling. Lastly, this book has a relevance for students interested in qualitative and ethnographic research. The long-term work of the group makes it relevant to studying how a research agenda develops and evolves as the context changes.

Acknowledgments

I am personally indebted to the Yup'ik elders who gave unselfishly of their time and energy in order that we, the teachers and myself, may learn and pass this knowledge on to the next generation. Although a book is an individual endeavor, this book was written from the perspective of being a member of a group. The number of elders involved are many and their contributions are numerous. I would like to thank Henry Alakayak, from Manokotak, Alaska, for his vision, wisdom, and leadership; Annie Blue, from Togiak, Alaska, for her wonderful storytelling and willingness to share; Joshua Phillip, from Akiachak, Alaska, for his teaching to "see the world," predict the weather, and his all-around knowledge of the environment; and Anuska Petla, from Koliganak, Alaska, for showing us how to dance and the meanings associated with those movements. Also deserving thanks are Anuska Nanalook, from Manokotak, Alaska, for her sense of humor, storyknifing, and storytelling; Lily "Gamechuck" Pauk, from Manokotak, Alaska, my "daughter's mother" within Yup'ik tradition, who got us started at our first meeting with the elders when she showed us how to "measure" with one's eyes; and Frederick George, from Akiachak, Alaska, the late Wassillie George, Sr., and Sam Ivan, both from Akiak, Alaska, for their incredible knowledge about how to make traps, travel in inclement weather, and survive under tough conditions. Elizabeth Jackson, from Akiak, Alaska, shared information about the heart beat and drumming, parka patterns, and bead patterns. Pauline Frederick and Ruth Liskey, from Akiachak, Alaska, shared information about grass baskets and measurements related to clothing. Mary George, from Akiachak, Alaska, and Marie Napoka, from Tuluksak, Alaska, brought traditional Yup'ik parka designs to our attention, which enabled us to see the connection between math and Yup'ik culture. Also from Tuluksak, Elizabeth Andrew shared information about parka patterns and the late Peter Napoka shared information pertaining to navigating, traps, and land forms.

Nick Gumlickpuk, from New Stuyahok, Alaska, shared his incredible sense of humor that made many meetings so enjoyable, as well as his wonderful Yup'ik dancing. Charlie Choknok, from New Stuyahok, Alaska, shared information about counting and the old village of Kulukak. Others from New Stuyahok, including Elena Gumlickpuk, "Humphrey" Qamiqurpak, and Moxie Andrew, offered their assistance in gathering information on Yup'ik place names.

Margaret and Willie Wassilie, from Togiak, Alaska, gave their support and commitment, and Mary Active, from Togiak as well, shared her knowledge on patterns and telling stories. Also from Togiak, Esther Thompson put into practice ideas gathered from the elders. Vera Gloko, Anecia Toyukak, and Grace Gamechuk from Manokotak, Alaska showed their commitment to teaching elders' knowledge. Gus Tugutuk, from Manokotak, Alaska, shared his knowledge of kayaks, measuring, and the "physics of the bay." John Pauk, from Manokotak, Alaska, shared his knowledge of hunting, trapping, and visualizing.

I thank Annie Andrew, from Dillingham, Alaska, for her storytelling and her ability to make the group laugh, and to Adam Chythlook for his drumming, singing, and laughter. Fred Andrew, from Dillingham, Alaska, and Lena Ilutsik, from Aleknagik, Alaska, although no longer with us, have left some of their spirit here. The elders' support and continued enthusiasm for our work has made this a most unusual and positive experience.

I am also indebted to the Yup'ik teachers for their continued openness and willingness to turn educational possibilities into reality. I thank Dana and Larry Bartman, Linda Brown, Dora Cline, Ann Edwards, William Gumlikpuk, Katherine Groat, Anecia Lomack, Sassa Peterson, Sassa Ruby, Ferdinand Sharp, Ina White, Jackie Wilson, and Anu Wysocki. The following educators' willingness to share their studies made this work possible: Vicki Dull, Esther Ilutsik, Fannie Parker, Nancy Sharp, and Evelyn Yanez.

To the many principals, teachers, aides, and cooks who allowed us to use their facilities and homes, as well as feed us, we owe a debt of gratitude. I thank, in particular, John Antonnen, the former superintendent of Southwest Region Schools, who had a vision for increasing the involvement of local Yup'ik teachers and forming the Ciulistet. Ben Cherry, former superintendent of schools, continued that commitment, and Don Evans, current superintendent of schools, continues to seek ways of improving schooling. I offer thanks to the late Dorion Ross, whose educational leadership and openness to school improvement served as a model to all of us. Kathy Schubeck and Janelle Cowan, of the Southwest Region Schools, continue to implement changes in the schools based on our long-term collaboration.

The University of Alaska, Fairbanks, under Gerald Mohatt, the former Dean of the College of Rural Alaska, supported much of the work in this book, both financially and spiritually. Ray Barhardt's pioneering work in Alaska through the Alaska Rural Teacher Training Program and the Cross-Cultural Educational Development Program enabled many of the persons in this book to become teachers. Without Barnhardt's persistence, these programs would not have existed and, without them, many of the current Yup'ik teachers may not have had an opportunity to get their degree and teaching certificate.

I thank professional colleagues who shared with us their expertise in sociolinguistics and research methodologies. Fred Erickson, in particular, helped us analyze videotape footage when we first began this enterprise. Similarly, Malcolm Collier assisted us in "seeing" body language, movement, and synchrony in classroom interactions. Terri McCarty, of the University of Arizona, and Arlene Stairs, of Queens University in Kingston, Ontario, gave their long-term support and encouragement. Claudette Bradley Kawagley and Claudia Zaslavsky helped us to see the mathematics embedded in everyday activity. Oscar Kawagley shared his insights into the science of everyday experience.

I am indebted to Esther Ilutsik for her courage and vision for what schooling could be, and for introducing me to the Bristol Bay region and its wonderful people. I am also indebted to the group, Esther Ilutsik, Sharon Nelson Barber, and Gerald Mohatt, who had told me, after I missed a meeting, that "by the way, we are going to write a book." I also thank Sue Mitchell for her editing, patience, and more patience, and Nastasia Wahlberg for translating, analyzing, and discussing "fine" points with me. Lastly, to my wife, Janet, and my son, Alan, and daughter, Leah, who endured when I traveled extensively to be with my "other family."

Although this is a collaborative work, I take full responsibility for any of the inevitable errors that may be contained in this volume.

—*Jerry Lipka*

Part I

1 Introduction: A Framework for Understanding the Possibilities of a Yup'ik Teacher Group

Jerry Lipka
University of Alaska, Fairbanks
Esher Ilutsik
The Ciulistet Group

In this book we show that an indigenous teachers' group has the potential to transform the culture of schooling. Here we present personal narratives by Yup'ik Eskimo teachers that speak directly to issues of equity and school transformation. We present these teachers' struggles, not simply to document their experiences but because these struggles represent the first in a series of constructive steps in which a group of Yup'ik teachers and university colleagues began a slow process of reconciling cultural differences and conflict between the culture of the school and the culture of the community. Here, in one small corner, far removed from mainstream America, these cases address the very heart of school reform. We believe our story goes well beyond documenting individual narratives and provides insights for others involved in creating culturally responsive education that fundamentally changes the role and relationship between teachers and schooling—and between the community and schooling.

According to Fullan (1991), school reform "contains ambivalence and dilemmas because, when we set off on a journey to achieve significant change, we do not know in advance all the details of how to get there, or even what it is going to be like when we arrive" (p. 345). This is all the more true when a marginalized group of teachers, such as the Ciulistet[1] or any other group, are the very first "professional" teachers from among their group. They are charting a new course.

---

[1] Pronounced "Jew-lis-tet," the word means "leaders."

As Lieberman (1995) noted, "...new structures put teachers and principals in different relationships to one another, changing expectations as power relationships are reconfigured. Working in unfamiliar groups and in unfamiliar ways with students [teachers] breeds insecurity and defensiveness" (p. 11).

As these cases show, the Yup'ik Eskimo teachers first tried to conform to the culture of schooling by, for example, not teaching in their language but teaching in English, and by requiring "hand raising" and "one speaker at a time." As the group began to analyze their own teaching and to discuss the context of their teaching, they increasingly realized that their cultural knowledge and ways of relating to students were being criticized both by their professional colleagues and by some members of their community. In effect, they were caught in a bind as the professional teachers expected them to "act more like a teacher," but if they did, the community would criticize them for "acting like a *kass'aq* [White]." Little (1993) showed that "conflict increases as the changing school culture begins to shift from superficial conversation to serious discourse about learning, teaching styles, modes of organizing the curriculum, and so on" (p. 11). In our case, these conflicts are exacerbated by the historical context of colonization, by the degree of cultural difference between mainstream and Yup'ik culture, and by issues of cultural continuity. Because these cases are about school change in a Yup'ik cultural context, their contrast to mainstream schooling highlights underlying processes that are common across schools and cultures and that have the potential to transform conflict into productive working relationships in many other school settings.

CULTURE AS A BARRIER

Typically, teachers from indigenous and other minority groups have found their knowledge and ways of relating to be a barrier to their success as teachers. Far too often, the present day result of a colonial legacy is schools that represent an alien institution in which indigenous teachers are asked to leave their culture and language at the schoolhouse door. (See a special issue on this topic in Watson-Gegeo, 1994.) Yet, teachers' groups such as Ciulistet form an important link between the culture of the school and that of their community. Empowerment begins with the Ciulistet forming a space to voice their frustrations and struggles, but empowerment substantially increases as Yup'ik cultural practices at first considered "out of bounds" become accepted practices that inform others.

The purpose of chapters 2 through 4 is to show the gradual resolution of personal struggles as these teachers slowly adapted to schooling and slowly adapted schooling to the culture of the community. In these chapters, we show how the establishment of a Yup'ik teacher group led directly to a discourse and an inquiry on learning, teaching, and school–community relations, which in turn led to a deeper contextualized understanding of the conflict between school and community. This discourse is reflected in each teacher's narrative. This inquiry began a slow process of reconciling cultural conflict, resulting in negotiation and adaptation. The process is not magical and these narratives are not Pollyana-ish. The teachers' experiences contained risk, and in fact, some of the teachers are casualties of these conflicts.

One experienced and two novice Yup'ik teachers demonstrate how they included their culture in the culture of schooling. The process of cultural conflict and cultural adaptation that they experienced and describe in this book begins to reverse the historical processes of education as colonization (Meriam, Brown, Cloud, & Dale, 1928; U.S. Department of Education, 1991; U.S. Senate Select Committee, 1969) and to slowly replace it with a process of democratization by which underrepresented minorities' access to the profession is increased, and their culture is included in the processes and content of schooling.

The teacher narratives presented in chapters 2 through 4 show how university teacher preparation can prepare teachers for specific cultural contexts. In addition, these insights can help school administrators who hire and evaluate ethnic minority teachers to overcome the tendency to apply monocultural conceptions of good and effective teaching as if they were applicable everywhere and for all times. Malin (1994) argued, "If, however, we as a society only accept those ethnic minority teachers who fit our culturally specific model of what is considered a good teacher, aren't we defeating the purpose in having Aboriginal [or other Native] teachers in the first place?" (p. 113). Teacher groups such as Ciulistet create an example for altering Eurocentric conceptions of teaching and schooling and the relationship between school and community. By rejecting "business as usual"—which too often leads to assimilative teaching practices with predictable consequences of Native language and culture loss—these groups raise the possibility of transforming the status quo.

In Yup'ik communities, schooling and its culture, which includes daily practices, rituals, legitimate bodies of knowledge, ways of teaching that knowledge, and ways of evaluating it, also include the historical context of the relationship of a dominant group to a subordinate group as well as the present set of circumstances. The important role of the community and its elders in indigenous contexts is an aspect of the culture of school that is central in the process of transforming the framework of schooling to become more inclusive and democratic. For example, basing curricular and pedagogical decisions on not only Western knowledge, but on Yup'ik ways of knowing and ways of interacting, creates new curricular and pedagogical possibilities.

We argue from evidence collected over a decade and a half that the contributions of indigenous teacher groups can be important tools for determining the what, how, and why of schooling, and that without these contributions, the powerful forces of assimilation—resulting in language and cultural loss and community alienation from schooling—will continue unabated.

Through the cases in this book, we show how the Yup'ik culture conflicts powerfully with cherished values associated with mainstream schooling and society. The conflict is part of a complex and evolving relationship between the school, community, Yup'ik teachers, and the university. The university was responsible for preparing more indigenous teachers through its Cross-Cultural Educational Development Program (X-CED)[2]; the school district supported this preparation with release time for teachers and travel to student meetings. However, support from the school district varied, ranging from establishing the Ciulistet to trying to terminate it, according to who was the particular superintendent of schools. The new and evolving role of Yup'ik teachers was viewed by many administrators and teachers skeptically, if not perjoratively. The community was mostly supportive but on occasion, powerful individuals aligned with the school district during times of conflict. For example, changing the language of instruction from English to Yup'ik caused a major rift between the school and the community and the school district and the university (see Lipka, 1994 for analysis of alignments). This conflict caused this author (a White male) to leave a project initiated by himself and the Ciulistet, a project accepted by both the school district and the university. Several years ago, Henry Alakayak (a Yup'ik elder and a key member of the Ciulistet) was outraged when he learned that I was asked to leave this project. He stated to me, "Whose school do they think it is?" Because I had strong ties with members of the local community, the local school district viewed my presence skeptically, at best[3]. In this book, I write from my own struggles and experiences gained while working with local communities, the Ciulistet teachers, and local school districts. Because our work spans almost two decades and documents the slow process of change, it is not simply about conflict between school and community, but it shows cycles of conflict, resolution, shifting power, and changing roles and relationships. The book documents not only the conflicts and power struggles involved in changing the culture of schooling in an indigenous context, but also shows a slow resolution of these conflicts as the culture of the school begins to change toward the culture of the community.

Because this book represents a long-term collaborative research and school change agenda, patterns of change that may not be visible in the short run become visible in the long run. In chapters 5 and 6 we show how Yup'ik teachers begin to transform schooling by altering classroom interaction routines, values, and content from western schooling to Yup'ik ways. These changes illustrate Sarason's (1996) and Fullan's (1991) claim that to change the status quo requires fundamental

---

[2]Pronounced "exceed."

[3]Because I was clearly aligned with the Yup'ik teachers, those preparing to become teachers, and many community members, I was perceived as a threat. In particular, in this situation, although we—school district, local school and community, Ciulistet, and university—agreed to initiate a feasibility study for the purpose of exploring the question, "Should Yup'ik be the language of instruction for elementary school students?" during community meetings, it was revealed that the school district was out of compliance with its own state-mandated bilingual plans. The plan stated they would be using Yup'ik as the language of instruction for grades 1 through 3. When this was revealed, the principal said, "I know we are not implementing this." This particular incident points out areas of conflict as roles, relationship, and power issues related to the culture of the school increasingly came to the fore. See Lipka (1994) for a more detailed account of this particular situation and see chapter 2 by Mohatt and Sharp who discuss this immersion program.

changes in the way teachers perceive themselves and their actual daily work, and changes in the relationship between community and school.

In chapter 5, a case study of Evelyn Yanez, we see an approach to teaching and student—teacher interaction routines that differs substantially from mainstream classroom discourse (Cazden, 1988) and that illustrates Sarason's point that the relationship between teachers, students, and knowledge must be altered to make it more dialogic and inquiring. The typical instructional routines of asking questions for the purpose of evaluating a student's response gives way to increased student-to-student interaction, conversation between teacher and students, and a drawing in of shared contextual and cultural knowledge. This culturally specific Yup'ik way of teaching also represents a concrete example of how teachers anywhere can use other adaptive approaches to classroom discourse specific to the cultural context in which they teach.

In chapter 6, we build on Yanez's and other Yup'ik teachers' ways of organizing their classroom space and interactions and begin to show how these processes and everyday Yup'ik knowledge can be connected to core academic content areas such as mathematics and science. Our work, like that of Moll, Amanti, Neff, and Gonzalez (1992), shows how everyday knowledge can have a place in schooling. We believe that the mathematics and science embedded in Yup'ik subsistence activities, language, and culture provide an ideal opportunity for developing curriculum and pedagogical approaches that simultaneously support the local culture and strengthen the teaching of mathematics and science. Students and teachers have the opportunity to view and solve problems from different cultural frameworks with the implication that understanding and approaching problems in two different cultural ways will strengthen each and build metacognitive awareness. Too often in the past, colonial forms of schooling provided an either/or situation in which the host community was "asked" to give up its language, culture, and ways of doing and being in exchange for formal education for their youngsters. We believe that our "both/and" approach presents a better alternative.

Developing curriculum and pedagogy cross culturally involves a series of dilemmas, particularly when the very context, the culture, and the language of the community, is in transition. The process of knowledge reconstruction, developing authentic pedagogy, and meeting the often differing standards of the community and the school is fraught with contradictions. Similarly, issues associated with local and situated knowledge, with transferring knowledge from one context to another (community to schooling), and with the problem of equivalence (that is, treating transferred and translated knowledge as if it had the same meaning) are some of the issues that curriculum developers, teacher educators, and principals must face when embarking on such school reform projects. We do not supply answers to these problems but only our experiences.

Much of the ethnographic research in indigenous and minority contexts conducted during the past two decades has evolved from a concern with "silenced voices" (Trueba, 1989) and invisibility (Malin, 1994; Philips, 1983) to an identification of cultural differences, particularly those that result in communicative discontinuities between teachers from one cultural group and students from another (Watson-Gegeo, 1994). We believe that our long-term approach to collaborative school change and research provides useful insights for other scholars and researchers who are concerned with their role in the larger societal issues involving dominant and subordinate groups. Our work involves insiders and outsiders collaborating in the research agenda, documentation, analysis, and writing. This collaborative approach to research includes, on occasion, three generations— elders, teachers, and their children. Interestingly, school change is occurring from the margins to the "center," from the Ciulistet and elders to the school district. This is most evident in chapter 6 in which we discuss how Yup'ik culture, language, and everyday experience can form a basis for developing math and science content and approaches to teaching it. The processes that we used in documenting and analyzing elders' knowledge and the process of translating it and adapting it to curriculum and pedagogy should be applicable to others engaged in documenting and interpreting local knowledge for schooling. It is through such processes that school and community relations can become more symmetrical, and classroom inquiry need not be limited to one knowledge domain and way of knowing.

We begin this book with a first-person narrative by Esther Ilutsik who is a founding member of the teacher group named Ciulistet. Ilutsik's narrative encapsulates many of the issues that this book documents, analyzes, and responds to. This chapter has three sections. First, Ilutsik establishes the need for the Ciulistet and describes its formation. She does this by representing her struggles and those of other Yup'ik teachers who feel isolated, criticized, and disrespected. However, through the Ciulistet, the teachers begin to identify and understand these feelings of alienation in relation to the larger context from which they emerged. Slowly, they see the potential contributions of their culture in ways of relating, in the values Yup'ik teachers bring to school, and in developing unique pedagogical approaches to the teaching of mathematics and science.

The second section describes the X-CED program and how it provided access to higher education for villagers interested in becoming teachers. In addition, this section provides a brief background on small rural villages and local schools.

The third section establishes a framework for understanding the importance of indigenous and minority teacher groups in coevolving the culture of schooling. As teachers and community members, we show how they are negotiating the larger context of school and community. From this constructivist position, we raise fundamental questions concerning school reform and reform in teacher education. What constitutes legitimate school knowledge? What is the role of the community, particularly a minority and indigenous community for whom schooling often represents a cultural discontinuity? How can insiders and outsiders work effectively in coconstructing curricula and pedagogy, and thereby transforming asymmetrical power relations?

Our work joins a growing body of research (Begay, Sells, Estell, Estell, & McCarty 1995; Kawagley 1995; Ladson-Billings, 1995; Lipka & Ilutsik, 1997; Moll, Amanti, Neff, & Gonzalez, 1992) involving insiders in the process of making cultural strengths visible that, at once, begins to extend what knowledge and ways of teaching are privileged and legitimate. Specifically, the what (the content), the how (the pedagogy), the who (the teacher), and the language of instruction become open to questions and discourse, potentially changing the nature of what constitutes legitimate knowledge and how that knowledge gets conveyed. Further, schooling viewed as a culture in the context of the community requires each to be responsible for and involved in coevolving schooling. This needs to occur in a way that alters the asymmetrical power relations of the past, with school and community becoming more equal partners.

We present a set of complex social and political relationships between "insiders" and "outsiders" in an educational community. In this sense, the book presents many voices and shifts from narrative to academic prose as the authors also struggle with how we are to represent ourselves in these pages. A word about how we view authorship, voice, and the multivocal presentation of this text: As we (insiders and outsiders) have worked together "to achieve one mind," we have gained a deeper understanding of cultural differences and the potential for conflict in cultural representation in text and in schooling. An elder clearly reminds us while telling a story that the story does not belong to them. As Morrow (1995) explained

> A common way for a storyteller to begin a Yup'ik narrative is to set himself, the recorder, the story, and those from whom he heard it in a web of relationships, a network of people, places, and events … this kind of opening is to invoke the collective authority of many storytellers … it reflects a timeless past and many retellings, rather than any individual's experience or authority. (pp. 32–33)

This importance of situating oneself among elders of the past, part of a web of relationships, extends to the meanings one is to draw from stories. Elsie Mather (1995), a Yup'ik teacher, writer, and traditional person, tells us that "old stories refer to the mysterious, that part of our life that cannot be interpreted … we can never really know exactly the message another person receives from hearing one of these stories" (p. 15). Questioning and interpreting meaning in a public display is not the way a Yup'ik audience responds to stories. Each individual draws out their own meaning from the story. As we write, as insiders and outsiders, we write in two distinct forms; a telling of one's own personal experience, allowing the listener to draw their own conclusions from these personal narratives and sets of relationships; and we write in academic prose, analyzing and drawing conclusions in an authoritative manner. This book is not a seamless collection but rather a series of stories within stories, conveying the struggles and dilemmas that we face as we work together. We hope this work provides insights to others as we work through some of these dilemmas.

ESTHER ILUTSIK—THE FOUNDING OF CIULISTET

I grew up in a Yup'ik-speaking home. My father spoke some English and my mother did not. We were taught to be afraid of the White men. Our parents would even warn us that the White men would come and take us away if we did not behave. The White men did come and take us children away. When I was the tender age of 3½, both my parents contracted tuberculosis and were sent away to be hospitalized. We were fortunate enough to be placed in a foster home in my home village. But it was like entering another world. We were placed into the local White man's house, where the habits of the two cultures were to clash. Although this White family had resided in the area for over 20 years, they had virtually kept to themselves. They didn't know the language, didn't eat any meat, and didn't subsist on the local wild plants, berries, or game that we were so accustomed to. They also had other strange habits that were totally foreign to us. I distinctly remember crying in the kitchen and clinging to my older sister, telling her in Yup'ik that she couldn't leave me to go to school, as I did not know the language and the habits of these people. I remember being torn from her and taken to another part of the house.

After 2 years, my parents were returned and we were returned to them, all of us virtually strangers to each other. My youngest brother would cry for the White man's home. It was great to eat meat again and to feel the strength return. It was also a discovery and education for my younger brother to be served a duck or beaver head to eat. He didn't have the slightest idea how to eat it. After this experience, we became more leery of the White man. When we saw them approach our island, we would run and hide up in the hills and watch these people from a tree until they left.

I remember one experience quite vividly. We happened to be home by ourselves, my four brothers, a neighbor friend, and me. We lived on an island. We heard a skiff (small boat) approaching, so we looked out the window and saw a White man coming toward our landing. We were afraid, remembering the warnings of our parents, and hid. We hid under the beds, in closets, and any place we could squeeze ourselves into. We waited and listened. We heard the skiff land on the beach, we heard the skiff being pulled up on the beach, then we heard footsteps approaching the house, the heavy steps on the porch stairs, then into the porch and then the dreadful, rapid, and loud knock, knock, knock. We held our breaths; all we heard was our slow intake of breath and then again, knock, knock, knock. My youngest brother could not contain himself. We heard him whisper, "come in" and then he yelled, "come in!" We were dreadfully frightened now. How dare he reveal our presence! The door opened, there was silence, then a voice asked, "Is anyone home?" And then he mumbled that he probably just imagined he heard something and shut the door. The footsteps faded away, and we heard the skiff being pushed out and the outboard motor start. We were so relieved. We all came out of our hiding places and attacked our younger brother for being so bold. We scolded him, telling him we could have been taken away, especially since our parents weren't there.

Eventually, we had to start school and encounter these White men again. We had to interact with them again. It truly was a frightening experience, but we survived.

We learned and tried very hard to understand and please White people and their strange ways. They always kept to themselves. These White people in the school were different from other White people we knew. I was confused. They did not eat meat, drink tea or coffee; they disapproved of movies, and went to church on Saturdays. It contradicted all the White men we saw in the fish canneries.

We were taught that the White men were to be respected, and we had to do what they wanted in school, or they would take us away; the threat was always there. At school and in their presence we could sense that we were never quite good enough for them. Therefore, we always blundered in their presence. Their word was over our word. We were the meek.

I was sent away to a Bureau of Indian Affairs (BIA) high school program located about 1,000 miles away from my home village. The enrollment was totally Alaska Native.

During high school, the realization came to me that I was Eskimo. At that time, I really did not care or even understand what "culture" meant. After all, my people were confirmed by the missionaries, and they had long abandoned their dances and other cultural celebrations. Otherwise, they continued with other cultural beliefs, which did sometimes manifest themselves to frighten the now deeply rooted religious people. It didn't matter to me at the time, but I still did not feel comfortable in the presence of White men.

Entering college in another state really brought the realization to me that I was an Alaska Native, an Eskimo, a Yup'ik Eskimo. And I had no knowledge of my own cultural background. Especially in light of the way others saw it; dances, ceremonies, rites of passage, and so forth. Other students, especially Native Americans, would ask me questions about Alaska and my cultural background. I really couldn't answer their questions seriously. I made a joke of it! I started reading and went to the library and tried to read as much as I could about Eskimos. The library was pathetically limited and all the authors were non-Native. Actually, I began to believe some of the things that were written about us Yup'ik people! So I just existed and joked about my culture!

The Native Americans could not believe the little knowledge we had about ourselves. It was a puzzlement to them and a void within ourselves.

Upon graduating from college with a degree in elementary education, I went home and fished commercially. Shortly after, I was employed with the Head Start Program administered out of Anchorage. I went to work for them, traveling to remote sites within Alaska and training teachers, directors, and parents on how to be "White." Teaching them "White" values, what foods to eat, what games to play with the children, what kinds of toys to make and play with, sleeping patterns, and even cleanliness. I was not comfortable with it; in fact, I was embarrassed but I did it anyway. It was a job. I was doing this job with my horrible conscience bothering me. I quit after a year.

The next year I got a teaching job in a remote village in the area where I grew up. Again, I experienced the awful feeling of not knowing about my culture. I knew that it existed, but did not know how to apply it in the classroom setting. I was accused of acting White. This really hit a special nerve. I left teaching. Fortunately, the Cross-Cultural Education Development Program (X-CED) with the University of Alaska, Fairbanks, had an opening for a field-based instructor. I applied and was called in for an interview. I was surprised to find a young White man, no older than myself, to interview me. I was insulted and a slow anger began to surface: What was his background? What qualified him for this position? During the interview I ended up asking him all the questions, and I bluntly told him that he shouldn't even be working for the program because of his inexperience.

This was the turning point in my life. With the cultural emphasis in the X-CED program, we, the Yup'ik people, were forced to look at ourselves and rediscover ourselves as a cultural group with our own values. I had to reeducate myself so that I could explain and apply this knowledge to future educators. After all, all my formal education and training was to make me become as "White" as possible.

During my employment with the University of Alaska, Fairbanks, Dr. Jerry Lipka was hired as a field coordinator with his unique and special interest and concern for the Yup'ik people. "We" (myself and the Yup'ik teacher education students) established a long and respectful relationship with Lipka. All of us learned and helped each other in this long and continuing struggle to understand ourselves as a Yup'ik people.

With the constant travel and demanding schedule as a regional coordinator with the X-CED program, I decided to move on to another position. However, I had a foundation, a Yup'ik cultural foundation, where I could begin to apply this knowledge to future generations, or so I thought. I applied for a teaching position with the Southwest Regional Schools but was hired as their bilingual/bicultural coordinator instead.

After much consideration, I decided to take the position. (I was leery as I had no administrative training, but the administrative staff informed me that I would be apprenticed.) I thought that I would make an impact on the educational system, but was I ever in for a surprise. I was laughed at, ridiculed, and even belittled.

At one point, I was called into the superintendent's office and told that I was not to put "ideas" into the board members' heads and that I could not talk to them about educational issues. I was shocked. After all, many of the board members were my friends and relatives.

After a few years, that superintendent retired and left, and Dr. John Antonnen came to take his place. What a change! He was much more open. But none of the other White administrative staff people liked him. Antonnen left in a couple of years, but before he left, he gave the certified Native Yup'ik teachers something for which they will always be grateful; an organization that they would feel comfortable with, where they would be able to express themselves without being jeopardized, an organization that would enhance their own positive image and classroom skills.

History of the Ciulistet

Antonnen organized the Ciulistet in 1987. The group was composed of all the certified Yup'ik Native teachers employed with the Southwest Regional Schools. They included Evelyn Yanez, Margie Hasting, Ferdinand and Nancy Sharp, Anecia Lomack, Miriam Olson, William Gumlickpuk, Mary Alexie, and myself, Esther A. Ilutsik.

At our first organizational meeting, Antonnen gave us the opportunity to empower ourselves by stating that we knew the educational system better than any educator coming into the area. He said, "You grew up in the area. You went through the educational system, and you even went further—you got certified! Now you are the teachers, parents, and community members. Who can better understand the educational system than yourselves? You should be the ones to advise the school board and the administrative staff on educational issues."

What a wonderful, positive feeling, to be thought of so highly by an outside educator. Yet, many of our own people and many other educators were painfully aware that we were different in a negative sense. In that respect, we had to get over our feeling of inferiority, especially if we were truly going to be the "leaders" in education, as the term "Ciulistet" implies.

As I mentioned, one of our first goals was for the group to work with the school board and provide them with direction in education policy. But what happened was miscommunication. Let me illustrate this with symbols. When I was a little girl, we did a lot of storyknife in the mud and snow. (Storyknife is telling stories in the snow or mud using a knife and specific symbols to represent the various characters.) The symbols we used for an adult male, for an adult female, for a male child, and for a female child are shown in Fig. 1.1. Figure 1.1 also includes the symbols for White people or strangers that came into the village; male adult, female adult, and so forth.

Many of us went outside the state to attend school for a bachelor's degree in teacher education. We came back as women like this because of our Western educational training and techniques that we used for classroom teaching. See Fig. 1.2.

The teachers that attended the Cross-Cultural Education Development Program looked like the women in Fig. 1.3; they were sensitive and aware of cultural

FIG. 1.1. Storyknife symbols.

FIG. 1.2. Western-educated female
Yup'ik teachers. Educated Alaska Native
female whose teacher training is totally
Western influence.

FIG. 1.3. Cross-culturally educated female
Yup'ik teachers. Educated Alaska Native
female whose teacher training was
sensitive to the cultural group.

differences within the classroom but most were not instructing from their Yup'ik culture in the classroom. See Fig. 1.3.

Although X-CED was respectful of indigenous cultures, it did not base educational methods on them. Models of how to integrate indigenous practices and knowledge into the classroom setting were not part of most teachers' educational experience. Student teaching and teaching in these schools, is, of course, dominated by the Western culture.

When Superintendent Anttonen asked us to help the board make educational policies or decisions, we didn't have the models or knowledge to recreate schooling. Anttonen's invitation and goals, although warmly welcomed, were difficult to achieve. Furthermore, our school board members usually sat in a square building, at a rectangular table (as noted in Fig. 1.4). The White man is displayed bigger because he controls these people (school board) and because our school board wants our educational system to look like a Western institution. We were trying to communicate with them, and communication was not good.

It drew out the negative powers from both sides. Fortunately, another "doctor" among us had worked with the majority of our teachers in the X-CED program. Dr. Jerry Lipka came up from Massachusetts to interview for the field coordinator position in X-CED, and he began working with us in 1981.

The group wanted to validate their own way of teaching. With the assistance of Lipka, Nelson-Barber (Stanford University), and Mohatt (University of Alaska Fairbanks and former dean of the College of Rural Alaska), we obtained resources to conduct research. These studies investigated Yup'ik classes (see Lipka, 1990a, 1990b, and 1991, and this book expands on this work) and showed how Yup'ik teachers organize their classrooms, how they relate to their students, and how they integrate Yup'ik cultural values into their lessons. Ciulistet teachers were heartened to see that others organized their classes in similar ways, that others spoke to students as a whole instead of "spotlighting" individual students, and that others expected students to become increasingly responsible for their behavior. The impact of these studies was so positive that we wanted to go a step further and look at how learning takes place in a natural setting. We, the group and Lipka, collaborated in obtaining funding from the University of Alaska Fairbanks, from the Eisenhower

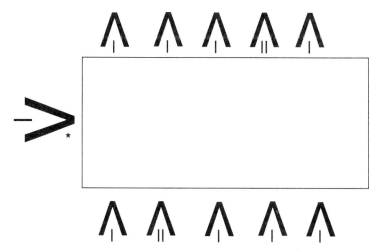

* Superintendent shown larger than school board members because of perceived differences in power.

FIG. 1.4. Western-oriented goals of Yup'ik school board.

Math and Science program, and from the National Science Foundation. These funds supported our investigation into how Yup'ik culture, language, and everyday practice contain science and math concepts. As Yup'ik teachers, we continue to strengthen ourselves and our identity, and we hope that we can pass these values on to our students. After all, with a strong self identity and language, we can do anything.

A new superintendent was hired, a White man whose total experience lay with minority people and who had been a VISTA volunteer, a teacher, principal, curriculum coordinator, a small school principal, an assistant superintendent, and a superintendent. The board was impressed with all his "bush" experience and hired him. However, even with his many years of experience in "bush" Alaska, he still had not crossed the bridge of respect and sensitivity for another cultural group. I left my position as bilingual coordinator, because I knew full well what lay ahead of me with this man in power. I did not want to go through the struggle I had gone through earlier, because now I had children of my own. I asked for a transfer to a teaching position in the village where I grew up, and that is where I am today. I have resigned myself to taking things slowly on a daily basis, trying to approach the cultural barriers more positively.

Today, I have begun working directly on developing curriculum in math and science based on the elders' knowledge. Funding from the University of Alaska Fairbanks and the National Science Foundation makes this a possibility. No longer must our culture remain outside of schooling. We have new possibilities.

BACKGROUND

Gaining Access to the Teaching Profession:
X-CED—A Program to Prepare Alaska Native Teachers

The small Alaska Native villages are typically located in remote areas of the state and are typically not connected to the road system. The University of Alaska Fairbanks developed the Cross-Cultural Education Development Program (X-CED) to serve those who are located in rural Alaska and to increase the number of indigenous teachers. Approximately 24 years ago, when the program first began, less than 1% of the teachers statewide and in the Bristol Bay region were indigenous. (See Fig. 1.5 below, which is a map of the state of Alaska and the Bristol Bay region.) X-CED was an outgrowth of the Johnson administration's Teacher Corps in which programs throughout the country were established to increase access to underrepresented minorities in the teaching profession. Today, with programs such as X-CED, the percentage of Alaska Native teachers in one Bristol Bay school district where the program has been operating continuously is approximately 25%. Statewide there are approximately 350 Alaska Native teachers; over 200 graduated

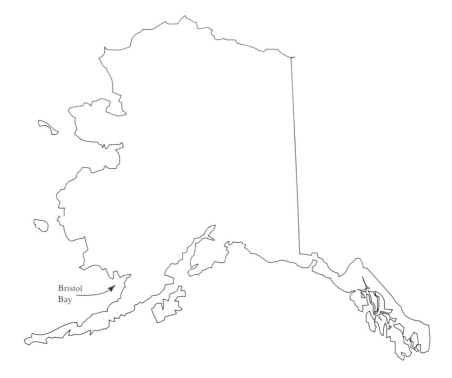

FIG. 1.5. Map of Alaska and Bristol Bay.

from X-CED (personal communication from the founder of the program (Ray Barnhardt, October 15, 1994).

The X-CED program allows students to take courses in their home villages through audioconferences, through site visits by field-based faculty, and through attending regional and statewide student meetings. Despite the hard work required to complete a college degree in a village, the program is perceived by some teachers, administrators, and campus-based faculty as being inferior to campus-based education. Two justifications are typically offered: First, because the program is not located on campus, it is inferior, and second, because it is a Native-oriented program, it is inferior. I was the X-CED field-based faculty member for 11 years in the Bristol Bay region of Alaska, between 1981 and 1992.

Access to Employment and Being Retained

No sooner did the program begin to alter the teaching demographics, increasing the number of certified Yup'ik teachers, than a new set of challenges faced the teachers; to gain access to employment as certified teachers. Fig. 1.6 shows that of the 23 certified Yup'ik teachers in the Bristol Bay region of Alaska, only 9 were hired immediately after graduating, and 8 were hired after 2 or more years. One waited 6 years, 4 were fired, 5 left the region to seek teaching opportunities elsewhere in the state, and 2 were never hired (one never applied). This occurred in a district in which teacher turnover rates ranged from 5% to 20% per year. The most insulting pattern that faced these qualified (certified) teachers who were actively seeking teaching jobs was the practice of hiring them as aides and hiring outside teachers with no Alaskan experience. These outside teachers typically stayed only 2 to 4 years.

One striking example highlights this pattern. One Yup'ik teacher was asked by the superintendent of schools to student teach in an urban area because she only had "village" experience working with Yup'ik students. Yet this student was a member of a different Alaska Native cultural and linguistic group and had only lived in the region for approximately 5 years. This rule of having prior teaching experience with other cultural groups was applied only one way: Alaska Natives needed experience in a White, mainstream context, but non-Natives were not required to have prior experience working in culturally different contexts. After successfully completing her student teaching in an urban area of the state, she was hired as an aide rather than as a teacher. Slowly, over a period of 3 years, she was hired as a half-time teacher. Two years later, she was a full-fledged teacher, yet in her second year of teaching, she was laid off as part of a reduction in staff. She was again rehired as a half-time teacher and a half-time aide. Four other Yup'ik teachers in the region have gone through a similar initiation process of being hired as aides after being fully qualified to teach school, despite the fact that most graduates of X-CED have more than 5 years prior experience as teachers' aides.

Yup'ik teachers reported that school administrators told them the district hires only teachers with experience outside the region. Yet, this was not a policy of this

Yup'ik Teachers	Hired Immediately as a Teacher	Hired as an Aide	Hired After Two Years or More	Left the Region	Not Retained	Never Hired
1		•	•			
2	•				•	
3			•			
4			•	•		
5	•					
6	•					
7	•					
8			•		•	
9		•				
10		•	•		•	
11	•					
12			•			
13			•	•		
14					•	
15		•	•			
16	•					
17		•		•		
18		•		•		
19	•					
20	•					
21						•
22	•				•	
23				•		
24						•
25	• *					
26	•					
27			• **			
28			• **			
29	•					
30	•					
31	•					

FIG. 1.6. Patterns of Yup'ik teacher retention and dismissal 1981–1996 in one region of Alaska.
*special certificate.
**returned to region.

district, nor was this rule applied consistently. Some Yup'ik teachers have not been told this and none of the White X-CED graduates have been told this.

Hiring Alaska Native teachers as aides whereas there is no pattern of hiring nonindigenous teachers as aides, expecting Alaska Native teachers to have experience with other cultural groups but not expecting the same of nonindigenous teachers, and having differential policies and practices of hiring by race can only be termed discrimination. The culminating effect of this discriminatory policy is a significantly smaller percentage of Yup'ik teachers in this region. These experiences and difficulties motivated Ilutsik and others to form the Ciulistet. At first the Ciulistet became a forum for understanding these conflicts.

The Changing School–Community Context

When we first began working together in 1981, there were less than a handful of Yup'ik teachers in the local school district, representing less than 3% of the teachers in this district. The curriculum and instructional paradigm were clearly based on standards and ways of knowing from the outside. This was already documented by J. Collier (1973), M. Collier (1979), and Krauss (1980). Furthermore, from our own experience, the discourse surrounding schooling did not include local issues, local knowledge, or local ways of instructing.

Small Schools and Villages.   The schools in the villages of southwest Alaska typically range in size from 1- to 10-teacher schools. The number of students typically ranges from 10 to 150 students. The schools and the communities of southwest Alaska are located off the road system, separated from each other by vast expanses of tundra, forest, and bodies of water. In 1981, most villages had only one telephone. The schools had radios for communication. At that time planning was under way for Rural Alaska Television Network to extend to the villages, however television was not a reality in southwest Alaskan villages.

The Economy.   The economy was and remains a mixture of subsistence hunting, fishing, gathering, commercial fishing, and employment in local government-supported institutions such as the school, health center, and post office. Today the cash economy has grown substantially from the government transfer of cash through the establishment of village corporations and businesses they have developed, including stores, air taxi enterprises, and tourism. The economy has shifted toward cash; however, the seasonal hunting, fishing, and gathering cycles continue uninterrupted and whole villages continue to move in the spring and summer to capitalize on the rich salmon and herring runs.

Today, television, telephones, computers, CDs, and other modern conveniences are part of the fabric of life in the villages of southwest Alaska. Traditional Yup'ik culture, modernity, and postmodernity all meet in rural Alaska today.

The Yup'ik Language.   Alaska's indigenous cultures and languages and Alaska's schools are at a crossroads. This intersection is beset by a historically situated dilemma that at once defines the problems and holds promise for a solution. The present dilemma is heightened, in Alaska, because of the critical decline in the number of fluent speakers and lessened numbers of children coming to school speaking their Native language. Krauss (1980) identified Yup'ik as the most viable of Alaska's indigenous languages; however, it too is subject to some of the same processes of modernization and marginalization experienced by Alaska's other indigenous languages. The decline in the number of Yup'ik speakers has been well documented (Krauss, 1974, 1982, and 1995): in 1974 there were approximately 32 Yup'ik-speaking villages (approximately 50% of all Yup'ik communities); in 1982, there were 24 Yup'ik villages (approximately 40% of all Yup'ik communities) in which most children began school speaking Yup'ik, but by 1995, this number had decreased to approximately 17 villages (approximately a 24% decline in the number of communities with children speaking Yup'ik) (Krauss, 1995). Figure 1.7 shows the changing demographic composition by population and the number of Yup'ik speaking people. In 1974, 88% of all Yup'ik people were speakers and by 1995 48% were Yup'ik speakers. Simultaneous to this precipitous decline in the number of Yup'ik speakers is the increase in the number of Yup'ik teachers. For example, when Ilutsik and I began working together no more than 3% of the local teachers were Yup'ik and today more than 20% are Yup'ik teachers.

At the very time that the number of Yup'ik teachers is increasing, the language is declining and the culture is undergoing rapid change. Becoming a teacher in such a shifting climate is at best a difficult task; being responsible for the next generation under such circumstances is all the more formidable.

When I began working with Ilutsik and the Yup'ik teachers-in-preparation, we and the university faculty involved in this process were quite naive about changing the culture of school. We thought that by simply increasing the number of indige-nous teachers, schooling would change; as Ilutsik's narrative indicated, that cer-tainly was not the case. To understand these struggles within a theoretical framework the concept of culture is advanced in the next section.

A FRAMEWORK FOR UNDERSTANDING
SCHOOL CULTURE

Contradictions and Possibilities in a Yup'ik Teacher Study Group

This section builds a theoretical framework based on Ilutsik's and other Ciulistet teachers' personal histories that capture the struggles, dilemmas, conflicts, and the hopes of the Ciulistet. Her narrative introduced many issues that this chapter and book explore; transforming cultural voids into cultural knowledge, changing frus-tration and anger into cultural work, and connecting Yup'ik cultural knowledge to schooling. Critical to the establishment of this framework is the establishment of the Ciulistet. As a formal ongoing teacher study and action-research group, it is the primary vehicle both for creating the climate for change and for change itself. It is the group itself, the kinlike relationship among its members that even extends, to some degree, to the "outside" consultants working with the Ciulistet. This grounds the teaching cases and research presented in this book. The remainder of this chapter

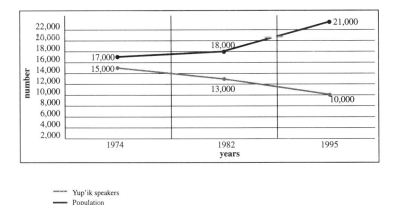

    Yup'ik speakers
    Population

FIG. 1.7. Changes in the population and number of Yup'ik speakers between 1974 and 1995.

situates the Ciulistet within the educational context of schooling in Alaska during the 1980s and 1990s.

Culture of School and the Culture of the Community

The concept of culture has been used by anthropologists studying "exotic" cultures, as in Mead's (1928) classic work. In the 1950s, the anthropological concept of culture gained saliency in schooling through the work of Mead (1951) and Spindler (1955), and by the 1960s, it was used as a way to understand school practice about the larger society in which it is embedded (Henry, 1960; Taba, 1962). Increasingly, the concept of culture was used by educators and anthropologists to understand differences between mainstream classroom practices and how those practices affected American Indian or Alaska Native[4] students (Darnell, 1972; Erickson & Mohatt, 1982; Philips, 1983). In Deyhle and Swisher's (1997) review of research in American Indian and Alaska Native education they found that other studies viewed "Indian culture" as a deficit and saw education's role as assimilation. In Alaska, the cultural distance and differences between Native and Euro-American culture resulted partially in two school systems (one for Whites and another for Natives) (Darnell, 1972; Ray, 1959). Likewise, Meriam, Brown, Cloud, and Dale (1928) found that Native culture, communities, and their wisdom were excluded from schooling in an assimilationist agenda. Increasingly today, as the context of education changes from an assimilationist to a pluralistic agenda, the concept of culture is more and more often from an insider perspective. Researchers from their own communities or cultural groups and in collaboration with university-based

---

[4]Throughout this book we will use American Indian/Alaska Native as the preferred terms when discussing the indigenous peoples of the United States. When referring to the indigenous people of Canada, the preferred term is First Nations and in Australia, it is Aborigines. However, whenever possible the specific indigenous group's name will be used. The above conventions follow those by Deyhle and Swisher (1997) in their extensive review of literature on American Indian/Alaska Natives.

researchers (Lipka & Ilutsik, 1995; Lipka & McCarty, 1994; Collins, 1986; Delpit, 1988; Foster, 1995; Hollins, 1996; Kawagley, 1995; Ladson-Billings, 1990; Lipka, 1990a, 1991; McCarty, Wallace, Hadley, Lynch, & Benally, 1991; Stairs, 1994; Swisher, 1993, 1996; Watahomigie, 1994; Wax, Wax, & Dumont, 1964) view the indigenous culture as having a place within schooling, contributing to both schooling and the local community. This more contextualized ethnographic research provides insights into how indigenous and minority teachers organize classrooms, how they view their relationships with students, other teachers, the surrounding community, and the larger historical and social context of education. Other research also indicates the important role local knowledge and pedagogy can play when teachers and researchers are of the community and have access to it, as well as to each other (Hollins, 1996; Kawagley, 1995; Lipka, 1994; Lipka & McCarty, 1994; Moll, Amanti, Neff, & Gonzalez, 1992).

This research also indicates both a culture and power struggle over the what (content), how (practice), where and when (space, place, and time), and who (identity) of schooling (Annahatak, 1994; Ilutsik, 1994; LaFrance, 1994; Sharp, 1994). These insider narratives underscore the struggle to be accepted by colleagues as legitimate teachers while being an authentic indigenous person (Annahatak, 1994). When it occurs, the inauthenticity is a response to the difficulty of being and acting as an indigenous person within the framework of an Anglo-European school. Feelings of inauthenticity heighten when many of these teachers teach in their second language, a language many were forced to speak as children in these same schools (William Gumlickpuk, a former Ciulistet member, personal communication, November 15, 1988). Or, as Nancy Sharp (1992) stated

> What made it difficult was that I was married to the curriculum and the Western style of teaching. I knew that my principal was looking at me and expected me to follow these guidelines. I taught in English even though my students were fluent in Yup'ik. I felt I had to present in English and explain in English because I was an English teacher.

However, for Yup'ik teachers to become legitimate teachers in the eyes of their colleagues and communities and to be authentic persons both in the school and in the community, then they, as cultural brokers and workers of Yup'ik language and knowledge, must extend the present boundaries of schooling. Further, they need to show that this knowledge can be perceived as beneficial to the goals of schooling while evolving Yup'ik culture. Simultaneously, outside teachers, to become more legitimate in the eyes of the community and local teachers, must also extend the boundaries of schooling.

THE CONCEPT OF CULTURE

In this book we have compelling reasons to use culture as a unifying concept. It is a tool that allows for a deeper understanding of teaching and learning in school and in the community. The indigenous teachers' narratives reported in this book and elsewhere indicate their struggles, and to the degree that these struggles are related to two cultures clashing, then schooling is contested space. Understanding these conflicts might lead to approaches that could reverse the situation. By understanding the beliefs and patterned ways of interacting, we might more clearly understand some of the causes of these conflicts. By viewing schooling as a cultural process, we can more effectively understand how it can change. Furthermore, each cultural group with its constituted ways of perceiving, valuing, and knowing represents a unique window into the world. The Yup'ik culture being no different, it then stands to inform schooling by sharing its wisdom of practice. Being, doing, thinking, and relating are shaped by this dynamic relationship between context and culture.

Culture is a difficult concept to grasp, because it is neither an object nor is it directly visible, but it can be inferred and discerned. By culture we mean the customary ways of relating (including such as taking turns speaking, forms of speech, and nonverbal behavior), organizing space and time, and values. Culture is the frame of reference that creates boundaries, categories, and rules in which meaning is negotiated. "The construction of meaning ... is realized through participation in the symbolic systems of the culture ... the very shape of our lives ... is understandable to ourselves and to others only by virtue of those cultural systems of interpretation" (Bruner, 1990, p. 33). Culture is not static; it reflects changes in the larger context surrounding a particular group and a group's response to those changes (McDermott & Verenne, 1995). School culture also includes the regularities, rituals, norms, values, and content of schooling. School culture is also more than a static conception of a school building or even a classroom. It includes the transactional nature of school and community relationships (Sarason, 1996). The cultural space between school and community, particularly in contested space, is unpredictable, variable, and creates options. Rosaldo (1989) reflected on such cultural space, "[it] enables a culturally valued quality of human relation where one can follow impulses, change directions, and coordinate with other people" (p. 112). This book's cultural frame of reference is neither Yup'ik culture per se nor Western culture and schooling. It is the culture formed between the two at the meeting place called school, and, hence, an evolving culture of "school and community."

Mediating the evolving culture of school is a set of historically situated power relations. In Yup'ik communities and most other indigenous settings, power relations are asymmetrical. Typically these asymmetrical power relations translate into cultural and educational discontinuities in school. These discontinuities often connote a severe break between the generations such as is occurring in rural Alaska at the present time. For example, the language of instruction in almost all Alaskan schools is English, regardless of whether that is the language of the students. Yet, school is one setting in which the dominant culture of the school and the local community culture have the potential to transform each other. The school community intersection is therefore viewed as an open, evolving, and complex system. It is this promise that extends the work of this book beyond the culture-specific information reported herein, and, thus is applicable to others.

Every culture is limited by its agreed-on conventions, although, of course, individuals vary greatly across any cultural group. Thus, the culture of school includes the way time and space are organized, typical ways in which lessons are presented (both their form and content), and the knowledge that is considered part of that cultural system. In a sense, school curriculum is a cultural artifact (Hollins, 1996); conversely, the null curriculum (the omitted curriculum) is those knowledge bases, ways of knowing, and ways of teaching that reside beyond the present boundaries of the culture of school. Schooling is ostensibly about transmitting knowledge from one generation to another, but in cross-cultural situations, what cultural knowledge ought to be transmitted and in what forms?

Ideally, the culture of school and the culture of the community are mutually reinforcing. In Alaska we have a situation in which the relationship of the culture of the school and the culture of the community do not reinforce each other. Quite simply, each represents a different cultural realm with different worldviews and different ways of relating—each has distinct purposes associated with their enculturation process. The school's culture, with its emphasis on abstract learning decontextualized from personal experience and organized in chunks to fit pre-scribed time, spaces, and places for learning, differs rather sharply from that of a society that values knowledge validated through personal experience—typically related to subsisting off the land. In addition, the language of knowledge transmission differs across these domains (although this is rapidly changing), which further sharpens the discontinuity between settings. Finally, culture and power are intricately related. School represents and reflects the dominant culture including the power to include or exclude bodies of knowledge and ways of transmitting that knowledge.

Our work in videotape analysis became a platform on which to understand these dynamics, the individual frustrations, and to begin to address them.

THE CIULISTET: THE ZONE OF THE POSSIBLE

The process of facing the cultural void, learning Yup'ik cultural knowledge and ways of being, and finding a place for this knowledge in school required a fundamental paradigm shift for the Ciulistet and the school system. At its core this shift required a more inclusive understanding of what constituted legitimate school knowledge and ways of transmitting that knowledge. Situating Yup'ik language and cultural knowledge and Western schooling, at the close of the 20th century, often shows that schooling is contested space with school and community often having contradictory and conflicting purposes.

When we began our video analysis (see Lipka, 1990a, 1991, and chapter 4 of this book), we were guided by the work of Hall (1973) on proxemics—how social relations are organized spatially—and, in particular, by M. Collier (1979) on how Yup'ik teachers and Caucasian teachers differed in their organization of space, rhythms, and use of voice. We observed how teachers used their voice in conveying messages, in creating public and private space, and how this related to school and community cultural norms.[5]

By viewing videotapes of outside teachers, and by using the dynamics of insiders' and outsiders' frames of reference, we gained a contrastive perspective on what constituted culturally patterned ways of doing schooling (see the Appendix for a fuller account of the methodology involved). Much later, we collected videotapes of community activities at fish camps and this was also used to contrast with schooled ways of transmitting knowledge. It was through this process that we slowly became aware of the deeper cognitive dimensions related to activity and contexts. We began to intuitively grasp not only a Yup'ik way of teaching, organizing lessons, spatial relations with students, and ways of communicating, but we also began to see the vague outlines of a distinct cultural system of meaning and cognition. Because culture is a unifying concept it enabled us to shift the discourse of schooling from deficits to existing assets.

In 1981, when Ilutsik and I first started working together in the Cross-Cultural Education Development Program (X-CED), the program's goal was to increase the number of Native teachers in Alaska. We did not set out to conduct research, just simply to graduate more Yup'ik teachers. However, as the graduates of this program became teachers, they struggled with doubts about their effectiveness as teachers and about their ability to be of service to their communities. It was the formation of the Ciulistet and our work to address these conflicts that formed the basis for our evolving research agenda.

These cultural conflicts were faced individually by the newly hired Yup'ik teachers. When superintendent of schools John Antonnen formed the Ciulistet, this provided an opportunity for individual concerns to be understood collectively. Because the Ciulistet was a group, we immediately changed the frame of reference from a psychological one of "Why don't I fit?" to a social and cultural one of "Why is it that we are having such similar problems?" No longer was it the lone teacher isolated in his or her classroom. As the teachers shared their experiences, they became aware of a larger sociohistorical and sociopolitical context and their place within this larger struggle. It was here that the very formation of the group created a zone of safety, and this represented a change in the context of schooling. Yet, it was more than just safety and comfort for the teachers; the group created a space that can be conceptualized much like that of Vygotsky's "zone of proximal development" (Newman, Griffin, & Cole, 1989). According to Newman, Griffin, and Cole, the zone of proximal development is "the locus of social negotiations about meanings, and it is, in the context of schools, a place where teachers and pupils may appropriate one another's understandings" (p. XII). The zone of proximal develop-

---

[5]Fred Erickson, Malcolm Collier, and Sharon Nelson-Barber all worked with the group and were particularly informative.

ment transferred to the Ciulistet becomes a "zone of possibility" where insiders and outsiders ferret out the meanings, conflicts, and confusions surrounding the practical question of how to negotiate Yup'ik cultural knowledge within a school context. Within this space, the teachers were able to vent their frustrations and see underlining connections, realizing ever so slowly that cultural differences need not be relegated to the margins or just accepted as a barrier to their teaching and to the students' learning, as some colleagues, principals, and even some community members suggested. Because we had established trust and had a safe environment in which to work, we took risks. We began to explore ways in which the Yup'ik language, culture, and everyday experience could be viewed as an asset. Once we made this connection, we immediately recognized the need to invite elders into the group. Our work began to accelerate because cultural voids, as described by Ilutsik, could be faced without ridicule in the relative safety of the group and with the expert guidance of the elders. The inclusion of elders also transformed the Ciulistet from a teacher group to a community-based collaborative research group. Because this community of learners has as its goal the inclusion of ancient knowledge, Yup'ik ways of knowing, and ways of connecting this knowledge to modern schooling, it slowly transformed schooling beyond the boundaries of the group. Here the concept of zone of possible development took on meaning as we began to translate the elders' knowledge into pedagogical practice. Some of the potential of the group has gone beyond the confines of the group into both the classrooms and the schools.

It is this meeting of modernity, postmodernism, and tradition in which opportunities and challenges present themselves, especially to teacher groups such as the Ciulistet. To reform education, elders, in collaboration with indigenous teachers' groups, must lead the way. In the community, elders—not students—are deemed wise, and elders are the keepers of the culture. Otherwise, efforts at educational reform may disrupt social processes at the community level. Therefore, learning from our own experiences that occurred when attempts at school reform resulted in misunderstandings because elders were not involved (Lipka, 1989), and recognizing the importance of accepting the community's precepts (of not replicating the status quo and of changing the context of education), we have included the elders in all aspects of our work, from recounting traditional stories, to making traditional crafts, to helping the teachers develop curriculum and pedagogy. Further, elders typically play a critical role within their villages and regions as members of local and regional educational boards.

Yet, no longer is it possible to simply transmit culture in an unbroken chain from one generation to another. Contemporary U.S. society has profoundly influenced traditional cultures. Instead, traditional cultures face a series of modern choices, and these choices open up new possibilities, including the potential for the school to serve the community, rather than continuing to siphon off the best of its resources.

For Alaska Natives, the very role of being a professional teacher is relatively new. The step from being a subsistence hunter, a member of a traditional group, to being a classroom teacher requires a major change in role and relationship to other community members. The traditional role of teaching the village's children was not typically the responsibility of a single expert, "the teacher," but the joint responsibility of the village's elders (Henry Alakayak, a Yup'ik elder, personal communication, October 10, 1992). In other words, parents and village elders had responsibility for teaching. Typically taught in the *qasg'iq* (men's or community house) and in situ, the group took responsibility for education; it was not relegated to one individual teacher (see Fienup-Riordan, 1995; Wahlberg, 1997).

Becoming a teacher in an alien context is difficult, and becoming a cultural broker is an even more difficult role. The historical legacy of colonialism is no mere fact recorded in textbooks, but the living history of many indigenous teachers (interviews with William Gumlickpuk, a former Ciulistet member, 1988; Sharp, 1994). More recently, Ciulistet teachers still felt threatened if they used their Yup'ik language in school (Lipka, 1994; Sharp, 1994). The complexity of the situation, its multiple pulls and pushes, places many indigenous teachers in a psychological double bind.

Cultural Brokers

To become a cultural broker between the Western school system and Yup'ik communities is to accept a role fraught with contradictions and dilemmas. As cultural brokers, such individuals must be effective members in the school and community; yet in taking on this role they risk losing their status as full-fledged community members and face the uncertainty of not being fully accepted by the school community. Motivating almost each member of the Ciulistet group is a profound sense of purpose; "[to] make a difference among my people" (Sharp, 1992). This desire, struggle to become authentic teachers are what enabled Ciulistet members to become cultural brokers. Furthermore, as Meade (1990) and Wahlberg (1997) reported, traditional knowledge is fragmenting, and the teachers' task must expand to include learning their oral tradition. Cultural brokers—who begin from a standpoint of understanding traditional and contemporary knowledge and who are willing to face the deep social conflicts initiated by colonizing institutions—will be in a powerful position to begin the long, slow process of reconstructing the culture of school.

The paradoxical task facing the Ciulistet is underscored by the historical and present day social context; that is, they must now accept the existing institutional school system as a partner in reversing cultural loss, and they must accept elders as keepers of traditional wisdom, learning how to transform schooling and ancient knowledge to create a contemporary and compatible system between the two. This must occur despite 100+ years of pedagogical policies and practices that have eroded indigenous culture and language (Krauss, 1980). Somehow, indigenous teachers must overcome the practices and policies they experienced as students (such as being forced to learn and speak in English) and as teachers (who sometimes report that they are "teaching against their will" in order to teach at all), to help the students they teach.

Simultaneously, many indigenous teachers feel scrutinized by "two pairs of eyes." Two pairs of eyes refers to the standards and scrutiny of the school and the standards and scrutiny of the village—which are often at odds with each other. Not only does the community view indigenous local teachers by different standards than those from outside, but in fact, some community members prefer mainstream English-only speakers to Yup'ik teachers whereas other community members are proud of having "teachers who eat seal meat" (Lipka, 1994; Sharp, 1992). The complexity of the situation, its multiple pulls and pushes, places these indigenous teachers in a psychological double bind. Denying one's language and culture is in part denying one's identity, which is a high price to pay for becoming a teacher. This is compounded when admittance to the profession is not guaranteed by conformity, as reported by minority teachers who may feel as "outsiders within," a state of belonging yet not belonging (Collins, 1986).

The Ciulistet teachers have became mediators between school and community, and thus cultural brokers. Ciulistet meetings, typically held in various villages, allowed different communities to participate. Community participation included elders teaching traditional knowledge and also learning from Ciulistet teachers. Ciulistet teachers would translate and accommodate what they learned from the elders. In this way elders were called on not only to teach in a way familiar to them, but to coconstruct curriculum and pedagogy. Through this process of formulating curriculum and pedagogy, inevitable political questions were raised and discussed. This created a dialogue not only between Ciulistet and community members but also between Ciulistet, community, and school. The discourse, often roughedged, has opened up areas of common interest.

Cultural Conflicts and Opportunities in the Classroom

The slow realization that historical and macrosocietal events influence classroom teaching and schooling is one major theme of this book. For example, the tensions between Yup'ik culture and mainstream culture over how one ought to organize classroom discourse and physical space, and how and what one should teach, are outgrowths of particular sets of relationships embedded in the larger social context. The realization that schooling is socially constructed, and the understanding that Yup'ik culture could be part of that constructive process, created new educational possibilities. These realizations led to the concept that schooling is not just a place for transferring knowledge but also a meeting place between cultures, and hence a site of cultural negotiations. Negotiating the culture of school holds promise for more equitable and inclusive policies that can change the context of schooling.

The conflicts and pressures of trying to be both a professional teacher and a community member are further accentuated by the different ways of organizing classroom space (the way physical and personal space and pacing are arranged) and classroom discourse (the culturally patterned ways of speaking in a classroom), as reported in a growing body of research on and with indigenous teachers (Annahatak, 1994; Barnhardt, 1982; J. Collier, 1973; M. Collier, 1979; Erickson & Mohatt, 1982; Lipka, 1990a, 1991; Malin, 1994; Van Ness, 1982). Commonly noted throughout this research are slower pacing and closer physical contact than that found in mainstream classes, as well as a discourse that includes a more even distribution of speech between students and teachers; speaking to a group instead of nominating individuals; allowing multiple speakers; and using content related to the local environment. At the risk of overgeneralizing, these differences in social organization reflect important indigenous values of individual autonomy and group harmony (Annahatak, 1994; Lipka, 1990a, 1991, 1994; Paradise, 1994). In contrast, classroom discourse in mainstream classes follows what Mehan (1979) and Cazden (1988) describe as the canonical discourse form of *nomination* (teacher calling individually on students), *elicitation* (teacher asking questions of students, usually individually, to elicit a response), and *evaluation* (teacher evaluating a student's answer as correct or incorrect). It is not difficult to imagine that yearly performance evaluations are possibly subject to cultural bias. The perceptions of principals and supervisors evaluating teachers have been criticized for 30 years (McNeil & Popham, 1973; Peterson, Deyhle, & Watkins, 1988) as not being a valid or reliable measure of teacher performance, and such measures cross-culturally can only be less valid indicators. This is especially true when forms of classroom organization and classroom discourse are unfamiliar to other colleagues and evaluators (Lipka, 1990b; Malin, 1994).

Yup'ik Culture as Content for Schooling

In addition to cultural differences in social discourse and organization (how one teaches) cultural differences exist between mainstream and Yup'ik knowledge. By concretely demonstrating how Yup'ik culture, language, and everyday experience could offer insights in teaching core academic areas, such as mathematics, the Ciulistet has slowly changed the discourse surrounding the value of indigenous cultural knowledge in schooling. This is similar to the work of Moll and his associates concerning "funds of knowledge" and what constitutes school knowledge (1992). Also, the work of Cole and Scribner (1974) on tailoring in Liberia shows how everyday experience relates to mathematical concepts. Bringing the knowledge of the community into schooling in ways that respect the local culture is referred to as "authentic culturally mediated cognition" (Hollins, 1996, p. 130). Hollins refers to the knowledge base and the activities that contain that knowledge as the *authentic context*. The work of Rogoff (1990) and of Lave and Wenger (1991) also views, out of the school, learning and knowledge in ways that correspond well with Yup'ik society. For example, the notion of "situated learning," children as apprentices within a learning community, and guided participation and peripheral practice all relate well to how Yup'ik adults instruct (Kawagley, 1995; Lipka, 1994).

However, in Alaska, as Meade (1990) warned, traditional knowledge is being scattered and now a gap exists between traditional knowledge and the next generation. The situation can be described as cultural discontinuity, meaning the next generation may no longer share the same language and cultural activities as their elders. This makes it even more difficult to use authentic cultural activities as a basis for developing culturally relevant curriculum and pedagogy. It is within such a complex arena that the Ciulistet teachers and other indigenous and minority teacher groups are being called on to transform the culture of schooling, adapting each to the other.

The future work of the group is to continue collaborating with school and community, to bring to fruition a curriculum and pedagogy that makes successful education and cultural authenticity possible. It is now possible to demonstrate that the teaching of mathematics can be based on Yup'ik culture; that Yup'ik culture can connect math to science and to literacy. (see chap. 6, this volume). In negotiating and coconstructing curriculum and pedagogy, community, and school, the Ciulistet can consciously make possible the what, how, who, and why of schooling. The processes and content of schooling can be clearly revealed as social constructions—based on the social choices that are made.

Culturally Negotiated Pedagogy

For far too long, the debates in anthropology and education concerning indigenous and minority schooling have been postulated in dichotomous terms. These arguments have been stated in the either—or terminology of "culture versus power" and "microanalysis versus macroanalysis." These bifurcated ways of conceptualizing the problems long associated with schooling in indigenous communities result in unfortunate typologies that blur the present situation. This either–or way of viewing the present scene in some ways continues the oppressive colonial legacy by suggesting that indigenous communities have to fully assimilate, that is, accept Western schooling "as is," or resist and be isolated in "traditional" indigenous learning. In the Sharp narrative (presented in this book), the author shows the deleterious effects of such either–or thinking, promulgated by the school district and accepted by some powerful community leaders. This mindset seriously constrains the educational possibilities, limiting and disempowering the community.

Neither Western society nor indigenous tribes are monolithic. The material presented in this book suggests there is no one way to conduct schooling (Holm & Holm, 1990, 1995). Our theories need to transcend overly simplistic structural explanations of school failure that both aggregate diverse groups of people and assume that their relationship to school and the dominant culture are similar (Ogbu, 1987, 1995). For example, categorizing groups along the dimensions of "primary and secondary cultural characteristics" creates unnecessarily rigid and unrealistic views of group and individual cultural identities. Theory must be derived from the experience of real people in real places. Indigenous groups are, as these cases suggest, making creative responses to what Stairs (1994) called "third cultural realities" (derived from Malinowski, p. 73, 1945/1961). Stairs stated, " A cultural negotiation perspective redefines education as culture-in-the-making at multiple levels" (p. 156). This third way implies a synthesis, a working through on the part of the community, to determine the meaning of schooling. Crossing cultural boundaries and creatively exploring the ways in which the culture of school could be formulated is one promising aspect of indigenous education. However, no two situations are identical. Different groups are negotiating both different aspects of their relationship between school and community and different aspects of the what (content), how (processes), and the why (meaning and purposes) of schooling. In all these contexts, communities are exerting their influence on the school as they struggle creatively to achieve a new synthesis.

Because communities are actively involved in the process of building a new synthesis, no longer is the paradigm of culture versus power adequate. Instead, culture and power are viewed in a both–and perspective, each contributing to the present circumstances. Establishing school norms, curricula, and ways of interacting in school is one nexus of power and culture. Carrying out policies that exclude community participation is another example of a meeting place for culture and power. One hopes that schools as institutions, as community institutions, have some autonomy in changing structural and cultural relations within the classroom and the larger school–community context. As an alternative to strategies derived from the deficit theory, the cultural difference theory, and the structural theory, we suggest culturally negotiated pedagogy. Such an approach is open to public debate and rational decision making. We are not so naive as to assume that power relations will automatically shift, or that local teachers and communities will simply identify curriculum and pedagogy that will be immediately implemented. But we expect an important discourse among indigenous and minority teacher groups and their communities will ensue, and a discourse across cultural boundaries will slowly evolve a shift in the context, content, and values of schooling. In this way, schooling can to some extent become a community institution, without, as Fishman (1984) described, undermining the community it ostensibly serves.

THEORETICAL IMPLICATIONS OF CULTURALLY NEGOTIATED SCHOOLING

The authors in this book propose culturally negotiated schooling as an alternative to the "culture versus power" dichotomy and to the dilemma of resolving modern and traditional tensions. This nascent theory, derived from the experience of indigenous and nonindigenous educators in various contexts, suggests that indigenous people are evolving their cultures, coevolving the culture of school, and increasingly making their schools community institutions (Begay et al., 1995; Watahomigie, 1995). One result is a variety of forms of schooling. Issues of indigenous language and cultural survival still predominate much of the dialogue (see McCarty & Zepeda, 1995). Culturally negotiated schooling is our attempt to formulate a theoretical construct that begins to capture some of the flavor of what occurs in these contexts. This construct extends beyond the work of Cummins (1986) and his theory of cultural inclusion. Cummins suggested that by including *more* local knowledge, social practices, and the community into the school this process would transform schooling. Although we find instructive the theories of cultural inclusion, such as Au's work on bringing local Hawaiian discourse patterns into schooling (Au & Jordan 1981); developing in school practices that are more culturally compatible (Jordan, 1985); making a cultural match between home and school (Mohatt & Erickson, 1981; Philips, 1972, 1983), they are far too simplistic. Besides neglecting power issues, they presume that communities *want* more and they neglect deeper cultural meanings of each culture. They neglect the challenging process of negotiating cultural forms and knowledge from one context to another. For example, within the Yup'ik storytelling tradition, the listener does not question the storyteller to learn the meaning of the story (Mathers, 1995). It is the listener's right and responsibility to hear the story and apply it to one's life. In many classrooms, using indigenous stories has come into vogue, but the difficulty of following the tradition of telling, not explaining, not discussing, and not analyzing presents a direct conflict with a cultural tradition of schooling in which discussing and analyzing are the major modalities. This conflict is not resolved by "more" of the local tradition. We suggest it may be resolved by negotiating the boundaries and meaning of schooling and the local culture. Further, the cultural inclusion approach assumes that indigenous communities will want more of the local culture in schooling; however, indigenous communities in their diversity will negotiate differently in different places and times. Cultural negotiations extend beyond dichotomous thinking by recognizing the dynamic interplay between culture and power and by recognizing the varied contexts and circumstances of different groups—hence acknowledging that cultural negotiations are multidimensional. To do less is to impose our thinking and our solutions on diverse groups who have specific sociohistorical contexts and who conceptualize their dilemmas and options differently. To do less is insulting.

Indigenous and minority teacher groups expand our concept of the contributions minority teachers can make in schooling. Beebe (1966) outlined a process that indigenous teachers go through, beginning with conformity to current norms and changing to being comfortable in using their language and pedagogical styles. From our experience, indigenous teacher groups appear to reduce isolation, conformity, and resistance. These groups also increase the awareness of their participants and assist in transforming feelings of inadequacy into collective understandings of the context of education. More slowly, these groups begin to tap the local culture and language so that each particular teacher can use his or her local knowledge in the classroom. Furthermore, these groups also have the potential to share their knowledge with all teachers; for example, by showing how local knowledge can apply to the teaching of mathematics and science.

In conclusion, the theoretical perspective of this book views the culture of school not as a static conception referring to physical buildings or even to what goes in classrooms, but views the culture of schooling as a dynamic, transactional process between school and community. In the case presented herein, and with many others in minority or indigenous contexts, this includes a set of historical and political relationships emanating from colonialism and its inherent asymmetrical power relations. Such educational contexts typically demonstrate severe discontinuities between the culture of school and the culture of the community. To reform schooling in such contexts includes evolving new sets of relationships, culturally negotiated pedagogy between school and community and intentionally affecting the regularities of schooling, its values and content. From a practice perspective, it means including elders' knowledge, ways of teaching, and ways of assessing that heretofore have been either on the margins of schooling or not even included in school discourse.

We believe that Yup'ik knowledge can not only enlighten Yup'ik students, but also that the unique and similar ways in which Yupiit[6] conceive of fundamental concepts can enrich others. Furthermore, if Yup'ik knowledge can be viewed as legitimate, others who perceive their knowledge as marginal to schooling can see these cases as exemplars. Similarly, Yup'ik ways of teaching, social organization, discourse routines, connections to community, and everyday knowledge provide additional examples about how schooling can be perceived as more representational and more democratic. The following cases explore the issues of who, what, how, and the purposes of schooling in depth.

For additional insights into the group's methodology and formal research methodology, see the Appendix.

REFERENCES

Annahatak, B. (1994). Quality education for Inuit today? Cultural strengths, new things, and working out the unknowns: A story by an Inuk. *Peabody Journal of Education, 69*(2), 12–18.

Au, K., & Jordan, C. (1981). Teaching reading to Hawaiian children: Finding a culturally appropriate solution. In H. T. Trueba, G. P. Guthrie, & K. Hu-Pei Au (Eds.), *Culture and the bilingual classroom* (pp. 139–152). Rowley, MA: Newbury House.

Barnhardt, C. (1982). "Tuning in": Athabaskan teachers and students. In R. Barnhardt (Ed.), *Cross-cultural studies in Alaskan education* (pp. 144–164). Fairbanks, AK: University of Alaska Fairbanks, Center for Cross-Cultural Studies.

Beebe, C. E. (1966). *The quality of education in developing countries.* Cambridge, MA: MIT Press.

Begay, S., Sells, D., Estell, D., Estell, J., & McCarty, T. (1995). Change from the inside out: A story of transformation in a Navajo community school. *Bilingual Research Journal, 19*(1), 121–140.

Bruner, J. (1990). *Acts of meaning.* Cambridge, MA: Harvard University Press.

Cazden, C. (1988). *Classroom discourse.* Portsmouth, NH: Heinemann.

Cole, M., & Scribner, S. (1974). *Culture and thought.* New York: Wiley.

---

[6]Plural form.

Collier, J. (1973). *Alaskan Eskimo education: A film analysis of cultural confrontation in the schools.* New York: Holt, Rinehart, & Winston.

Collier, M. (1979). *A film study of classrooms in Western Alaska.* Fairbanks, AK: University of Alaska Fairbanks, Center for Cross-Cultural Studies.

Collins, P. (1986). Learning about the outsider from within: The sociological significances of Black feminist thought. *Social Problems, 33,* 14–32.

Cummins, J. (1986). Empowering minority students: A framework for intervention. *The Harvard Education Review, 56,* 18–36.

Darnell, F. (1972). *Education in the North.* Fairbanks, AK: Arctic Institute of North America and University of Alaska.

Deyhle, D., & Swisher, K. (1997). Research in American Indian and Alaska Native education: From assimilation to self-determination. In M. Apple (Ed.), *Review of Research in Education.* Washington, DC: American Educational Research Association.

Delpit, L. (1988). The silenced dialogue. *Harvard Educational Review, 58,* 280–298.

Dumont, R. (1972). Learning English and how to be silent: Studies in Sioux and Cherokee classrooms. In C. Cazden, V. John, & D. Hymes (Eds.), *Functions of language in the classroom* (pp. 334–369). New York: Teachers College Press.

Erickson, F. & Mohatt, G. (1982). Cultural organization of participation structures in two classrooms of Indian students. In D. G. Spindler (Ed.), *Doing the ethnography of schooling* (pp. 132–174). New York: Holt, Rinehart, & Winston.

Fienup-Riordan, A. (1995). *Boundaries and passages: Rule and ritual in Yup'ik Eskimo oral tradition.* Norman, OK: University of Oklahoma Press.

Fishman, J. (1984). Minority mother tongues in education. *Prospects, 14,* 51–56.

Foster, M. (1995). African-American teachers and culturally relevant pedagogy. In J. Banks and C. Banks (Eds.), *The handbook on research on multi-cultural education* (pp. 747–759). New York: MacMillan.

Fullan, M. (1991). *The meaning of educational change.* New York: Teachers College Press.

Hall, E. (1973). *The silent language.* New York: Anchor Books.

Henry, J. (1960). A cross-cultural outline of education. *Current Anthropology, 1,* 267–305.

Hollins, E. (1996). *Culture in school learning: Revealing the deep meaning.* Mahwah, NJ: Lawrence Erlbaum Associates.

Holm, A. & Holm, W. (1995). Navajo language education: Retrospect and prospects. *Bilingual Research Journal, 19*(1), 141-167)

Holm, A., & Holm, W. (1990). Rock Point: A Navajo way to go to school: A valediction. In C. Cazden, & C. Snow (Eds.), English plus: Issues in bilingual education. *Annals of the American Academy of Political and Social Science* (pp. 170–184). Newberry Park, CA: Sage.

Ilutsik, E. (1994). The founding of the Ciulistet: One teacher's journey. *Journal of American Indian Education, 33*(3), 6–13.

Jordan, C. (1985). Translating culture: From ethnographic information to educational program. *Anthropology and Education Quarterly, 16,* 105–125.

Kawagley, O. (1995). *A Yupiaq worldview: A pathway to an ecology and spirit.* Prospect Heights, IL: Waveland Press, Inc.

Krauss, M. (1995). *Inuit, Nunait, Nunangit, and Yuget.* Fairbanks, AK: Alaska Native Language Center.

Krauss, M. (1982). *Native peoples and languages of Alaska.* Fairbanks, AK: Alaska Native Language Center.

Krauss, M. (1980). *Alaska Native languages: Past, present, and future.* Fairbanks, AK: Alaska Native Language Center.

Krauss, M. (1974). *Native peoples and languages of Alaska.* Fairbanks, AK: Alaska Native Language Center.

Ladson-Billings, G. (1995). Multicultural teacher education: Research practice and policy. In J. Banks & C. Banks (Eds.), *The handbook on research on multicultural education* (pp. 747–759). New York: MacMillan.

Ladson-Billings, G. (1990). Like lightning in a bottle: Attempting to capture the pedagogical excellence of successful teachers of Black students. *International Journal of Qualitative Studies in Education, 3,* 335–344.

LaFrance, B. (1994). Empowering ourselves: Making education and schooling one. *Peabody Journal of Education, 69*(2), 140–153.

Lave, J., & Wenger, E. (1991). *Situated learning: Legitimate peripheral participation.* Cambridge, England. Cambridge University Press.

Lieberman, A. (1995). Restructuring schools: The dynamics of changing practice, structure, and culture. In A. Lieberman (Ed.), *The work of restructuring schools: Building from the ground up* (pp. 1–17). New York: Teachers College Press.

Lipka, J. (1989). A cautionary tale of curriculum development in Yup'ik Eskimo communities. *Anthropology & Education Quarterly, 20,* 216–231.

Lipka, J. (1990a). Cross-cultural teacher perspectives of teaching styles. *Kaurna, 1*(1), 33–46.

Lipka, J. (1990b). Integrating cultural form and content in one Yup'ik Eskimo class. *Canadian Journal of Native Education, 17*(2), 18–32.

Lipka, J. (1991). Toward a culturally based pedagogy: A case study of one Yup'ik Eskimo teacher. *Anthropology and Education Quarterly, 22*(3), 203–223.

Lipka, J. (1994). Language, power, and pedagogy: Whose school is it anyway? *Peabody Journal of Education, 69*(2), 71–93.

Lipka, J., & Ilutsik, E. (1997). Ciulistet and the curriculum of the possible. In N. Hornberger (Ed.), *Indigenous literacies in the Americas: Language planning from the bottom up* (pp. 45–68). Berlin: Mouton de Gruyter.

Lipka, J. & Ilutsik, E. (1995). Negotiated change: Yup'ik perspectives on indigenous schooling. *Bilingual Research Journal, 19,* 195–207.

Lipka, J. & McCarty, T. (1994). Changing the culture of schooling: Navajo and Yup'ik cases. *Anthropology and Education Quarterly, 25*(3), 266–284.

Little, J. W. (1993). Teachers' professional development in a climate of educational reform. *Educational Evaluation and Policy Analysis, 15*(2),129–151.

Malin, M. (1994). What is a good teacher? Anglo and Aboriginal Australian views. *Peabody Journal of Education, 69*(2), 94–114.

Malinwoski, B. (1961). The dynamics of culture change: An inquiry in race relations in Africa. New Haven: Yale University Press. (Original work published 1945.)

Mathers, E. (1995). With a vision beyond our immediate needs: Oral traditions in an age of literacy. In P. Morrow, & S. Schneider (Eds.), *When our words return* (pp. 13–26). Logan, UT: Utah State University Press.

McCarty, T., & Zepeda, O. (1995). Special issue: Indigenous language education and literacy. *Bilingual Research Journal, 19*(1), 1–215.

McCarty, T., Wallace, S., Hadley Lynch, R., & Benally, A. (1991). Classroom inquiry and Navajo learning styles: A call for reassessment. *Anthropology and Education Quarterly 22*(1), 42–59.

McDermott, R., & Verenne, H. (1995). Culture as a disability. *Anthropology and Education Quarterly 26*(3), 324–348

McNeil, J., & Popham, J. (1973). The assessment of teacher competence. In Traveers, R. (Ed.), *Second handbook of research on education* (pp. 218–244). Chicago: Rand McNally.

Mead, M. (1928). *Coming of age in Samoa: A psychological study of primitive youth for Western civilization.* New York: Morrow.

Mead, M. (1951). *The school in American culture.* Cambridge, MA: Harvard University Press.

Meade, M. (1990). Sewing to maintain the past, present and future. *Inuit Studies 14*(1–2), 229–239.

Mehan, H. (1979). *Learning lessons.* Cambridge, MA: Harvard University Press.

Meriam, L., Brown, R., Cloud, H., & Dale, E. (1928). *The problem of Indian administration.* Baltimore, MD: Johns Hopkins University Press.

Mohatt, T., & Erickson, F. (1981). Cultural differences in teaching styles in an Odawa school. In H. Trueba, G. Gutherie, & K. Au (Eds.), *Culture and the bilingual classroom: Studies in Classroom Ethnography* (pp. 105–119). Cambridge, MA: Newbury House Publishers, Inc.

Moll, L., Amanti, C., Neff, D., & Gonzalez, N. (1992). Funds of knowledge for teaching: Using a qualitative approach to connect homes and classrooms. *Theory Into Practice, 31*(1), 132–141.

Morrow, P. (1995). On shaky ground: Folklore, collaboration, and problematic outcomes. In P. Morrow, & S. Schneider (Eds.), *When our words return* (pp. 27–52). Logan, UT: Utah State University Press.

Newman, D., Griffin, P., & Cole, M. (1989). *The construction zone: Working for cognitive change in school.* Cambridge, England: Cambridge University Press.

Ogbu, J. (1995). Understanding cultural diversity and learning. In J. Banks, & C. Banks (Eds.), *A handbook on research on multicultural education* (pp. 582–593). New York: MacMillan.

Ogbu, J. (1987). Variability in minority school performance: A problem in search of an explanation. *Anthropology and Education Quarterly, 18*(4), 312–334.

Paradise, R. (1994). Spontaneous cultural compatibility: Mazahua students and their teachers constructing trusting relationships. *Peabody Journal of Education, 69*(2), 60–70.

Peterson, K., Deyle, D., & Watkins, W. (1988). Evaluation that accommodates minority teacher contributions. *Urban Education, 23*(2), 133–149.

Philips, S. (1983). *The invisible culture: Communication in classroom and community on the Warm Springs Indian Reservation.* New York & London: Longman, University of Arizona.

Philips, S. (1972). Participant structure and communicative competence: Warm Springs children in community and classroom. In C. Cazden, V. John, & D. Hymes (Eds.), *Functions of language in the classroom* (pp. 370–394). Columbia: Teachers College Press.

Ray, C. (1959). *A program of education for Alaska Natives.* Fairbanks, AK: University of Alaska.

Rogoff, B. (1990). *Apprenticeship in thinking: Cognitive development in social context.* Oxford, England: Oxford University Press.

Rosaldo, R. (1989). *Culture and truth: The remaking of social analysis.* Boston: Beacon Press.

Sarason, S. (1996). *Revisiting the culture of the school and the problem of change.* New York: Teachers College Press.

Sharp, N. (1992, May). *Indigenous pedagogy and languages: Integration of community and school.* Paper presented at Circumpolar Language Development Conference, Whitehorse, Yukon Territory, Canada.

Sharp, N. (1994). Caknernarqutet. *Peabody Journal of Education, 69*(2), 6–11.

Spindler, G. (1955). *Education and anthropology.* Palo Alto, CA: Stanford University Press.

Stairs, A. (1994). The cultural negotiation of indigenous education: Between microethnography and model-building. *Peabody Journal of Education, 69*(2), 154–171.

Swisher, K. (1993). From passive to active:.Research in Indian country. *Tribal College, 4,* 4–5.

Taba, H. (1962). *Curriculum development: Theory and practice.* New York: Harcourt, Brace and World.

Trueba, H. (1989). *Raising silent voices: Educating the linguistic minorities for the twenty-first century.* New York: Newbury House.

U.S. Department of Education (1991). Indian nations at risk: An educational strategy for action. *Final report of the Indian Nations at Risk Task Force.* Washington, DC: U.S. Department of Education.

U.S. Senate Select Committee (1969). *Indian education: A national tragedy, a national challenge.* Washington, DC: U.S. Government Printing Office.

Van Ness, H. (1982). Social control and social organization in an Alaskan Athabaskan classroom. In R. Barnhardt (Ed.), *Cross-cultural issues in Alaskan education* (Vol. 2, pp. 165–191). Fairbanks, AK: University of Alaska, Center for Cross-Cultural Studies.

Wahlberg, N. (1997). Teaching and preserving Yup'ik traditional literacy. In N. Hornberger (Ed.), *Indigenous literacies in the Americas: Language planning from the bottom up* (pp. 19-44). Berlin: Mouton de Gruyter.

Watahomigie, L. (1994). Bilingual/bicultural education at Peach Springs: A Hualapai way of schooling. *Peabody Journal of Education, 69*(2), 26–42.

Watahomigie, L. (1995). The power of American Indian parents and communities. *Bilingual Research Journal, 19*(1), 189–194.

Watson-Gegeo, K. (1994). *Educational Foundations* [Special Issue], *8*(2), 3–80.

Wax, M., Wax, R., & Dumont, R. (1964). *Formal education in an American Indian community.* [Special supplement]. *Social Problems, 11*(4).

Part II
Becoming a Teacher:
Overcoming Cultural Barriers

In chapters 2 through 4, we document the struggles of novice and experienced Yup'ik teachers as they find their niche. Each narrative embodies the conflicts between the culture of the school and the culture of the community, establishing schooling as contested space. This conflict occurs at the primary level of the teachers' identity.

These cases show quite vividly how school reform must not only include access to the teaching profession for underrepresented groups, but must go further to include the teachers' culture in schooling. Inclusion of the local communities, particularly elders, strengthened the teachers. Case after case shows how these teachers individually adapted to the culture of school, and at the same time, how the culture of the school slowly adapted toward the local culture.

Although these cases are culturally specific, they challenge fundamental beliefs concerning instruction. For example, these cases raise questions about and present alternatives to conducting the typical classroom discourse routine of "initiate, response, and evaluate" (IRE; Cazden, 1988).

CULTURE AS A DEFICIT

Mohatt's introduction to the first two cases situates them within the field of indigenous educational research and its impact on practice. In the 1960s, when he first began his professional career, the dominant research and school improvement paradigm was "culture as a deficit." Sometimes the students from this "other" group were represented as the "disadvantaged." This meant, quite simply, that minority students, families, and communities, and, by implication, minority teachers had deficits that compensatory education would remediate. (For a similar discussion, see Ladson-Billings, 1994). The cases in this book show that teacher preparation and school leadership, to a degree, continue to adhere to this outdated model of theory and practice. But more important, they provide guidance to school and university scholars by showing how the school must not only accommodate to the other but fundamentally change its culture to include other ways of relating, inquiring, and evaluating. In chapter 2 by Mohatt and Sharp, issues of language continuity and the place of Yup'ik language in schooling are the dominant themes. Elsewhere (Lipka, 1994; Sharp, 1994) we analyzed a university–community–school partnership, concerning the feasibility of Yup'ik being the language of instruction. This relationship burst asunder when Lipka, the principal investigator of the project, was asked to leave because he challenged the school's being out of compliance with its own bilingual plan (Lipka, 1994) and because he strongly supported local people's efforts to gain an immersion program. Despite this or possibly because of it, the school district established a Yup'ik language of instruction program. This program continues to this day. Sharp's perseverance with the support of others has translated into numerous changes in her classroom and in the school's relationship with the community.

In particular, chapter 3 by Mohatt and Parker shows the power of the specific school context and culture. Here we compare an indigenous-controlled school with an Alaska state–controlled school. This reveals fundamental differences in the two schools' culture. These differences show the need for school change that authentically connect indigenous and minority teachers with their students and community.

In chapter 4, Dull's narrative and Nelson-Barber's analysis explores Dull's initiation into the teaching profession. Her attempts to be a "teacher" result in a deepening personal and cultural chasm between herself, the students, and the community. Eventually she finds ways to be "Vicki" and establishes a more authentic relationship with the students. Germane to these cases is the establishment of the Ciulistet teacher's group. It was only within the private and safe space of the group that the teachers were able to collectively discuss their individual teaching concerns. This sharing led inevitably to some of the common problems they shared. They struggled with how to be both an authentic Yup'ik person and a professional teacher. Although the group provided a safe zone, this work was and is not without its risks for the persons involved (Lipka & McCarty, 1994). The very presentation of these cases involves risk because the very telling of this story is a critique of schooling, and most are still teachers living in their respective communities.

In summary, school reform in schools and communities such as the ones this book reports requires more than Sarason (1996) and other school change "experts" suggest. Such fundamentally taken-for-granted expectations such as speaking in one's first language, using everyday knowledge, and relating in ways acceptable to the community. As the history of American Indians/Alaska Natives indicates, these are the very essences of one's identity, yet all of these were challenged by the place called school. This story is not new; what is new is the perseverance of the group and the individual teacher's narratives that show how a marginalized group can reshape the culture of school.

REFERENCES

Cazden, C. (1988). *Classroom Discourse*. Portsmouth, NH: Heinemann.

Ladson-Billing, G. (1994). *Dreamkeepers: Successful teachers of African American children*. San Francisco: Jossey-Bass Publishers.

Lipka, J. (1994). Language, power, and pedagogy: Whose school is it anyway? *Peabody Journal of Education, 69*(2), 71–93.

Lipka, J., & McCarty, T. (1994). Changing the culture of schooling: Navajo and Yup'ik cases. *Anthropology and Education Quarterly, 25*(3), 266–284.

Sarason, S. (1996). *Revisiting "The culture of the school and the problem of change."* New York: Teachers College Press.

Sharp, N. (1994). Caknernarqutet. *Peabody Journal of Education, 69*(2), 6–11.

2 The Evolution and Development of a Yup'ik Teacher

Gerald V. Mohatt
University of Alaska, Fairbanks
Nancy Sharp
Ciulistet Group

GERALD MOHATT: LEARNING TO SEE AND FORMING RELATIONSHIPS

The first time I traveled on an airplane was in November of 1968. I went to the Rosebud Sioux Indian reservation in South Dakota, in order to discuss with the principal of the Jesuit school what I would teach in January when I would become a replacement middle school teacher. He said that I would teach math, religion, and social studies. I returned to St. Louis for my final exams and thesis defense for my M.S. in psychology. In January of 1969, I flew for the second time in my life, from St. Louis to Pierre, South Dakota.

I arrived on a Saturday and drove the 110 miles to the Jesuit Mission. Excited and full of energy, I met with the principal to check my schedule. To my shock and chagrin, he told me that I would teach math, religion, and Sioux History and Culture. I was prepared for the first two, but I knew nothing—and had no clue of what to teach—about Sioux History and Culture. I prepared and prepared, read every book I could in 2 days, and was ready for Monday's class. The children listened to my stories about a certain event in the Lakota history. Eyes were glued on me. Their interest seemed high, but then the first day was over and the future confronted me. How could I teach what I did not know?

As the semester moved on, I discovered that prepared or ill prepared, I simply could not engage the children in conversation or discussion. We would complete a math game during which they vied for a chance to take a turn. They ran to the blackboard to answer the problem or correct a fellow student. They chattered to each other about the correct solution to a problem. As soon as I stopped the game, had everyone return to their rows and seats, and began to query them about the concepts, I met silence. This became the characteristic pattern—silence, dropped heads, no physical movement, and not a word. I spoke to the other teachers and they told me that this was the "Sioux way." Some told me that the Sioux were shy and reticent people. Others told me that there were many troubled children in the class. Some said that the children could not delay gratification and think of the future, so they just did not want to learn. I found myself reading contemporary theorists on minority education, trying to understand what was happening in my classroom. They all viewed the minority cultures as the problem. They spoke of economic, social, and cultural disadvantage (Coleman et al., 1966). According to these writers, minority children lacked the English language, books, adults reading to them, stimulating toys, privacy in their homes, the ability to travel and exposure to the wider world, and many other advantages associated with American mainstream culture. Children lacked a good self-concept and saw themselves as negative and worthless. They experienced significant anomie (Bryde, 1977). They almost all argued that schools and the government should build both compensatory programs to make up for these deficits by building early skills and advantages in the society, and early educational programs such as Headstart.

During my first semester, Fuchs and Havinghurst (1973) and their graduate students were studying Indian children and schools throughout the United States, and our school was in their sample. I was able to talk to the social scientists involved in the project for their views. Their data began to challenge some of the prevailing "deficit views" of education. They discovered that Indian children in fact may not have had low self-concepts. In self-concept tests that related to questions about future opportunity, such as "I have a good chance to finish high school," the children realistically appraised their opportunities and knew what their chances were in certain spheres of activity. Poor self-concept was not some internal psychological state arising because of disadvantage; but instead, a social situation in which Indian children were involved in a complex interaction between societal circumstances, power relationships, and individual perceptions. I, however, continued to vacillate between an outsider perspective based on prevailing notions of psychological states as outcomes of oppression or disadvantage and some incipient views that questioned this perspective.

Then an event happened that changed my views about why my students were so silent and reticent in my class. I taught in a classroom that had two doors. One went outside and one went into a small gymnasium where the children play basketball. One day during recess, I went back into the cloak room on the gymnasium side to get some papers, and I heard conversation in my classroom. Being curious and snoopy, I decided to listen before I walked in. I looked through the crack in the door. At the front of the classroom were three of my quietest students. Two were sitting in desks in the front of the class and the other was teaching them. The one that was teaching was imitating me perfectly. She spoke my form of standard

English. She used my gestures, including my characteristic pulling up of my pants, which always seemed to be too loose. The other girls asked questions of her about math problems, and then they switched to Sioux history and asked questions in very clear, voluble standard English. I was shocked. Why are these adolescent girls so competent in this play situation, and not in my class? I remembered that they always came up to me after class and talked and talked with no reticence whatsoever. What was it about my classroom that prevented them from demonstrating to me their knowledge of English, math, or their own history and culture?

I attended Harvard in the summers and worked on my research when I returned to my teaching and school psychology position during 1968 and 1969. My work was focused on the psychological variables of self-concept, time formation, early childhood memories and pathology, and interactive style. In this research I found no significant self-concept problems. I also found that the interactive style of Sioux adolescents was instrumental rather than cooperative or cognitive/abstract. In simple terms, they were more interested in figuring out how to solve a problem by doing and getting it done than by talking about it to other people and working it out with them. I did not publish this work because at the time it did not appear to me to say anything of significance. I was wrong. It pointed to the problems that plagued our thinking about the whole area of inquiry. I was still looking at deficits and not focusing on assets and differences. I still failed to see the power of context in preventing children from opportunities to function instrumentally.

I began to see the importance of context and that the children and their families seemed to lack the power to shape the institutions that served them. In 1970, I turned to working in communities to change the power relationships at a macro level and to build indigenous institutions. The Jesuit school had already decided to turn over control to a Lakota board by 1969. My focus was on other community projects. With the leadership and encouragement of a Sioux group of elders, I helped begin an Indian college. I taught in the college as we struggled to finance it and to gain accreditation. In these classes, I experienced with adults many of the same behaviors characteristic of the younger children. Watching the Jesuit school change from Jesuit control to Indian control gave me a dose of realism. It certainly seemed that the more the school changed the more it remained the same. The Indian board chose to keep the same name that history had provided. The teachers seemed to come from the same places as they had before. The discourse about classrooms and ways of teaching remained the same. Superintendents were all non-Lakota. When a Lakota principal came to the school, he precipitated a rash of suspicion on the part of both the community and the school. He seemed to be held to a different, higher standard. The level of incompetence tolerated among non-Indian administrators did not seem to raise the same ire.

It was not until 1973, when I returned to Harvard as a doctoral student and met Frederick Erickson, Peter Lenrow, and Vickie Steinetz, that I was exposed to a literature and a way of thinking about culture and institutional settings that began to answer my questions. I knew that the administrative and board composition of

Indian schools was changing, but discovered from Sarason's (1971) work the concept of the culture of the school. Sarason focused my thoughts on the perduring nature of the culture of teachers and their classrooms. I discovered from Erickson that cultural differences impacted the way in which teachers organized their classrooms. Culture was more than language and material culture; it was social and interactional. I saw for the first time that classrooms were social organizations with rules for how one demonstrated that they were communicatively competent. The idea of communicative competence was new to me. It made the link for me between what I saw in Sioux homes and what I experienced in my own and colleagues' classrooms. In everyday Sioux life, children spoke frequently, joked, demonstrated subtle word play and humor, and had a beautifully descriptive first language. Adults told them stories in their home. They had a whole prairie on which to play, and they constructed interesting toys out of materials in their homes. I began to see that they listened in ways I didn't understand. Their lack of movement when they listened made me repeat what I said, because I thought no one understood. What I did not know was that I continually communicated to the students that I thought they were incompetent. They felt uncomfortable with my continual questioning. I felt uncomfortable with their refusal to speak quickly and directly after the question or their immobility while they listened—no head nodding from these children or adults. Erickson's powerful videotapes of cross-cultural counseling dyads in Chicago and of a multicultural classroom in Newton, Massachusetts, forced me to examine these phenomena as differences in culture rather than as deficits in the children.

I learned to try to adapt my teaching, but I realized that I would never have the facility that a person within the culture had. I wondered what differences actually did exist between a classroom taught by Indian and non-Indian teachers. If, as I believed, the hypothesis of cultural differences in social organization was central to how Indian students perform and demonstrate their competence in a classroom, one should see differences in the way classrooms were organized by Indian or Caucasian teachers. There were no active Indian teachers on Rosebud at the time, so I looked other places and found a school in Ontario where Native people had been teaching for years. There was a Native principal, and the control of the school was rapidly transitioning to local control. Erickson and I initiated a study in 1978 of two teachers in this school (Erickson & Mohatt, 1982; Mohatt & Erickson, 1981). It was one of the first pieces of sociolinguistic and microethnographic research applied to Native contexts and has helped to raise issues of cultural compatibility in classrooms as a key element in school reform by discovering consistent differences between the way in which a Native and a Euro-Canadian teacher organized teaching and learning.

Critical to this research was the commitment to apply it to the education of teachers for Native schools. For five summers I taught a course to teachers of Native students (the majority were First Nations teachers or preservice teachers) based on this research. Many in-services were done both in Canada and the United States using this early research as a point of departure for discussing how to structure instruction for children of various cultures. The work in Canada continued in many different iterations as the relationship between myself and this community continued and continues. Simultaneously with the attention to the sociolinguistic context of classrooms, I read Seymour Sarason (1971) who called my attention to schools as organizations in which the problem of change was a problem of culture. Focus on massive changes on the organizational level often ignored the culture of the classroom and its perduring, if not intransigent, character. A focus on reform had to deal with this shared, transmitted culture that was reinforced and passed down by generation after generation of teachers. Sarason's work helped explain for me why the process of change at the St. Francis Indian School seemed so powerfully stuck in time. His work on the development of settings and the problem of change provided critical concepts for why we, who were creating this new college, found it so difficult to create new models for teaching and learning. We felt intense pressure to replicate the failed models of organizational structure and classroom interaction of mainstream universities and colleges. In order to gain credibility we seemed to embrace conformity (Mohatt, 1978).

For a variety of family and professional reasons, I left the Rosebud in 1983 after 15 years and came to Alaska to serve as Dean of the College of Human and Rural Development of the University of Alaska Fairbanks. Part of the attraction of this job was the strong tradition of sociolinguistics, anthropology, and education applied to Native schools in Alaska. Faculty members Scollons, Barnhardt, Kleinfeld, Van Ness, Esmailka, Orvik, and Oleksa all conducted projects that posed questions about how Native children learned in their everyday lives, and how these methods applied to the ways they learn in school. All of these researchers tried to find ways that schools could work better for Native people. My purpose was to help to develop a setting in a mainstream university that could serve Native people in a way that other schools had not. It would need to honor the cultures, the ways of knowing and seeing, and the knowledge by integrating it into the university knowledge base. The bifurcation of Western and indigenous knowledge could yield to a synthetic, at times, and parallel, at other times, process of cross-cultural education.

As Dean I met a talented faculty, many of whom lived and worked in rural Alaska, preparing Native peoples to become teachers through the Cross-Cultural Educational Development Program (X-CED). One of these individuals, the principal author of this volume, Jerry Lipka, introduced me to his students and graduates in the Yup'ik region of southwestern Alaska. I attended his student meetings and discussed with the students their work in these schools. Later, after observing some Yup'ik teacher aides at work, I was struck by the ways in which their strategies differed from those of the Odawa, Sioux, and Caucasian teachers I had known. The Yup'ik aides utilized more direct questioning techniques and often praised the students more than I had experienced with Sioux or Odawa teachers, yet they also were slower paced, and they organized classrooms around small group and individual work more than the Caucasian teachers did.

Lipka proposed building a support and research group of Yup'ik teachers and current education students in his area, in order to differentiate the unique pedagogical methods of Yup'ik teachers. He asked me to assist in this project, both through personal involvement and funding from the college. Through this group, Nancy Sharp, Fannie Parker, and I came to know each other and finally to collaborate on the chapters in this book. We began to videotape classrooms, discuss the methodology we observed, and ask consultants to present their work. Lipka and Ilutsik became the core leaders of the group. I was able to support it and engaged in the sociolinguistic research that I enjoyed. On a personal level, this time was an oasis in the midst of a busy and intense administrative position. On a professional level, the work allowed a relationship between Yup'ik communities and teachers and me to grow and allowed for my own practice of collaborative and participatory research. Rather than being a remote dean committed simply to administrative efficiency, I hoped to model a leader who could engage in a type of practice with Native communities that would both inform me and model collaborative research for those with whom I worked.

The research we conducted was truly collaborative in nature. It went well beyond models of action or ethnographic research to become a process of human and community development. Yup'ik teachers were only beginning to enter the school system. They were both welcomed and treated as objects of suspicion. Administrators feared that if they hired Native teachers, they could never dismiss a poor or unsuccessful teacher. Teachers from outside feared that they would lose their job security. Community members wondered if the Yup'ik teachers could ever be as good as White teachers. The existing culture of the schools had formed over nearly a century of church and state collaboration. The model was assimilation. I have called it "virtuous assimilation," because it seemed that the policy of the state as a whole agreed that the most virtuous Alaska Native was the fully assimilated one, who would then be equal. Equality was defined as linguistic and cultural sameness. The goal was to supplant the language of the community with English. Yup'ik and Yup'ik culture was the province of the home and community; English, the "standard form," was the province of the school. The community had accepted this model and, although uneasy with it, they were suspicious of change (Darnell & Hoem, 1996).

In this context, Lipka prepared indigenous teachers. He had lived in the region 11 years and had become part of the families and communities. He and the X-CED program tried to prepare them to become not "teachers," but "Yup'ik teachers." This created, and continues to create, suspicion among educators both in the school districts and in the university. The predominant feeling among many educators is that a good teacher and good teaching are not ethnically or contextually specific, but universal. Cultural differences are eschewed as surface factors. Lipka and the group of Yup'ik teachers, the Ciulistet group, refused to accept this model. Their work inevitably became a process of personal, social, and institutional change. The following case, written by Sharp and myself, presents these processes in her life. I have been fortunate to work with her and the group in bringing this study to readers interested in finding ways to build schools that develop the human potential of indigenous children.

Context of the Current Work

Nancy Sharp is a Yup'ik teacher who has taught in southwestern Alaska for 19 years. This chapter describes her struggle to achieve a way of teaching she can call her own. After her narrative, we examine in more detail what factors helped shape her as a teacher. These include the indigenous methods of teaching and learning she acquired at home and in her village, how she was expected to learn and perform in school, what she was exposed to in teacher education, and what she learned from her years of experience both as an aide and as a teacher. Her development was not one of simple dichotomies between home and community or home and university. University courses helped her differentiate her own way in contrast to the Euro-American way of teaching. Her professional formation highlights a complex journey of personal and cultural development that does not end with the day she became a teacher or with this telling. Rather, she tells of a continuing struggle to be a Yup'ik teacher, to maintain Yup'ik as the language of the community and the children, and to insure a strong Yup'ik identity for all her students. Because this telling took place over many years, interviews, and meetings recorded and transcribed, this chapter is a compilation and synthesis.

We began recording our discussions to reflect on the microethnographic aspects of Sharp's teaching and the social organization of her instruction. As Sharp, Lipka, and I talked among ourselves, we found her story resonated with what we had heard from indigenous teachers throughout Yup'ik country and in other indigenous contexts. Many have repeated that the institutional setting in which they teach demands that they put away their cultures in their most basic and primary forms if they wish to become and remain teachers. One Native teacher recently told me that she was encouraged for years to become a teacher, but now finds that the schools invariably hire an outside non-Native teacher rather than her. She is perplexed and frustrated.[1]

With only a few exceptions, such as the Lower Kuskokwim School District, Alaskan school districts have characteristically considered it unadvisable or unnecessary to use Yup'ik as the formal language of instruction. Sharp shows us that she used her language while teaching in order to clarify material, even though the institutional culture of the school discouraged the use of Yup'ik either as a medium for clarification or for informal social interactions between children. The culture of the school is defined by the teachers and the school leaders, who are very often outsiders, non-Natives who do not speak or understand Yup'ik. They are uncomfortable when students speak in their own language, and at times suspect the children are talking about them. Additionally, many teachers, policymakers, and parents believe that speaking the Native language interferes with the children's formal learning.

---

[1]Mrs. Vera Weiser, an Athabascan teacher, cannot find employment although she has taught for years. Wendy Esmailka has written a moving story about Vera and three other Native Alaskans' struggles to achieve a university education as her PhD dissertation at Michigan State University.

The school where Sharp teaches demanded that Yup'ik teachers teach like non-Native teachers. This "ideal" way of teaching consists of behaviors considered universal by the school administrators and by outside teachers. The contention of this chapter and, ultimately, this book is that they are far from universal. Rather, the so-called "ideal" way of teaching is constructed from the everyday social interaction of Euro-American cultures, which have formed the pedagogical theory and curricular methods of American schools.

However, the conflict is not only at the intercultural level. Sharp vividly presents the conflict she experienced in becoming a professional in her own community due to the reactions and expectations of that community. She expands our understanding of the ways Yup'ik communities and families have changed and are changing; the ambivalence of many to retaining their own language; the fear elders feel that the bedrock of their culture is eroding; and the sense of ambivalence the community feels toward the evolution of their own professionals.

This chapter focuses on the evolution of one Yup'ik teacher's ability to teach in a way that she defines as fitting herself and her students. The tools she used to grow as a Yup'ik teacher are multiple; the support of a family and village; that of her husband, Ferdinand, already a teacher; and her formal Western education, including her relationship over many years with her mentor, friend, and colleague, Dr. Jerry Lipka. Sharp also possesses a tenacity, or psychological strength, and an intelligence that allowed her to apply the needed political leverage to force change in the schools.

A Note on Methodology

This first person narrative by and about Sharp was created from interviews conducted sometimes by Lipka, and sometimes by myself, from transcriptions of Ciulistet group meetings, and from case materials she wrote for this chapter. Sharp commented and revised several drafts of this text. Meetings with us allowed her to review the materials, insuring that the sequence and form were accurate and true to her voice, and that the text reflected her psychological sense of her evolution and development. Because the story was collected over time, this synthesis and collaboration were essential to a coherent and progressive presentation.

It is important that this research occurred in the context of a field-based teacher education program with over 20 years' commitment to the people of the southwestern Bristol Bay area, Alaska. Lipka served as the only university faculty member living within this region. His and the college's commitment to developing a cadre of Yup'ik teachers that could transform the context of schooling in this region are the backdrop for the story. This research is part of a collaborative process of change and development, not simply researchers coming in to work with informants over a short or long period of time. In fact, without the relationships existing between Lipka, Sharp, and the other members of the Ciulistet group, and without X-CED in the region, my own work would never have occurred. This process, then, of research, teaching, professional and social support, and professional development were reciprocal activities. They occurred in the context of efforts to change the composition of the teaching force in the local district in order to increase the numbers of indigenous teachers and to improve schools for Yup'ik children.

Sharp presented the following narrative with some trepidation. It is impossible to completely disguise people and places, and she feared that political repercussions might occur as a result of putting her story on paper. However, the risk is worth the telling. Sharp felt that the future can and must learn from the past, and that the persistence of her language is the key to the vitality of her people's future.

NANCY SHARP: CAKNERNARQUTET[2]

I am happy to have an opportunity to share this. My education has been a struggle. I have been climbing a mountain and overcoming a mountain; only then I would find another mountain, then a valley.

I entered school at a late age. I was 7 years old and spoke Yup'ik. My early years of schooling were in English. In grade school, I was taught only in English and hardly had a chance to speak, because this language was not my language. My language was Yup'ik. At home our family spoke fully in Yup'ik. My parents spoke Yup'ik, so the only time I heard English was in school. In school, my own tongue was shunned. As a result, my involvement in learning was not full fledged. Some days I would want to ask the teacher a question, such as what she meant by a word. However, before I could ask her, she would go on in her lesson. So my grade school was entirely in English. I really wish now it could have been in Yup'ik, because I could have been further along in my learning and I would have had a more complete education.

High school was also all in English. I went to a private boarding school. However, high school was not as much of a struggle—one of those valleys, or going down the mountain, I think. There I had friends I could go to and ask questions in Yup'ik to find out about the content. They were older, or understood the material and could explain it to me. During high school, my peer group would say that I was a "pure Yup'ik" because I would pronounce hometowns using their real Yup'ik pronunciation. When my peers did this I would ask myself: "Who do they think *they* are?" It made me proud of my own language, but mainly made me wonder who did they think they were—*kass'aq* or Yup'ik or something in between. This was interesting because it came up again later.

After I graduated from high school, I was asked if I was interested in becoming a bilingual instructor. I took the offer. I had met my future husband in 1970 and we were married in 1973. I worked one year after we were married and then moved on to other villages. Because my husband was a teacher, we had to move to where the

---

[2]A shorter narration with the same theme and material (Lipka, 1994) appears in the Winter 1994 version of the *Peabody Education Journal of Education*. The literal English translation is "the things that struggle me or that make me struggle."

jobs were available. We went to Platinum. My husband had graduated from X-CED and was the first Yup'ik person to teach in Platinum. The community was all Yup'ik, but they had lost their language, or were on the verge of losing it. The older folks were all speaking Yup'ik, but the children spoke only English. I was startled that they claimed themselves as *kass'aqs*, but were pure Yup'ik. They were ashamed to try to speak Yup'ik. We lived right next to the school, and my sister lived with us for the year. We spoke only Yup'ik in everyday life between my sister, my husband, and me. The students would hear us speaking Yup'ik all of the time, so by the end of the year many of the students were no longer ashamed either to speak, or learn to speak, Yup'ik. My husband and I felt we had really done something good for those students because they began to identify themselves as Yup'ik and acquired their own language.

In Platinum we had another experience that was sort of funny. In Platinum there was a geologist. He came to the school one day after we had begun to work there. He knocked on the door and asked: "Who is the principal?" My husband isn't really tall and he looked very young. My husband said: "You are looking at him!" I guess the geologist was looking for a tall *kass'aq* teacher and thought Ferdinand was a student. This is pretty typical of my experience in the schools and with many *kass'aqs*. They just could not imagine a teacher and principal who was Yup'ik.

It seemed to me that the only way I could change things is if I were to become a teacher. As the years went by, my aide jobs varied from year to year. I was a teacher aide, classroom aide, Title I aide, and special education aide. I was asked, during this time, if I wanted to join the X-CED program to become a teacher and study both in the village and on campus as well. While I was an aide I used to yearn to have a class of my own so that I could try out what I had learned. I wanted to handle some of the things that were happening in the classroom in my own ways. As an aide, I felt I had no strong voice in the educational process. I felt pushed around to do whatever pleased the certified teacher who, obviously, was never a Yup'ik.

Sure, while I was an aide I did what I was directed to do; however, I questioned the methods and approaches to teaching. As an example, I did not approve of the DISTAR approach. I just could not stand their idea of time. They forced one to rush through the lesson. Nothing was done on the student's pace, but the lesson forced the students to work a given amount of time and finish all of the material whether they were tired or not, ready or whatever. There was no variation to this. It was rigid.

As a result of these experiences, I decided that I would become a certified teacher. I entered X-CED. When I began to work on my certification, I began to understand the way that students learned. I became more aware that I needed to be more on the pace of students if I wanted to really help them. This was very important to me culturally. My teaching had to base itself on the students and their way of learning. Yet I held back my cultural view, or the methods I knew, even when I wanted to implement them. As an aide I had been pressured to use the Western style and approach. I still felt, during my days as an X-CED student, that I had to learn these Western ways, and I was hesitant to teach in my own cultural way. I studied in X-CED for 8 years and struggled again. It was mountains and valleys and back up the mountains. I struggled with English, and in some years, I wanted to drop out. But I had people that backed me. The person that really helped me was Jerry. He really helped me and never gave up on me.

One of the problems was from my own people. By going to college, some of the people would comment that I was becoming a *kass'aq*. That was hard to take. But in order to help the people, I had to learn the ways that the village people thought and I had to be a common person. There were also doubts from other people—the staff at the school. The staff, teachers, and administrators did not value and even doubted the worth of my learning. They would say I should teach in a city before I graduated, and afterwards. I would say, "I am not qualified to do so." I am qualified to teach in my own village where I can understand the children, have good connections with the people, and can relate well to the students. So I continued to work in X-CED and serve as an aide. After 8 years of studies taken in my village, I was certified in May of 1983. I felt a great sense of accomplishment—another valley. Now I would apply for my own classroom.

I applied for some positions to teach and to have my own classroom. I did not receive them. Rather, I was first hired as a special education aide, and then I asked for a contract as a teacher, but was not given one. That year I felt put down. I became frustrated because I had worked so hard to become a teacher of my own people and I could not get a job. So, I decided to politic for my position. I talked to school board members and the community advisory council members.[3] I told them I would like to have a chance to work in my own classroom.

At last, in the fall of 1985, I was hired as a regular classroom teacher. With much enthusiasm I prepared my classroom and lessons in the ways I was taught. What was good about it was that I could do what I longed to do—be on my own and make a difference among my people.

So I followed the district curriculum and taught in the Western tradition. What made it difficult was that I was married to the curriculum and the Western style of teaching. I knew that my principal was looking at me and expected me to follow these guidelines. I taught in English, even though my students were fluent in Yup'ik. I felt I had to present in English and explain in English because I was an "English" teacher.

This continued for quite a few years. In the first few years, I mainly tried my best to teach like I had been taught so I would be accepted by all the other Western teachers. I feared teaching in my own way because I would be labeled as an unqualified teacher, or a nonteacher. So I put away my culture for a few years. I rewarded students by copying the Western teachers.

---

[3]Community School Committees or CSCS were established as the link between the community and the school. Each village has one. In addition there is a school board for the entire regional school district, in this case the Southwest Regional School District. The CSC has significant power in hiring and retaining teachers. At times, a regional school board member was also a resident of the community in which Nancy resided. She therefore had a number of ways in which she could influence the hiring decision.

One area that bothered me was the ideal way I was supposed to reward children. This was with great amounts of verbal praise. I felt this way of rewarding with bubbly praise was too much, but I felt I had to do it to be accepted by them and the principal. I wanted to show my colleagues that I too could have input and influence in raising the students' test scores. The other area was all of the content that just did not relate to our situation. For example, the reading books, they would use the word "lot" to teach different things in a story. Well, we don't have a village set out in lots so it was very hard to explain to them what a lot was. I don't think I truly understood it myself until I went to Philadelphia a little while ago and saw an empty lot. I immediately thought of the story in the book that was all about a lot. To me, we needed more content that related to the children's environment and culture so they could learn rapidly. *Kass'aq* people would probably be mad if all their reading books had material that their kids knew nothing about.

As the years passed and I got to know my colleagues, I was more able to voice my own views and the values of my culture. I began to believe and know my ideas about teaching were different from other educators around me. I began to practice my culture and language. For example, I didn't really stress to the students that they all sit and perk up their ears and watch me. When students enter the classroom, they work on whatever I encourage them to do or they feel comfortable doing. This almost always relates to what they had done in previous classes. It is my view that people want to get to their work when they enter. Waiting for a lesson to begin seems to kill the child's willingness to learn or work. In our community, some elders do not like to wait. They want to get to work or do it right away. Because of this cultural tradition—I believe it is in our blood—I begin my day in this manner.

I give my students choices with this free time. This, then, is also part of my reward system. In the area of rewards, I stopped all of the sticker awards and started to talk to the students in Yup'ik about their work. I gave them free time, so their reward would be an opportunity to learn more, to get to work, and to make their own choices.

As we changed the school and began the new immersion program, things really began to progress. Now I can converse with the children in their mother tongue and explain lessons in the language they know well. I can now get feedback from students in their own language and know if they understand the concept. In a sense, I feel I have a rich learning environment going on in English and in Yup'ik, choices and free time, group work and lessons. I feel very comfortable in this situation that I have created. It is more mine than what I had previously.

My relatives have shown respect that I am a teacher of their kind. For example, my aunt says; *elitnauristet maklagtutulit* (teachers who eat seal meat). So I am a bridge for my people. Also, I know that when I deal with my students in my Yup'ik way, I feel more comfortable and not so stressed, because I am not afraid to implement my Yup'ik way. My students communicate more freely and openly participate because there is commonality. As the years have progressed, I have read and been exposed to other cultural traditions, and with the help of these outside researchers I am beginning to feel more empowered. For example, Kathy Au's KEEP project really helped me in this area, by making me have a sense that other traditions can value their culture, use it to create ways of teaching, and base a classroom on the children's pace and values.[4]

But there is still a fear or a portion of my heart that tells me not to tell totally the honest feeling or truth of what is happening to us as Native teachers. I still fear putting forth our true style of teaching, because we fear that we will lose our positions. Also, we hold back some of our voice because of this fear.

You know, there is a difference between the old culture and the new. I'm in between and must combine those differences and see in what ways I can be a better teacher for my students. Some of the things they did a long time ago people don't do anymore, but there is a connection behind how we do things, even if we don't need to do it. The children need to know this. A good example was how I taught the students about hunting squirrels and making squirrel parkas, and how the principal interacted with us. I asked my mom to come in and she did. I also asked the principal to come in and observe us. I knew my mom was uncomfortable, but I told her she could tell the students how they used to use the hides and the whole process. But she got turned off because of the way the principal came in to videotape. It looked like it was for his own benefit. He asked us questions and interfered with the students' learning. He took over the classroom and the students started to pay more attention to him. These were first graders. I did the same thing with the second graders and he was not there, so it went a lot better. They asked many questions. Mom answered them, and the kids learned how to kill and skin a squirrel and about making a parka. I did not even know how to skin a squirrel so we all learned, and we learned the deeper meanings. Well, not only did the principal videotape the first graders for his own benefit, but he commented afterward that I must not really be a Yup'ik because I did not know how. That really put me down.

It is part of this problem we always face in both the school and community, that as teachers we should know everything. If Ferdinand didn't know a certain thing, an elder would say "you should know because you are a teacher." But there is a different system now. Teachers used to do everything for the village, and the people got the idea that teachers know everything. So it is difficult to have the community making these demands and the principal expecting that you should know everything about your culture. No one knows everything.

But back to the squirrels: I think Mom would have been much different if the principal had not been asking questions for his own benefit—if it was for the school, rather than for his own tape. He did not show, or offer to show, his tape to us. In essence, I guess it is back to the principal's school.

Now, if we had a Yup'ik principal, maybe he would not have schedules with certain times for the people to come to the school. They could come whenever they were ready to share with the students or teachers. Unfortunately, most of the time,

---

[4]Kathy Au, who was one of the leaders in creating the Kamameha reading project in Hawaii, visited the region and Manokotak, and worked with the Ciulistet group during 1992.

it is a set time. This is not a real welcome. The elders feel now that they would disturb the class. We need to get them to the point that they can work alongside the children. This would really encourage the students. But many of the parents have this idea that if you come to the school to help, you should get paid. Teaching is *your* job, they think. They have not really seen that the learning is not just in the school, but at home too. But I think some are slowly seeing that they have to start at home.

Now there once was another principal that really bridged the gap between community and school. He did more because he would go to birthday feasts. He would go to lunch and eat in the birthday places. He was the only one who would go out and spend time with the men. He even went to the homes to pick up the students. He was actually more strict, but also more open. Although his wife did not go out, he really went out and the people were more open.

Too many of the teachers still stay in their compounds and keep their curtains closed and don't even open their windows. They only go for special education reasons, like to set up an Individual Program Review (IPR). This is not really open communication. When the principal was open and visited the village, I think the people came more because, I guess, they felt more welcome there. He was a common kind of person. Even in the school he treated all of the teachers as a whole and met with us at times as a group. He did not always split the elementary from the secondary. We had a chance for input about the high school, and they about the elementary. I think this is more on the Yup'ik people's side, more like our way.

There are other things about teaching that are more Yup'ik. Now that I teach in Yup'ik, I see that we teach by repetition, by doing it over and over. I do not like the phonetics way of teaching, with things broken out step by step, teaching the vowels and then the consonants, and so forth. Rather, I teach it with the content. You teach the language while you are learning about something relevant, or even when you are doing math. For instance, I teach handwriting to the kids while they are learning Yup'ik, not as a separate lesson. Also, I don't teach the alphabet separately, but while they are learning words, sentences, how to write something that expresses something.

To me it is slowing them down to do it separately. I think I'm teaching them at a faster pace because it is not just teaching sounds and writing, but assuming they have the sounds. It is their own language. They may not have the connection, but I think they will start seeing it as they hear it over and over in different words, instead of pinpointing it as this or that.

I think that the base in Yup'ik must come first, before they get to English. The children need one language as a base and they are Yup'ik. If the community wants it, then they should be taught in Yup'ik. I think they have no identity without their language. Just like with my relatives; I tell them "you should learn your language, you're not a *kass'aq*."

Well, now it is beginning to change in our community because of the Yup'ik immersion schooling. Even in the community, now we hear comments about how the children can sing fully in Yup'ik. The students seem to be really opening up and the community is really impressed. Yup'ik also has very long words. In fact, a sentence is contained in one verb. When we do math in Yup'ik, the students will learn a word problem and comment, "Wow, that's a long word. Write it up there." They want to count the letters. They had one word with 26 letters that they could write and pronounce. They are very proud of their accomplishments in this area. In the second grade, we are spending time saying all the words beginning with an A. We make up stories. We write sentences, paragraphs. They are having fun. So, to me, English will become easier because of this experience. I see it in one of the students I know well. She seems to make more progress in her one hour of English than students used to when they had all English.

We do have continuing problems getting the immersion program started and on firm ground. We need more in-service in second-language learning. The school has been reluctant to do this. We need materials, so we need time to develop curriculum or to go to other places, like LKSD[5], and find good curriculum to use. It is hard to do it all at once.

We still have some doubts from the other teachers, but actually the experience of the principal's children in Yup'ik immersion helped. The principal's wife learned to sympathize with Yup'ik children when her daughter came home and told them how difficult it was for her to learn when she had to ask the teacher all of the time how to pronounce a word or what a word meant. She told her mother how she understood now how tough it was for the Yup'ik children to learn in English. It is this type of understanding we need. But too often, the teachers blame us Native teachers. They blame the behavior of the kids on us, or on those children who are not learning. They blame it on the children's language and say that it is interfering with their learning. Like Evelyn said, (another Yup'ik teacher), they never complained when the kass'aqs were teaching the kids in English and they were not learning. The children enjoy being with us and also being taught in Yup'ik. We do not shout and holler. Another Yup'ik teacher, Margie, said, shouting and domineering turns the kids off. I agree with Evelyn that it makes the kids feel dumb. Like she says, the classroom teacher is screaming, as if he is angry. The kids almost whimper and the teacher can't really hear them, so then the teacher complains about the kids. I don't see why. It's wrong to teach like this. Margie told us in the meeting once that a teacher must be able to confront the problems in the classroom and not send the kids off to the principal all of the time. She never sent a kid to the office. It would be as if she was a mother and sent her own child away to be treated harshly. It is not our style. Another Yup'ik teacher, Vickie, made a nice comparison at the meeting. Parents don't send their kids to a babysitter to fix a problem. They fix it. We have to accept the kids and believe in them. We counsel the children in our own

---

[5]LKSD stands for Lower Kuskokwim School District which is in Southwestern Alaska and serves the largest number of first language Yup'ik students in Alaska. They have distinguish themselves in both Yup'ik immersion programs and in developing local Yup'ik paraprofessionals and high school graduates for teaching positions.

classrooms. The fact of the matter is that the children just don't trust *kass'aq* teachers. The principals and *kass'aq* teachers have to trust the Yup'ik teachers to help them. They need to seek some advice from us.

This year they seem to have begun to tolerate Yup'ik being spoken in the classroom more. Before, the *kass'aq* teachers felt like they were being talked about, and they corrected the kids and told them to speak English. They think that only practicing English over and over from the first day of school will teach the students English. We see a different way, and when our way is used, the students will speak both languages well. They will know who they are as Yup'ik and speak English without shame or confusion. I have become less fearful. Even if I hear comments, I feel they just don't understand what teaching is. I don't mess around because I don't want to get into arguments or anything like that. Sooner or later they may change. I think there are some who still think that teaching in Yup'ik is slowing the children down, but I have seen the positive outcomes. That's why I really keep fighting, even if others aren't pressing forward for immersion and teaching in the Yup'ik way.

At present, having taught in my own classroom since 1985, I know I have great opportunities to enhance the learning of my own people. I can help the children open their eyes and minds so they can go on in education with fewer obstacles. However, since 1990–1991, the improvement of our schools has really begun. We had a number of meetings that year among international experts in bilingual and multicultural education, our top administrators of the school district, and our principal. These meetings opened their eyes, and they saw that our town needs to comply with Title VII by creating a true bilingual program for Yup'ik-speaking children.

So we began a bilingual Yup'ik immersion program. We teach the children all subjects in Yup'ik and have English one period a day. I have always known my people should be taught first in the language they understand, so they can learn English with more confidence.

I have no fear of fighting on for the survival and use of the language even if I am labeled a pure Yup'ik person. I am a pure Yup'ik, educated a little to understand the world around me, and still acquiring knowledge about what and how I should teach. I will continue to learn. I will continue to teach in my own tongue, whether it is in school or at home. I have no shame in speaking my own language.

My classroom now is totally in Yup'ik, with the exception of English words that can be translated into Yup'ik and some English that cannot be translated into Yup'ik. Some Yup'ik can't be translated into English without losing the meaning or flavor, so I use Yup'ik. But the students hear me speak in English in the hall to them or someone Yup'ik, and they tell me "*yug'tun*" in Yup'ik. So I know that they realize that there are two languages and that we can learn and use both. This is the way it should be, with students understanding that they can learn and speak in different languages and feel strong in their own.

The second and third graders who have begun this new immersion program in Manokotak are now fluent in speaking and writing Yup'ik. They write in a 5 minute fast writing exercise in a smooth flow that is unbelievable. It is readable writing with less misspelled words than they had in English. Students are wearing out pencils faster than when I taught in English. Students are writing with a nonstop pencil in Yup'ik, in contrast to English, in which the pencil used to pause in search of the next English word to use. So I call my students "little professors" because they are writing with such a smooth flow.

There are some who say that technology will take over teaching. But I say that the students must be self-confident, speaking, writing, and reading with people talking their own language. This is the first year that I have had special education children in my classroom. You can see them write and compose. They had been sloppy and now have become neat. I really wonder what these children would have been like if I had them all the time. Some *kass'aq* teachers are placing Yup'ik-speaking children in lower levels because they do not see that the children do not understand English. These teachers don't understand the students' responses, or why they do not answer at all. So some of the *kass'aq* teachers say they are dumb, label them as "handicapped," and place them in special education.

Some of the kids I see in my classroom who are considered slow are very fluent in our language, and I know they are smart. The boy who wrote this story about the mouse hunting for food because he had nothing to eat, is smart. His guardians don't speak English and it is not his first language. Yet this boy, who is in special education, responds in the old Yup'ik language when I talk about Yup'ik stories. When I have a question, he tells me the answer. He is a tremendous help in teaching Yup'ik, but because he is slow in English he is labeled as "handicapped." Now the special education teacher sees these changes and wants Yup'ik teaching for all of her children.

Yet there are still obstacles along the way from people in the village and district who speak only English or parents who don't really understand the education of a child. Once when I was explaining ptarmigan snaring as a way of teaching science in one of our bilingual conferences, one of the school board members from our district left without hearing all I had to say. After that particular session, I met him outside our hotel. He said, "Because I can get lots of ptarmigan with a gun, I left without listening." He did not listen to all of my speech on teaching how to snare because he has the use of a gun to obtain game.

I responded to him: "But you did not listen on how it is taught and how it can be helpful to the students. I know you can get game with a gun and catch lots. But to teach the old ways—if something happens to them in the wilderness they will know how not to be hungry. That is why we are teaching."

For the school, we now have to document what we teach, what materials we use, how we use them, when, and so forth. Also, blocks are put in the way of asking elders to teach. We must go through the principal and he tells us that we must write a "need." But I have broken this chain of command and gone ahead and invited an elder to help me teach. It went very well. As a result of this experience, I believe that the community needs to be educated about the contribution they can make to the school, about what they can teach or the information they can give that will benefit the students. This is really important for the elders to do before it dies with them.

Another problem area that I consider a put down to both the program and me is that the top ranking people in the district will tell me that I will not be teaching bilingually all of my life. I disagree. I *will* teach bilingually all of my life because it is in my blood. I may not be a teacher or working in a school all of my life, but teaching in Yup'ik sure will be in my home.

Today my language in school is not a "Jack in the box." It is "out of the box." I appreciate my language more now because I am proud to see the confidence in my students' learning. They know when to switch languages and types of speaking in terms of to whom they are speaking. So I strongly believe I am helping my own people become educated. In fact, one of my colleagues who speaks Yup'ik commented that she too is almost understanding or having a little glimpse of the way we can teach and the culturally unique way of our teaching.

In conclusion, I want to thank everyone that has educated me and helped me see the two worlds of my educational system. I am a very rich person. I have my education in my own language and another in English. I say, "But they have learned a lot because they have learned two languages. In the future they can learn more." I tell my students, "You have learned your own language and you have learned this other language. Because of it, you will go to college, or even get a doctor's degree." They will be able to obtain diplomas or write books. These children have a good chance.

GERALD MOHATT: DILEMMAS AND STRUGGLES

Implicit in Sharp's use of the metaphor of valleys and mountains is that success and problems, as well as relief and struggle, coexist. Sharp teaches currently in Yup'ik, but her achievement feels very fragile. It is juxtaposed with the lukewarm reception of the school administration and their failure to provide the time, materials, consultation, and training necessary to guarantee a serious effort and the commitment of the school to bilingual and bicultural literacy. Some members of the community continue to be ambivalent. Struggle is constant and cyclical.

A major theme in Sharp's life has been commitment and service to her Yup'ik people, her role and contributions as an insider. She desired to teach in order to make a difference for the children. She could connect, network, involve the families, and understand the children. While she was a student in school and later as an aide, she understood how school impacts the children's sense of Yup'ik identity. She experienced, particularly in one community, how she and her husband could make a difference in the children's sense of identity and their pride in that identity.

Her story repeats her desire to help students value themselves as Yup'ik. She used culturally oriented content, helped students connect school with their everyday life, disciplined and rewarded in ways that fit the children as Yup'ik, and taught in Yup'ik. Sharp believed that if she taught in this manner, the children would learn all subjects faster and become proud of themselves.

However, she did what only a Yup'ik teacher could do—taught in a Yup'ik way and modeled the best of being a Yup'ik—and all the while the village communicated doubts about whether she herself was acting like a *kass'aq*. They seemed to see her as being, or trying to become, better than the people of the village and, at the same time, as remaining inferior to a kass'aq teacher. She vividly communicates her sense of confusion.

She recalled that this confusion began with her earliest experiences with schooling. As a student, Sharp confronted an alien system called a classroom that was decontextualized, not shaped by her village. Both the village and the school can be considered a mirror for differentiating and forming new aspects of the self. Lacan (1977), Muller and Richardson (1982), Muller (1996), Winnicott (1971), and Sullivan (1953) considered the earliest formation of the self as being based on the reflected appraisals of significant others. However, as Lacan noted, these reflections can be like a mirror that is concave and, therefore, not true to a person's visage, but reflecting a distortion. The idea of the mutual recognition through the intersubjective process of interaction with significant others, such as the "gaze" and the recognition of a smile, and how this process has the power to construct the self, to become the experience of empathy is well described by semiotics (Muller, 1996).

Becker (1974) similarly discussed character as a "vital lie" designed to protect our cultures from the truth of mortality. The self then is formed around a distortion; the truth of the "other" is substituted for finding one's own sense of the world. As a result, human beings struggle to remove these distortions in order to form a sense of coherence (Antonovsky, 1980) that is derived from the views, appraisals, and desires of others and balanced with each person's idiosyncratic desires. However, most of the psychoanalytic literature ignores the application of these concepts after the formation of the self in infancy and early childhood. Becker, in contrast, described how culture, national ethos, and family systems influence the continual reinforcement and development of mirror experiences throughout life. Such experiences either reinforce or conflict with the earlier formation of a coherent system of self in context. This fundamental dynamic of self-definition, involving a struggle of the outside to define interior perceptions and establish the ways in which a person relates to the world, is pivotal for understanding the confusion and pain experienced by Sharp. Her experience with the principal and his videotaping of her classroom with her mother teaching shows the way in which mutuality and sharing are denied and how the "gaze" becomes one way.

The contexts and cultures of her home, community, the university, and the school competed to define who she was as a person and as a teacher. It would appear the struggle was over which institutional culture would define her, which one would mirror and form her role identity as a teacher. Could this sense of a coherent self in the context of a school resonate with her identity as a Yup'ik? Could she create a new role as a Yup'ik teacher, or would the culture of the school or the fears of the community define her, a "Yup'ik teacher," as alien? Would the institutional culture say that Yup'ik teachers cannot have a coherent self congruent with who they are as a cultural being? We must realize that one becomes a coherent self in many contexts and that many "selves" exist. The question should be not who one is but where one is or with whom one is. But if Sharp and other Yup'ik teachers cannot be simultaneously in school and Yup'ik, then they are asked to change both the definition of their culture and their personal identity. The problem of identity is, therefore, not simply intrapersonal. Rather, it is social, interpersonal, and cultural; there is no institutional mirror called Yup'ik teaching and no Yup'ik institutional culture to define the Yup'ik teacher.

A theme throughout this case is not simply "Who am I?" but "What am I doing in this school?" and "Can this school change to accommodate me and my culture? Do I belong, and, if I do, can I only belong if I become behaviorally Caucasian? Can a school exist in this community and become a Yup'ik school?" In contrast to Ogbu's (1987, 1995) notion of school conflict being at the level of secondary culture, Sharp's experience was of conflict at the level of primary culture. This theme of conflict permeated her struggles while she attended college and graduated through X-CED, became a teacher, and built a Yup'ik classroom in content and process. Sharp saw a congruence between her struggle, that of the children, and that of Yup'ik teachers. Both groups were not simply being asked to behave in what social psychologists (Asch, 1946; Heider, 1958, Jones, Davis, & Gergen, 1961) call in-role behavior, (i.e., student and teacher), but they were pressured to change their definitions of self. Definition of the roles of teacher and school were not equally open to potential change by community and Native teachers. They, Yup'ik teachers, legitimately felt that schools did not want the teaching role to include the cultural knowledge, behaviors, and language of the indigenous community.

However, Sharp pushed the issue beyond intercultural conflict and resistance: She spoke clearly about how the Yup'ik community was split over the value of making culture and language part of the school.

This latter experience makes the issue of role and identity even more complex. Some villagers defined her in a way that placed her in a double bind: She should not act White, but if she acted as herself (Yup'ik), she was not considered a "real teacher," or not as good as the White teachers. She found the same bind in her dealings with other teachers and the administration of the school. She tried to teach the children to make a parka and was made to feel she failed because she was not "Yup'ik" enough. On the one hand, she should value the old culture, and, on the other, she was told the ability to hunt with a gun makes the old ways anachronistic and irrelevant. And Sharp knew that if she chose to teach like a *kass'aq*, she would teach in a way and in a language that failed to educate Yup'ik children successfully for the past century.

Given the context of schooling in Alaska, such pressures seem inevitable. The Alaska Department of Education report on assessments (1991) identified indigenous language speaking as correlated with low assessment test scores. Many of the school leaders blamed Yup'ik teachers, who speak a local English dialect, for these low scores, saying that they speak to the children in a nonstandard and accented English. Both the first language and the dialectical language are seen as impediments to learning good English. However, the nonstandard, accented, and dialectical English of Caucasian teachers from various regions of the United States is not questioned.[6] The pervasive message Native teachers received from Euro-American school leaders, reinforced by ambivalent community attitudes, is that to speak like *kass'aqs*, to behave like *kass'aqs*, to sit and pay attention like *kass'aqs*, should become their goal for students.

THE YUP'IK LANGUAGE IMMERSION PROGRAM

A detailed description of the development of the Manokotak immersion program is in Lipka (1994). Its development came out of meetings of the Ciulistet group as they thought about and debated the challenge—to not let their language die but to work to retain and develop it—given by Canadian Native people at the Mokakit conference. Ciulistet decided to develop a partnership with the school district and university to establish the immersion program. Funding was requested and received from the Alaska Schools Research Fund of the College of Rural Alaska, University of Alaska, Fairbanks. During a year-long process, the group brought in a number of outside consultants with expertise in bilingual and immersion programs to meet with the teachers, community, and school district. Deep rifts, which had always existed, became apparent in the discussions, such as "How can our children learn English through Yup'ik?; Yup'ik is only a community responsibility and should be taught in the home, not the school; What will happen to our non-Native teachers if we teach in Yup'ik?" Certainly these are only some of the questions revealing the tensions and rifts. The process became so polarized at one point that the school officials accused Lipka of "stirring trouble" among the local people. They asked him to leave the project. Although he left it "officially," he continued to work with the Ciulistet Group and community. Sharp and other members of the group and the elders took more responsibility and persisted in creating the program. The project continues today and now the group, the community, the school, and Lipka are working openly in a collaborative process. The content of the program is described fully in chapter 6.

---

[6]During a meeting of the president, chancellors, and leaders of the state school administrators in June of 1989, one of the superintendents stated this as one of their main problems with the way Native teachers were educated at the university. They came out of the university programs and still spoke dialectical (or "village") English and interacted socially in culturally patterned ways. They were not likely to model standard English and, therefore, the children would not learn it. He, and the others who spoke in support of this position, delivered this judgment in an accented, "cowboy" twang, sprinkled with their own nonlocal and nonstandard dialects.

Sharp has seen good reasons why the primary culture and language of her home community, in contrast to that of the majority culture, can serve to organize teaching and learning, as well as school governance and structure. Her successes with children in the immersion program substantiates this conviction. Although it is a fragile innovation, she knows that the immersion concept has created confident children able to shape their own and their community's future. Sharp points with pride to the on-grade-level and above-grade-level results of her students on the Central Yup'ik version of the Stanford Early School Achievement Test (SESAT) and how they maintain such achievement over time. Table 2.1 presents the Manokotak students' scores on the Yup'ik version of SESAT in environment, math, English letters, Eskimo sounds, and aural comprehension of Yup'ik. The scores reported in Table 2.1 are grade-equivalent scores for 1992–1993.

In 1994, the students continued to score on or near grade equivalent on the Yup'ik test: kindergarten was one year above the normed grade equivalent with a mean of 2.0, 2 months above in grade one with a mean of 2.2, and 3 months behind in grade two with a mean of 2.7. Sample size continues to be very small; therefore, changes are quite susceptible to skewing if one or two students have lower scores. The results confirm Sharp's belief in an image of student competence in contrast to that of the ITBS scores.

Further data on student growth and competence within a linguistic context that is appropriate for student learning comes from Yup'ik writing samples of first graders. The following stories were written as an exercise when Sharp talked to her students about the picture of the ptarmigan, a pigeon-like tundra bird:

> *Una yaquleq a' parkalam' angnituq tuai-i aiparkaminek piuq tuai-i tailininluni yaqu'gem house-aminun tuai'i irutalratek uliguayulim ulilglukek yaqulgek arpagalitek a-a-a-a-ikayki.*
>
> This bird does not have a partner. He is unhappy. He found his partner then he came to the bird's house. Then when they played hide and seek, a ghost who has a blanket covered them. The birds yelled a-a-a-a, help us.

Sharp stated that the children are becoming literate in Yup'ik because they know the language structure. They can present complex ideas such as in the story with multiple images and concepts. She believed they would be better able to contrast English with Yup'ik, and English would then become easier to learn. She felt that

TABLE 2.1

Manokotak SESAT/Yup'ik Test Results 1992-93

Pretest			Posttest	
Norm Actual	*n*		*Norm Actual*	*Change*
K 0.2	0.4 12		0.8 1.8	+1.4
1 1.2	1.6 13		1.8 2.1	+0.5
2 2.2	2.3 11		2.8 2.7	+0.4

the clear letter–sound relationship of Yup'ik would create less confusion for the students in becoming linguistically literate. She believed that every person, every child had the right to become literate in their home language and that that would build linguistic capacity in other languages.

Sharp saw her students blossoming, able to "move smoothly and quickly forward" with their writing. Some of the children were labeled incorrectly as "special ed" because the teachers lacked an understanding of Yup'ik. She believed these special children were also growing and becoming competent in communicating beyond what had been expected of them. In each case, whether it was a mainstreamed student with a learning disability or a student at the highest level of performance, they were all growing. Sharp noted that "these students are thinking in Yup'ik … when reading a story to them in Yup'ik they can tell the story back in sequence. Ask them a question about the story and they respond with a higher level of question."

After a 20-year period, the Yup'ik teachers, aides, and students have their own language as the language of instruction. It is surpassing a "transitional" bilingual program as more time is dedicated to students, including those in higher grades, speaking in Yup'ik. Teachers can now use their mother tongue with pride to teach the highest concepts.

YUP'IK SCHOOLING AND PEDAGOGY

In the next section, we examine how Sharp defined Yup'ik schooling; the social organization of the classroom, the relationship to school and community, the language of instruction, the way that subject-specific content should be framed and taught. What we can discover in the changes that Sharp and other Yup'ik teachers have forged are changes in the culture of schooling (Sarason, 1971, 1996).

Relationship to the Community and Leadership

Sharp contrasted a number of school principals in terms of leadership and connectedness to the community. Principal number one extended himself out to the community. He went to birthday parties and visited with the people in their homes. During his time as a principal, he was seen as becoming part of the community; the community responded by finding the school welcoming. In contrast, Sharp too often found the teachers and principal walled off from the people. The closed curtains in the teachers' houses implied to the Yup'ik people fear, disinterest, even hostility. Sharp described a second principal's behavior when an elder visited her classroom to teach parka making. To her it appeared that this outside professional acted like a tourist. He asked to tape the class, but he did not explain what he intended to do with it, nor did he share the tape with the participants. He also alienated the teacher by criticizing her for not knowing how to make a squirrel parka. This one instance symbolized for Sharp the characteristic pattern of outside teachers; they remain distant from the people and appear unapproachable and temporary. They perceive themselves as outsiders as well; Sharp saw teachers repeatedly exhibit suspicion that they were being talked about when children spoke in Yup'ik. The contrast between the school leadership of a principal who connected to the people and one who did not is dramatic. Her most recent experiences of feeling the school as supportive and a lessening of the struggle was due to the new school principal and his support.

This theme of connectedness, implied inclusion rather than exclusion, is continued in Sharp's discussion of the principals' administrative practices. She indicated she found it distressing when a principal met separately with elementary or secondary teachers. Rather, she valued the principal who brought them together, including everyone in order to solve problems and keep them informed about each other's needs. He encouraged both levels to see themselves as part of the same school. To Sharp, a Yup'ik school would connect people within and outside of the school. Although noting that domains do exist in which each group must work on questions specific to elementary or secondary, the leadership she favored is one that fosters inclusion and connectedness and reduces exclusion, fragmentation, and isolation of teachers, students, staff, and the community.

Social Organization of the Classroom

Rewards, Praise, and Verbal Interactions. Sharp described her reward structures as less verbally effusive than those of her *kass'aq* colleagues. She did not say she refuses to praise, but she rejected the "bubbly" praise she heard used by outside teachers. She preferred to praise privately and only once, rather than in multiple verbal iterations. In our analysis of tapes contrasting Native and non-Native teachers, we have seen repeated examples of this. One will find a Western teacher using valuative praising (e.g., "good," "great," etc.) more frequently in a 10-minute period than a Yup'ik teacher in an entire class period. The data are so striking that one does not have to do percentages, ratios, or tests of significance. Sharp believed that the student should receive rewards such as free time at the beginning of the class, opportunities to work alone on projects if one gets one's work done, and encouragement through subtle nonverbal responses, such as raising of the eyebrows (meaning yes in Yup'ik), a single verbal praise, or repeating the correct answer.

Choice, Rhythm, and Responsibility. In analyzing tapes of Sharp's class, Mohatt and Lipka found that as the year progressed, it was difficult to determine when class began, because the children came into the room, went to their seats, and began immediately to work on projects. She would circulate, and at a certain point, begin a new segment of the lesson or a new lesson. She might signal this by a brief explanation at the front of the class or by separating the children into two groups and working with one group while the other children continued work at their desks. She quietly built an expectation in the children that the classroom was a time for work. This expectation was routinized to the point that she managed it with few verbal directions. As she indicated in her narrative, this use of time was both part of a reward system and of her sense that students could decide for themselves how to begin the day, and do so in an orderly manner without her verbal guidance. We observed a highly contextualized way of organizing classroom management that implied that the children on their own could learn and internalize a daily organization of the class without frequent verbal directions. Sharp provided them with the freedom to decide. She was, therefore, able to focus on each child's needs rather than wasting time making everyone follow her time frame through constant directions.

Sharp repeated the theme of how and who controls learning when she talked about her objections to DISTAR. It is based on directed instruction using an operant conditioning paradigm. Students must repeat correct answers quickly after the stimulus question and receive a reward with rapidity. Sharp's objection to DISTAR was twofold; pace and rigid homogeneity are controlled by the teacher. In contrast, she believed that space and time of the Yup'ik classroom should become the students'. The teacher must learn how to build a space for work to be done within the students' time frame while avoiding demanding that the students "sit and perk up their ears and watch me" (the teacher).

Verbal Control.   Another related theme is the use of the voice in controlling the classroom. A Yup'ik classroom teacher would not "holler or scream," but Sharp and the other Yup'ik teachers considered the voice tone and rhythm used by outside teachers as hollering and screaming. In addition, the Yup'ik teachers, including Sharp, felt that outside teachers use too many verbal directions. In our tape analysis, it was interesting to note that outside teachers who spoke softly, who had a well-organized routine in which the children knew what to do without being told, and who spoke in private face-to-face situations with the children received praise as good instructors from the Yup'ik teachers. Also interesting was that the perceptions of screaming seemed to have as much to do with the number of directions as with the volume of the speech. Phillips (1974) spoke of a similar phenomenon in the Warm Springs Indian Reservation in which students seemed saturated by so many verbal directions that it caused the children to become agitated. Sharp believed one should organize and manage a classroom with a parsimony of verbal directions. The rules should be clear, the routine predictable, and the children should be expected to follow this routine without continual direction by the teachers. One then organizes beginnings through having engaging activities waiting for the children and by moving from student to student to insure the organization is reestablished each day. Within this routine the children should have the flexibility to make decisions and the freedom to move to a different activity or to take a short time-out.

Sharp saw her work as building a predictable learning environment that maximized the children's responsibility for their own learning, that was verbally nonintrusive, that allowed the teacher to maintain connection with each student individually, and that paced speaking to be like what the students experienced at home.

It is important to note that her organization of the classroom included strategies used by both Euro-American and Yup'ik teachers. Sharp taught to the whole group. She had activities that they did in both small and large groups. She had students as a group observe, listen, recite, and answer questions. Sharp and the other Yup'ik teachers in the Ciulistet group saw the major contrast between Euro-American and Yup'ik teachers to be when, how, and why they, in contrast to Euro-American teachers, spoke to the children and how they demanded that the children speak to them; whether it was within an individual or group context and with a long or short pause between question and answer.

Content Teaching

Connections and Relationships.   In describing her criticisms of phonics-based reading programs and how she was taught to teach language, Sharp stressed that language was decontextualized. One taught sounds, words, and sequences with little reference to meaning. To her this method made language seem useless. She wanted to teach sounds in the context of words, sentences, and stories. Sentences should become part of something larger, and connections and relationships should rule the teaching. The purpose of language learning is so that the students can "write something that expresses something."

One must realize that within the context of the educational system, the new emphasis on whole-language learning and the writing project are all recent developments. Sharp's reactions, which are based on her cultural perspective, preceded these developments. The critical point is to realize that embedded within her primary culture was a linguistic and sociolinguistic system that accentuated context and relationship. It is an interesting side note to realize that more recent developments in the teaching of reading seem to resonate with her view.

Using the Context to Teach Depth.   Sharp contextualized her teaching to create meaning: Teaching the class about making the squirrel parka is a good example. Her lesson focused on both method and meaning: Students learned about the relationship of the animal world to humans, how the animals gave themselves so the people could stay warm, the way to treat and respect the animals, and how the people used these skins. She encouraged them to learn the whole process and the "why" of the process. She reiterated this same point in her statements that math must be made relevant to the children's world, and stressed it again in her discussion of their problems understanding the word lot. Connections between the familiar and unfamiliar are critical if the children are to understand subject matter.

SUMMARY: WHOSE SCHOOL WILL THIS BECOME?

Sharp's dilemmas are not simple, nor are they easily categorized. She tried to make her classroom and the school a place in which Yup'ik children can learn and graduate as Yup'ik. The place called school must welcome and sanction Yup'ik teachers to teach in the ways that are comfortable for both the teachers and the children, it must teach them literacy in both languages, and it must allow them to come of age proud and confident. She saw the process of schooling inextricably dependent on the existence of a cadre of Yup'ik professional educators.

Yup'ik teachers are related to the children and parents, and are part of the community and culture. Yup'ik teachers teach both Western and Yup'ik content. Yup'ik teachers use Western curricula, such as "Math our Way," computers, and so forth. Yup'ik teachers work with Euro-American colleagues and want to build relationships with them and to their world for the children. Indigenous ways of knowing and learning are valid and part of the school's norms. Domains mix, but the point of departure and the goals set rest on Yup'ik people creating a new synthesis of all of these aspects. This new synthesis will become their school. Western authors (Harris, 1992; Lipka, 1994; Stairs, 1992) have advocated that indigenous schools must be seen as third realities where all aspects of schooling are negotiated.

Through this process, the tradition of formal schooling and the traditions of the indigenous people will find coexistence and reciprocal nurturance. Steele (1991) called this type of schooling "wise schooling," if it is linked with demanding programs of study for African, Asian, Spanish and Native American children. When schooling is unwise, it submerges the traditions of these children, making them invisible. It reinforces stigmatization through low expectations and programs that label the children as slow, in need of remediation, or as only able to learn one language. In wise schooling, the culture, the child's competence, and the child him- or herself becomes visible. The wisdom of the home culture shapes the teaching and learning and the culture of the classroom, to create wise classrooms.

It is striking that Sharp's struggle on a personal level was marked by the threat she perceived: Unless she behaved as a Euro-American teacher she would become invisible. She would become a nonteacher. The image of the mirror is again helpful. Her perceived choices appeared to be: Look into the school's mirror and see a teacher who is not you, the Euro-American model—or teach as a Yup'ik teacher and see nothing. In this scenario, the mirror is controlled and dominated by images of Western teaching practices. It functions as the societal definition of the self in this context; outside this paradigm and setting it does not exist. Until recently, Yup'ik teachers have not had the freedom to create new images of teaching, new ways of organizing a school, and new ways to relate to the culture and community. It sounds simple to say "Well, one can change one's role and still be one's self at home." This severely limits the learning potential for the children, as Sharp so succinctly noted when she indicated that she was being encouraged to teach in a way that had historically failed her people.

The alternative rests in answering the question, "Whose school will it become?" This is linked to the creation by Yup'ik teachers, community, and the "outsiders" of a negotiated third reality—of a wise contemporary Yup'ik schooling and teachers. Our sense is, the defining quality of this type of school within the Yup'ik context is kinship and relatedness. Kinship within a village accentuates connectedness and relatedness. This connectedness and relationship will become the guiding principle for building a Yup'ik school that creates a place where the teachers "understand the children, have good connections with the people, and can relate well to the students." As Sharp related here, creating this type of school implies significant control and work at the site level. It demands what Sharp described as a "strong voice in the educational process." Much significance lies in Sharp's story. At a time when the stated demand remains high for minority teachers, the numbers are dwindling or flat at best. Her story gives us clues as to what schools and teacher preparation programs must address if the context of schooling and higher education is to welcome and graduate minority people. But the contribution of Sharp's success and struggle is to show how a place like school can change when a new culture of teachers and teaching can evolve. Reform takes places at the classroom level, supported and encouraged by the school leader. Such a simple process does focus the efforts on the key area in which change must occur—the classroom culture of schools.

REFERENCES

Alaska Department of Education. (1991). *Basic skills performance of Alaska's students.* Juneau, AK: Office of Data Management.

Antonovsky, A. (1980). *Health, stress, and coping.* San Francisco: Jossey-Bass.

Asch, S. (1946). Forming impressions of personality. *Journal of Abnormal and Social Psychology,* 41, 258–290.

Becker, E. (1974). The denial of death. New York: The Free Press.

Bryde, J. (1977). Indian students and guidance. *Guidance Monograph.* New York: Houghton-Mifflin.

Coleman, J. S., Campbell, E., Jobson, C., McOareland, J., Mood, A., Weinfeld, F., & York, R. (1966). *Equality of educational opportunity.* Washington, DC: Government Printing Office.

Darnell, F., & Hoem, A. (1996). *Taken to extremes: Education in the far north.* Oslo: Scandinavian University Press.

Erickson, F., & Mohatt, G. (1982). Cultural organization of participation structures in two classrooms of Indian Students. In G. Spindler (Ed.), Doing the ethnography of schooling (pp. 132–174). New York: Holt, Rinehart, & Winston.

Fuchs, E., & Havinghurst, R. J. (1973). *To live on this earth: American Indian education.* Garden City, NY: Anchor Books.

Harris, S. (1992). "Soft" and "hard" domain theory for bicultural education in indigenous groups. *Peabody Journal of Education, 69*(2), 140–154.

Heider, F. (1958). *The psychology of interpersonal relations.* New York: Wiley.

Jones, E., Davis, K., & Gergen, K. (1961). Role playing variations and their informational value for person perception. Journal of Abnormal and Social Psychology, 63, 302-310.

Lacan, J. (1977). *Ecrits* (Alan Sheridan, Trans.). New York: Norton. (Original work published in 1977)

Lipka, J. (1994). Language, power, and pedagogy: Whose school is it? *Peabody Journal of Education, 69*(2), 71–94.

Mohatt, G. (1978). *Final report: Study of Odawa and non-Native teachers.* Canada: Canadian Government, Department of Indian and Northern Affairs.

Mohatt, G., & Erickson, F. (1981). Cultural differences in teaching styles in an Odawa school: A sociolinguistic approach. In H. Trueba, H. Gutherie, & K. Au (Eds.), *Culture and the bilingual classroom* (pp. 105–120). Rowley, MA: Newbury House Publishers, Inc.

Muller, J., & Richardson, W. (1982). *Lacan and language: A reader's guide to ecrits.* New York: International Universities Press, Inc.

Muller, J. (1996). *Beyond the psychoanalytic dyad.* New York: Routledge.

Ogbu, J. (1995). Understanding cultural diversity in learning. In J. Banks, & C. Banks (Ed.), *The handbook on research on multicultural education* (pp. 582–593). New York: MacMillan.

Ogbu, J. (1987). Variability in minority school performance: A problem in search of an explanation. *Anthropology and Education Quarterly, 18*(4), 312–334.

Philips, S. (1974). Participant structures and communicative competence: Warm Springs children in community and classroom. In C. Cazdan, V. John, & D. Hymes (Eds.), Functions of language in the classroom (pp. 370–394). New York: Teacher's College Press.

Sarason, S. (1971). *The culture of the school and the problem of change.* Boston: Allyn & Bacon.

Sarason, S. (1996). *Revisiting "The culture of the school and the problem of change."* New York: Teacher's College Press.

Stairs, A. (1992). The cultural negotiation of indigenous education: Between microethnography and model-building. *Peabody Journal of Education, 69*(2), 154–172.

Steele, C. (1991). *Race and the schooling of Black Americans.* The Atlantic Monthly, 68–76.

Sullivan, H. (1953). An interpersonal theory of psychiatry. New York: Norton.

Winnicott, D.W. (1971). Playing and reality. London: Tavistock Publications.

3   Two Teachers, Two Contexts

Gerald V. Mohatt
University of Alaska, Fairbanks
Fannie Parker
Ciulistet Group

The current volume contends that relationships of power and culture shape teaching and learning outcomes in schools that serve indigenous children. The experiences related by Native teachers in these cases present the barriers they have experienced in defining themselves and their roles as teachers, the factors that lead to their persistence, and their frustrations in constructing indigenous schools in today's world. Our goal has been to sort out the relationships between the domains of classroom, community, culture, and the larger societal context of the school in order to better differentiate the factors that can make schools in indigenous and minority communities belong to these communities and work for more students.

Much literature on the schooling of minorities has debated the differential contribution of factors within the school in contrast to those outside the school. Ogbu (1987, 1995) articulated one of the strongest criticism of microethnographic approaches to explaining school failure among minorities. This project and similar research focused attention on changing the culture of the classroom to increase its compatibility with that of the students' cultural rules, particularly those for organizing learning and participation. Harris (1994), Ogbu (1987, 1995), Stairs (1994), Villegas (1991) all pointed to the limitations of this conceptualization, given the paucity of empirical data on its effectiveness in improving educational performance of minority children. They argued that the theory ignores the influence of factors outside the school and implies that significant change in methods of teaching minority children would in and of itself improve school performance. In contrast, these researchers pointed to the importance of understanding the relationships of power, status, and stigma (Steele, 1991), and how complex interactions of these factors influence the way children behave in school and thus create a culture of schooling. Although they do not ignore classroom variables, these researchers believe that these factors are created more from relationships external to, but represented in, the classroom than from primary cultural differences between classroom and home culture. They believe sociolinguists or cultural compatibility theorists, as they have labeled them, ignore these domains and the relationships between them. Therefore, they claim cultural compatibility theorists focus on only one aspect of schooling—one that has little chance to create significant change or to improve schools.

The following two cases delineate the teaching situations of two Native teachers in their respective classrooms. The case material describes, first, the lessons and why the teachers taught in the manner detailed, and, second, the context of each school in terms of the sociopolitical relationships of the school to the community. The results of the teaching were almost identical, even though the two teachers represent two different indigenous groups, two different epochs, and two different social and political contexts of schooling. Both lessons failed in the judgment of the respective teachers. The two teachers and their situations show how each defined how one should teach, who one must please, and a sense of who had the power to define the act of teaching. The cases show how their teaching was affected by who controlled the school and how the influence of the indigenous community was perceived by each teacher. The act of teaching and its results were analyzed microethnographically. Finally, this chapter describes fundamental ways in which the social organization of the classroom was structured and it relates the sociopolitical context of the school to how the teachers defined their roles.

The potential for building an indigenous pedagogy and a culturally negotiated school are both limited by power relationships at the societal level as well as enhanced by these relationships. We argued that culture in schooling and teaching is a constructed system, which is neither old nor new, Western nor indigenous, but a third reality in process. Social and political power and their influence on schooling are also not merely defined as an either/or. It is not simply a "we versus them" situation, a stark dichotomy of who controls the school. Rather the exercise of power and control is in the process of construction and evolution. We examine how it is either limited or enhanced when the power relationships between the school and community are either symmetrical or asymmetrical. This chapter argues that when differences between school and community exist both at the level of primary culture and political power, these differences maximize the conflicts experienced by both Native students and teachers in creating indigenous schools.

METHODOLOGY

Parker and I have known each other for the past 8 years. As noted in the previous chapter, I had worked with the Ciulistet group for 8 years. Parker agreed to work on the case with me and she furnished a tape of her teaching of the lesson she considered ineffective. We reviewed what did not work in the lesson and she related her experiences as both a student teacher and as a teacher. We met again in the spring of 1994 to discuss ways in which she had changed over the past 4 years of teaching and how she now structured her classrooms. She presents both past and present versions of herself as a teacher. Her experiences as a student teacher and as a teacher show that she possesses a new sense of power and control.

The Odawa teacher, Gertrude Trudeau, was videotaped as part of a Canadian Department of Indian and Northern Affairs grant (Mohatt, 1978) to study the social organization of classrooms of Indian and non-Indian teachers. The project also aimed to develop a series of summer courses for cross-cultural education of teachers in northern Ontario reserves. Additionally, interviews with Trudeau and the non-Native teachers were designed to identify reasons why they used particular strategies. Discussion of Trudeau's case is based on notes of interviews, as well as on my own recollections of the lesson. The cases are presented in two sections; first, the description of the lesson and its background for each teacher and, second, their responses to it. Parker presented her background as well as her analysis. It is, therefore, presented in this chapter, like her analysis, in narrative form.

FANNIE PARKER: A YUP'IK STUDENT TEACHER

I am a full-blooded Yup'ik Eskimo from Togiak, Alaska. My elementary years were in the Togiak school and secondary school was in Mt. Edgecumbe High School in Sitka, Alaska. I decided to become a teacher when I saw that helping my fellow Yup'ik people would be the most beneficial work I could do. I wanted to model what they could become. I had seen only *kass'aq* (White) teachers growing up and I wanted my people to know that we could do whatever we wanted. I also did have some teachers, when I was young, who were really nice to me and made me feel good. I knew I could do the same and even better. I also wanted to stay in my own village and live there. I did not want to move away and become a city person forever. Rather I wanted to work at home, and teaching was a wonderful opportunity to work right at home. When I decided to become a teacher, I already had a family with children. I saw that moving my whole family to Anchorage or Fairbanks to attend college would be too costly, so I looked into the Cross-Cultural Educational Development Program (X-CED). This is offered by the University of Alaska Fairbanks in the Bristol Bay region with an office in Dillingham, Alaska. This wonderful program allowed me to go to school in my village without leaving behind my family to attend a university.

I worked in the village as a secretary for the local corporation while taking the required courses. It took me 6 long, challenging years. The course work was more difficult in a way because my professors were hundreds of miles away and there was no face-to-face interaction, except through audio conferences and periodic student meetings. Learning to manage my time, to form a support group with fellow X-CED students, and studying were constant. My husband and family were the backbone of my schooling; my husband gave me 150% support and the whole family helped out with the household chores.

Finally, at the end of those 6 years, I was ready for student teaching. I was fortunate to be able to do this in Togiak. The Togiak School had 12 certified teachers (5 high school teachers and 7 elementary teachers). I was the only student teacher and Evelyn Yanez was the only Yup'ik teacher. Now I am a teacher and there are four Native teachers. To me this is progress, even though I look forward to the day when most of the teachers are Yup'ik. The main language spoken among the students was Yup'ik, with 70% Yup'ik and 30% English. From the first day of class as a student teacher I encouraged my students to speak to me anytime in Yup'ik. When they did this, I would always interpret it for my supervising teacher who was a non-Yup'ik and did not speak our language. Today this has changed. Now most children who come to school do not speak Yup'ik. They can understand it, but not speak it. This happened in only 4 short years.

My supervisor, the entire time of my student teaching, never left the classroom. He observed me daily and wrote a day-by-day journal, which he shared with me to let me know how I fared. By the end of my student teaching career, you can imagine the amount of papers my folder was full of.

I present a case from my student teaching in the fall of 1990. The three groups I student taught were the eighth-grade class, the ninth- through twelfth-grade English classes, and a beginning art class. I had two supervising teachers, but only one stayed in the classroom all of the time. In the classes there were approximately 11 eighth graders, 37 English students, and 12 art students. The study that I concentrate on is with the eighth-grade class. That classroom was a beautiful room with two eye-catching bulletin boards. The room was fully carpeted in a medium blue color, and classroom rules were written out in big, bold letters for all to see. The desks were set up in normal rows when I first entered. I immediately changed the desk arrangement to a half-circle with the teacher's podium in the middle. I describe two situations. The first is teaching of vocabulary words and the second is the review of vocabulary words and reading comprehension.

Lesson: Vocabulary Words

This followed a section during which a student presented the vocabulary words. They would write the word, definition, and one sentence down on the chalkboard using the word correctly. Then they would act it out in a play by choosing the students who would act out the play they created. My supervising teacher picked the best play and the winner was awarded a prize of goodies, like candy and gum. I structured this episode with the advice of my supervising teacher. Both this section and the following section on vocabulary word review and comprehension used the elicitation technique. I was instructed to use this technique by my supervising teacher. He gave me examples of how to do the technique, which was to call on the specific student and put them on the spot to answer a question.

[Transcription: T = teacher; S = student]

T: Okay, let's do a little review on vocabulary. If the police were coming here and took me away to the jailhouse, what, what would they be doing? Norine?

[Eight-second pause and no response.]

T: If you take someone, take them away, what's the word? Amy, you want to help her out?

S 2: [Amy whispers, "galleries"?]

T: No, it's not galleries. Sharol?

S 1: Confiscate.

T: Confiscating. Okay, if I worked really hard and just got my house spotless, the house would be very ... Emma, what's the word?

[Six-second pause with no student response.]

T: When it's really clean, it's ... ?

[S 1: No response.]

[S 2: She shrugs her shoulders to indicate her answer. This takes about 5 seconds.]

T: Merlin, do you remember the word?

[Four-second pause.]

S 3: No response from Merlin.

T: Amy?

[Twelve-second pause.]

S 4: Fastidiously?

T: Immaculate, fastidious is, is when, is when you're in a market place like Esther's mom who whenever she is out her hair must be in just a certain way. That was why she was fastidious. Okay, if I go into the gymnasium and am doing a lots of exercises, what am I doing, Mirth?

[S 5: No response and shakes her head.]

T: I run in place, I do jumping jacks, Jamie?

S 6: Calisthenics.

T: Calisthenics, okay ...

Vocabulary Review and Reading Comprehension

I came into the class and brought my chair to the center of the room and placed it in the front of the class. I then walked over and handed a student a piece of paper, then went back and sat down and began to teach.

T: Okay, so far in our book, Esther and her family have been captured by the Russian soldiers. What happened after that?

[Three-second pause.]

S 1: What?

T: What happened after they were captured by the Russians?

[Four-second pause.]

T: Okay, they were taken to another country. What was that country?

[Three-second pause with some verbalizations that are not intelligible.]

T: Siberia. Siberia is in Asia. Okay, Emma, when that really one quiet guy came in (takes about 5 seconds looking in the book). It starts with an M. Conrad Alexander Ivanova M. This guy is in charge. When he comes in and tells people where to go. Where are they told to go? Jamie?

[Six-second pause with no answer.]

T: They are given two places to go, either to the farm or to the mine. Where were Samuel, Anraya, and Esther told to go? [Looks over at the student to the right and says] Cheryl, do you remember?

[Two-second pause.]

S2: The mine.

T: The mine. What kind of mine was it? Mert?

[Four-second pause with no answer.]

T: It starts with a G. You didn't bring your book. You can share a book with Cheryl. Steven, What kind of a mine was it? It starts with a G. It's used in plaster; when I get hurt and if I break my leg and I'm taken to the hospital, the doctor puts this on my leg. Yeah, what's the name of it, it starts with a G. Remember the book told us what it was in chapter 4?

[Eight-second pause.]

T: Merlin, do you remember? Did you read your book, Merlin?

S3: Someone took it.

T: Someone took it? Okay, it was gypsum. Gypsum was a grayish-white powder dug out of the desolate land by a people in despair. [At this point the student teacher gets up and goes over to a student and says:] I need for you to sit up.

Teacher's Comments on the Lesson

Personally, I felt calling on the specific students and putting them on the spot was not a good idea because this was and is not a normal style of interacting in Yup'ik culture. The outcome held true, as one can see on the videotape. All of the students except one were called on, actually six students, but no responses were made by them.

I was not surprised when the students did not respond when called on individually and spotlighted, because it was obvious they were not used to this style of interacting. I felt it was not my place to be telling the supervising teacher how to teach. I was the student teacher. What did I know? I did not express any of my feelings because I thought it was not my place to say anything. My supervising teacher was the type of person that was very outspoken. Once he set his way, it must be done that way. Watching the videotape, I could say that the elicitation technique was not appropriate and another method should have been used with Yup'ik Eskimo children. The method should have been closely related to what they were used to or to something that was in their cultural way of speaking.

Initially, the Yup'ik way of communicating begins when someone has something of importance to say to the audience as a whole. Usually, the speaker starts by telling a story with a moral either hidden or shown. There is no one raising his voice or clapping hands to draw attention. Everyone respectfully sits down and gets ready to listen to the speaker or leader. Usually in the Yup'ik culture, when one wants a response from anyone in the audience, a question is asked to no one in general. Whoever answers the question correctly is accepted by the speaker or leader.

In contrast, the elicitation technique demanded that a particular student speak when called on. The results were clear when I used it. The students shrugged their shoulders, shook their heads, mouthed out "I don't want to answer," smiled, put their heads down, or simply refused to answer. My supervising teacher wanted this elicitation technique done his way because he felt those students were not outspoken enough and would not get a chance to speak unless a specific student was called on. He did suggest another method I used in the first segment. It was called "slotting," which simplified the clues to the vocabulary word. He showed me this and I thought this method was satisfactory. It broke the ice for most of the students who were nonverbal in the classroom.

Today, I feel that methods such as the elicitation technique are still considered the best ways to teach in our school. I sense that I am supposed to teach in this manner. But I have changed and my role is quite different. Now I am a teacher.

It was a struggle to become one. I remember vividly the 8th or 9th of May, 1991, the superintendent interviewed me for a teaching position. I had known him for many years. We were sitting there and he was asking questions, very casually, like how did you like your courses, what have you been doing? Then all of a sudden, he asked me "Are you fluent in English?" I thought he was kidding, so I asked him "Do you speak Yup'ik?" in a joking way, since I really thought he was joking. Then he asked again, "Do you speak English fluently?" I said "Yes, I do my best." Then I felt very uncomfortable. I wondered how he could ask me this question. We were sitting having a conversation in English! He had known me for many years!

He went into great detail comparing Yup'ik X-CED graduates with Anglo on-campus graduates. He gestured with both hands. He put his right hand higher than the other and said, "Here is an on-campus Anglo graduate." Then he lowered his left arm and said, "Here is an off-campus X-CED student."

I sat there for a few moments, said nothing, and then I said, "I am really surprised of this coming from you, because you helped start the X-CED program. I thought you really wanted to encourage us to stay in our homes and take the courses." I thought to myself I was very proud of being an X-CED student, proud of my accomplishment, of what I knew and could do.

Then he tried to get out of it by saying, "Oh, I don't mean you; it is not a bad program." But I assumed he meant we were dumber and stupider than the new kass'aq teachers.

So we sat there and completed a very long interview, 3½ or more hours. He asked things like, "If you are going to teach in a regular classroom will you use a literature-based curriculum?"

I said, "Any teacher has to look at the curriculum guide and teach what's in it. Then they can adapt it and supplement it with local knowledge."

He asked me about what I would teach. I told him that I likely would teach works such as Grapes of Wrath, Shakespeare's works, A Tale of Two Cities, and other American and international literature. I tried to give him a broad range. He kept asking me for more specifics. I thought I had been very specific. He then asked me about what I would teach of Yup'ik stories. I told him about the Yup'ik stories I would use, those that my parents and grandparents had told me, like how the beaver had gotten a flat tail. But he appeared to not believe I had enough knowledge, because he asked me the same question over and over. He seemed to test me continually. I had expected a test, but this was more than what I had expected.

So we went on and on. I felt terrible. I was exhausted. He grilled me repeatedly and when his questions finally dwindled down to talking about the weather, he still sat. He just continued to sit and talk. I finally got up, shook his hand, and told him thanks for all he had done for me and us. I left.

After it was over I felt truly awful. Jerry Lipka was in town so I went to talk to him. I felt like I had been demoted to a lower level of intellect. I wondered if that was why our Yup'ik teachers all had to begin their teaching careers in noncertificated positions even though they had their teaching certificate, whereas new *kass'aq* teachers came into the certificated positions. I wondered if he and the school thought of us as inferior, dumb, and stupid. But I survived, I got a certificated position in resource classrooms.

Now there are four of us in the school who are Yup'ik and we have the backing of the community so I feel comfortable. Even though I have only taught for 4 years on my own, I have begun to have much more confidence in myself and in my position. I am a real teacher and have the rights of any other teacher. So I teach the way I think best fits my students. Actually today I use the same technique, elicitation, with confidence. I have made it part of my teaching because I want my students to get used to spotlighting and rapid fire answering. They do not have to do this all day and change their whole way of behaving, but I tell them if they are going to make it in college or other places, they must be ready for this. So today I use it and feel comfortable with the technique. But when I had no power, I didn't like it. When I couldn't structure it the way I thought fit my students, I did it without confidence and you see what happened. I was lost and they were lost. Certainly today we are changing and my classroom reflects the changes. I use lots of different ways of teaching. I use Yup'ik and English. I think we have to prepare our students to be themselves and to be confident without feeling so shy when called on. That means I have to employ many techniques and some of them are not what we do at home. I think that is ok now, and I know that the parents want this also.

It is not always so supportive. Still there are criticisms of us, but for the most part, people here agree with this way of teaching. Maybe the school will become more and more of what we want. You know, I tend to be an optimistic person.

GERTRUDE TRUDEAU: AN ODAWA TEACHER

Gertrude Trudeau was a teacher with over 20 years of experience when I met her in the summer of 1974 while I was teaching a course on psychology and education in which she was enrolled. She was a member of the Wikemikong Unceded Band, an Ojibwe-Ottawa First Nations Reserve on Manitoulin Island, Ontario. The following fall she was asked to participate in a video project analyzing teaching from a sociolinguistic paradigm. Trudeau agreed because she wanted to learn more about her teaching. She asked me for assistance in other areas, such as the identification of dyslexia, as reciprocity for her work with us. The following year of 1976–1977, through a grant from the Canadian Department of Indian Affairs, the project was expanded to compare the way in which Trudeau organized her teaching with that of a Euro-Canadian teacher. The project taped over 40 hours of Trudeau and two Euro-Canadian teachers. Additionally, children were taped in home settings, and researchers visited public meetings and formal gatherings in the Native and Euro-Canadian communities, and interviewed the teachers in order to compare school and everyday settings. The two teachers taped, one Indian and one Euro-Canadian, were picked by the local Odawa principal who was asked to chose two good teachers. Both were successful in engaging the students and stimulated learning and growth in the students. Two "good" teachers were chosen in order to identify how culture influenced the ways teaching was organized.[1]

After each series of videotaping, the researchers and Trudeau met to view tape and discuss the organization of her classroom, why she did certain things, what were her underlying constructs for organizing teaching. During the first series of viewing sessions, I did not notice any lessons in which the first graders were taught reading. I wondered if I had missed them, so I asked Trudeau if the next time we scheduled taping, we could do so when she was doing a reading lesson. The following is a description of this lesson. The tape of this lesson was lost during an office move, so the verbatim transcription is unavailable. As indicated earlier, it is reconstructed from notes and from viewing other similar lessons. It is, therefore, a construction of the author.

Reading Lesson

The class was a group of eight grade-one[2] Ojibwe-Odawa children. The children were at a large table, which was created by arranging a number of desks. The children sat around this table and Trudeau stood in one location at the corner of the tables and carried out the lesson. She did not move during the lesson. The lesson taught the meaning of who, what, where, and when as applied to a particular story that all the children had read. Trudeau would ask the children individually and by name to identify which of the interrogatives was the right one for a particular piece of information. Prior to the questioning, she would read a sentence and identify the

---

[1]It is important to note this given that some critics mistakenly identified the differences examined in this research (Erickson and Mohatt, 1982; Mohatt & Erickson, 1981) as secondary differences. In these articles, the authors did not attempt to deal with the complex issue of culture and school success, but to find instances in which primary cultural differences were used to organize a classroom. These earlier articles, however, did raise questions about culture and school success that would bear further investigation. By choosing two teachers who were both successful, we were trying to look at school success in order not to confound our attempt to find cultural differences by choosing teachers who were mediocre or ineffective.

[2]During the description of the Canadian lesson, I refer to the grades as grade one, eight, and so forth, which is the Canadian convention.

appropriate interrogative. She would say, for example, "Johnny went home at 3:00 in the afternoon. I want to know WHEN did Johnny go home?" She would slightly raise her tone on "when." After a number of examples such as these, she began to question the children. She would say, "John ate the apple. Do you ask who, what, or when John was eating? Junior?" Another example was: "April went to the store yesterday. You want to ask April who, what, or when did she go to the store?" Trudeau then read the sentence and asked the child to identify whether this was a who, what, where, or when sentence. Jack slept all night. "Jack is ... ? Yvette? All night is ... ? Jimmy?"

The lesson was organized in the following way:

T: Question with name of student.

(No response, with typically a pause between 4 and 8 seconds.)

T: Rephrase the question and then ask another student.

(Same response pattern and pause period.)

T: Answer the question and explain: for example, "Jack is a who" or "all night is when" or "in the forest is a where."

This sequence was repeated throughout the lesson, which went on for about 30 minutes. During the lesson, Trudeau publicly chastised the students as a group for not paying attention or for not knowing the material. She never moved from where she was standing. This was in sharp contrast to Trudeau's typical teaching style in which she moved frequently and coordinated her movements with her voice in order to organize the classroom. In all of the other tapes we observed during our analysis, Trudeau seldom chastised the group as a whole. She also taught, typically, in very short segments to the whole group and used choral questioning and answering rather than individual questioning and answering.

When Erickson and I first viewed this tape, we were perplexed. We discovered that she had spent the whole lesson questioning individuals, only received the correct answers a fraction of the time, and only from someone other than the child queried. Unlike the smooth routinized teaching we had seen in earlier tapes, the children were confused and did not seem to understand the questions. With these questions in mind, I interviewed Trudeau to ask her what was happening and why it happened the way it did.

I asked her what she thought of the lesson, how she felt about it, and her general impressions. She indicated that she thought nothing had worked in the lesson. She said she felt ill at ease and stiff, and thought the students felt the same way. She knew they understood how to use the interrogative and understood the sentences in the book, but they appeared on the tape to look lost. I asked why she felt so sure of this, and she said she had given a worksheet, explained how to use it, went around to each student to review the process, asked questions about the content, and then returned to each child and found that they had identified the correct interrogative for the sentence. At this point I asked Trudeau why she thought the taped lesson went so poorly. She said she felt that the individual questioning and probing by calling on the children were methods they were not used to, and she did not feel comfortable using them. She indicated she too did not like this strategy of teaching.

I became more and more perplexed. Why was she doing something she obviously did not agree with or see as effective. Finally, I asked her why she taught this lesson in this manner. She indicated: "I thought you wanted me to teach reading." I said: "Yes, but I wanted you to teach it like you always taught reading." She then said: "I figured that you were asking me to teach reading like teachers are supposed to, like I was taught in teacher's college. So I just taught like I thought you wanted me to teach."

My next question was whether she ever used this technique normally. She said that she did not, nor did she intend to do so in the future. She explained that she typically did individual reading in small groups, asked the group questions about the reading, and then circulated to each student privately to do comprehension work or an exercise like the one on interrogatives. She said she often paired the students to work with each other in identifying the correct interrogative. I asked her how she had the freedom to teach in the way she considered best for the students, a way that contrasted with what she had been told in teacher's college. She said that all the faculty in the school were encouraged to arrange their teaching in ways that stimulated the children to speak. She said: "Sara, the principal, would not let us keep teaching the children the way I was. It puts them down."

She also said that she would use group questioning at times to do the entire comprehension part of the lesson, but she did not call on individual students. I asked her why she preferred these situations, and she responded that she had found that these were the situations in which the children spoke and showed her when they knew or did not know the material. I asked her if she thought this was based on her culture and the way she saw children taught at home, but she said she didn't really know.

During the project, we videotaped home situations such as an older sibling baking a cake and the younger ones watching her, children and adults interacting after school, or a family at dinner and watching TV. We found that in the home adults seldom called out to individual children, especially if they were across the room. Additionally, local teachers indicated that Odawa styles of teaching and learning allowed for private testing and experimentation after watching someone do something, such as baking a cake, fishing, and so forth, rather than forcing them to demonstrate their competence immediately after or during the teaching. They indicated that learning took place through less directive forms than those often seen in classrooms. Individuals were expected to learn by watching, without an adult singling out an individual.

Hardy, the husband of the local principal, told a very funny story that illustrated both this culturally based learning, as well as a little about local perspectives on the more Euro-Canadian and American style of teaching. One day he noticed Erickson teaching his son to fish. He related how Erickson explained that "this is a rod, this is a string, this is a hook." Erickson showed the child how to string the rod, bait the hook, and throw it out, explaining each step. As he told the story, Hardy imitated and changed Erickson's speech, slowing and drawing out the words. He considered this a very strange way to teach someone, and he wondered why Erickson didn't simply let the child do it independently after watching him do it for awhile; that, he said, was how his own children would learn to fish.

In short, evidence does exist from participant observation, videotapes, and interviews that spotlighting and the "elicitation" technique is culturally foreign to most Odawa children. In the case described here, Trudeau chose the teaching strategy, thinking it was the socially correct thing to do, an idea that originated from her perception that the power of the researcher took precedence over her definition of the teacher's role in this situation. She wanted to cooperate with the researchers by using an "appropriate" teaching technique. The context and occasion for the taping triggered a powerful set of social norms for her. This set defined the behavior of a teacher, even for a teacher with 20 years' experience. This old standard returned at the moment when the researcher used a set of words, "reading lesson," which she perceived meant the same thing for the researcher as it had for her instructors in the teacher's college. However, once the researcher left, she defined her role in a way that fit the children, and felt confident doing so. I asked Trudeau and her principal why she was able to teach in this way. Trudeau told me that she was supported by her principal. The principal told me the following story to illustrate the expectations—to create a culturally appropriate way of teaching—that existed in the school.

An experienced Euro-Canadian teacher came to the local Odawa school and began to teach. (He is in fact the second teacher compared in the 1981 Mohatt and Erickson study.) Early in his first week, the local principal observed him and noted that he had arranged the children in desks and rows, was lecturing, asking them questions, and having them go to the board to demonstrate their knowledge. She called him in after school and told him that "in their school the children did not sit in rows, but sat in circles." She advised him to rearrange the classroom so the children were in groups at tables. She indicated that teachers were expected to teach in a way that maximized student-to-student interaction. She said that the other experienced teachers would be good resources for him to observe and from whom he could learn. He returned to the classroom, changed the seating, and began to observe teachers, both Native and non-Native, who had taught for years in the community. His methods of teaching gradually changed over the years to resemble those of the indigenous and more experienced local teachers. The norm for the school had been set by the principal. She stipulated that the classroom should approximate the ways in which children learned in their home community and that children should feel comfortable in their classrooms. She expected teachers to organize their teaching to meet these goals, and she specifically suggested people from whom they could learn about the appropriate way to teach.

DISCUSSION

The Context of Schooling

The Yup'ik school and Odawa school each had local advisory boards whose members were predominantly indigenous, but there similarities ended. The Alaskan school functioned within a context and institutional culture in which much power was invested in the school superintendent, his administration, and a districtwide school board. Locally, the Alaskan school was in a village in which an advisory group had limited powers that did not allow it to govern the school. Instead it was one school among many in a large rural district.

In contrast, between 1974 and 1980, the Odawa school was controlled by the Department of Indian Affairs, which was beginning to relinquish more and more control to the local band council. In this particular school, the school council was also advisory, but had significant power over teacher retention and school management. The superintendent had much less power. He served more as a broker between the department and band than as a final authority. He also was charged with facilitating the process by which the local band took increasing control of the school at the community level. Although the larger geographic area had many bands in it, each was independent. There was no megadistrict formed to unite the various bands under one school board. Therefore, the exercise of power and leadership at both the building and community level was local.

In the Alaskan school, the principal was an outsider, as were the majority of the teachers. There was only one Native teacher in Togiak, but there are now four. In the Odawa community, the principal was Native and the faculty composition approached a 50–50 balance between Native and non-Native teachers. The difference in these contexts is best illustrated by comparing the two teachers in terms of their perceptions of power and control over what and how they taught—what was possible in their classroom. In Parker's case, she perceived correctly that power was lodged in a supervising teacher who represented the school. She believed that what she experienced as a student teacher was the norm for the school. She knew that she had, as a student teacher, very little freedom to create her own strategies for teaching, whether they reflected her Yup'ik culture or Euro-American culture. However, she also knew that there was no avenue to raise the issue of cultural compatibility, because the school defined itself at the instructional level by Euro-American standards for classroom organization. The context did not allow her to learn about culturally compatible teaching.

Today, she teaches the way she thinks is best, but feels that it is still contrary to the norm set by the principal, the superintendent, and the majority of the *kass'aq* teachers. However, she now feels that she has the power to organize the classroom in a way she thinks best fits the children. Her goal is to create a culture in the classroom that reflects the current demands placed on Yup'ik children. Her methods of teaching include both those she feels are rooted in her Yup'ik culture and those she has adapted from Euro-American pedagogy.

What has changed for her is both her role, from being a student teacher to an experienced teacher, and the context of schooling. More Native teachers are working in the school. She indicated that they support each other. The districtwide Ciulistet group supports Yup'ik-defined methods of teaching. Parker feels enough support and power from the local school advisory committee to risk being the kind of teacher she believes is best for Yup'ik children.

In Trudeau's case, she chose to teach as she thought we expected. This fact demonstrates the immense power of the expectations for the teaching role that non-Native professionals can trigger. She stopped teaching in this manner the minute the taping was over. Her sense of what she could do was structured by what she knew her school context expected and demanded.

The Context of Power

School norms are created through the interaction of many factors. Every school possesses a culture with historical precedents that have a life beyond the situation of the particular community in which it is situated. One is able to visit schools throughout the United States and Canada and find similarities that mark the national culture of each country's formal educational system. This is a formidable culture and one not easily changed. One must only read the literature on school change and improvement to understand the difficulties inherent in the process of changing such a culture through school reform (Brookover & Lazotte, 1979; Chubb & Moe, 1990; Coleman et al., 1966; Good & Brophy, 1986; Sarason, 1971, 1986; Stedman, 1987). Within Alaska, the culture of the school and its normative paradigm was well documented by Darnell in his 1979 report: " ... the premise was that members of western society knew what was best for indigenous minority people. The concept of cultural replacement, in one of its forms, was the prevailing reason given for initiating most programs" (p. 29).

The current cases point to the persistence and strength of this school culture, and they help to differentiate how it affects teaching in a cross-cultural situation. In the Odawa case, the teacher assumed that the teaching of reading meant the teaching of reading in a Western manner. The Yup'ik case elucidates how such an assumption could develop. Parker was instructed in the "correct" way of teaching, and no alternatives were presented. Once the lesson was completed, she was left alone to analyze why it did not work. Feedback she received focused on the application of the method. She felt that she was at fault. The method itself was not challenged by her cooperating teacher. The conflict between cultures was not considered, nor were the power relationships that existed between the majority institution and the community. Such consistent communication from supervisors—who symbolize and exercise gatekeeping power—that culturally incompatible methods are appropriate leads to the situation in which even a person with many years' experience, such as Trudeau, succumbs to its demands. The cases provide a window into how schools control the culture of teaching. They also show that indigenous teachers and student teachers possess cultural knowledge that can point to better ways of teaching. The tragedy in Togiak was that no one in the system even posed this as a question.

As Lipka indicated in an unpublished manuscript in 1991, the issue is not simply one of unequal and one-way control. Control is a prerequisite for negotiation between community and school. Such a process is necessary for teachers and students to create an indigenous school. An open-ended forum must develop in which school and community together construct a learning and teaching system in which questions about culture and teaching can serve as one of the central organizing principles. The unfortunate situation in most Alaskan districts is that indigenous teachers find themselves in schools in which little negotiation is taking place and the prerequisites for change and control at the community level still do not exist.

Control in Alaska typically exists only at a macro or district level. Parker's case shows that Native control is not simultaneously at a district, village, and classroom level. Only 4 of 17 teachers are Yup'ik. The local council is advisory. There has never been a Yup'ik principal in the history of the school. The mandate of the state and district, often accepted within the community, remains one of assimilation. Under this banner the state promises, implicitly and explicitly, that modernization and success in English schooling will make the community economically and politically self-sustaining and powerful. As a result of these factors, a systematic process of school development among all interested parties does not take place.

Currently, Parker and other Native teachers in Togiak are working to begin such a process. Discussions are beginning between teachers, the school board representatives, the principal, advisory council members, and the elders and parents of Togiak. Certainly differences exist. Some Yup'ik people believe the language and culture have no place in the school. Others believe all students should learn in Yup'ik as the language of instruction. Disagreements are inherent in any process of negotiated change. The question remains as to whether the power and control from the centralized, Euro-American school leadership will limit the range of alternatives that can be considered in this process of community-based school reform. Clearly, once Native teachers grow to a significant number, they have the potential to stimulate a process of such reform.

Trudeau's situation was very different from Parker's. In the late 1970s, local bands (the Canadian term for First Nations Tribes) in Canada were becoming more involved in the control of schools. A major report of the Minister of Indian Affairs called for bands to increase their control over all aspects of their political and social institutions. Local leaders on the Wikemikong Reserve were aggressive and strongly committed to this process of self-determinatioh. When the videos of Trudeau's class were made, it was clear to the local superintendent of education for the Department of Indian Affairs (DIA), that the band should control the school and that any decision made without their involvement would lead to resistance and conflict. He had served in another Indian school as it had become Indian controlled and understood the importance of such power issues. As a result of these social changes, a first step, the political context for exercising control, was present. The local Native leadership and a farsighted superintendent both simultaneously encouraged and supported this process. It was not without conflict, however; both the superintendent and the local Native leaders disagreed. They experienced great pressure and much conflict due to both double messages and resistance from the DIA. In addition, many local Native people suspected that establishing band control of the schools was another attempt by the government to eliminate local schools and send their students to area non-Native schools. In any case, the ethos of the political situation was different from what Parker experienced in Togiak. The goal of shifting from band-based control was acknowledged and in process at the community level in Ontario.

Therefore, the Native community in Ontario went beyond achieving control symbolized by the existence of a board or council. The band successfully advocated the hiring of Native teachers and a Native principal. The building leadership shifted from Euro-Canadian to Odawa. New school cultural norms were created, with the assistance of a cadre of Native and non-Native teachers who were encouraged to create learning that fit the children. They adapted and changed Western theories of pedagogy. The principal encouraged all teachers to use culturally appropriate classroom organizations. DIA administrators tried to support these policies and practices. The exercise of this control included board meetings and band council discussions; Odawa teachers organizing classrooms to reflect teaching methods congruent to styles and the organization of learning used in the Odawa community; and an Odawa principal socializing new Native and non-Native teachers, pushing them to examine their ways of teaching based on the culture of the community. Certainly a mix of more familiar Western forms of pedagogy and that of an indigenous pedagogy existed. All the participating teachers had been educated in Euro-Canadian universities. These critical events allowed change to occur through negotiation over time among all groups involved in the school. This process gave them a local mandate and a freedom to create new forms of schooling.

In contrast, the school leadership in Togiak reinforced and continues to reinforce a norm of Western-oriented teaching methods and curriculum, such as elicitation, Math Our Way, clinical teaching, cooperative learning, and whole language. In this context, we advocate for a process by which a school creates a mutually constructed learning system. Without such a process in place, Parker and other Native teachers in Togiak will continue to teach in their own ways, but they will find that these are discontinuous and anomalous with both the school's and the community's norms, and that their careers are often more difficult because of this choice.

Cultural Compatibility and Negotiated Schooling:
Limits for Compatibility

In two failed lessons, we have seen the persistence in each person of cultural forms of teaching. This is instructive given the tendency for some to believe that the consequence of cultural compatibility is effective teaching. Rather, we see that even when the method is culturally inappropriate, a Native teacher will structure it in a way that is culturally appropriate. Both teachers tried to make the methods work by interacting in a culturally appropriate way. However, the organization of the lesson did not fit the ways they interact. They created a culturally compatible interaction in a culturally incompatible organization and it failed. Compatibility at the level of social interactional style was insufficient in and of itself to produce an effective lesson. Parker provided long pauses rather than rapid intervention. She gave the spotlighted student time to think and to generate a response. She corrected the children privately by leaving her seat in the front and moving to talk to them about opening a book. She did not criticize the student for not having a book, but suggested sharing with another student. In Trudeau's case, she also called on and gave long pauses in contrast to the typical pause time of the non-Native teacher (Mohatt, 1978; Mohatt & Erickson, 1981). She did chastise the group, but did not criticize or correct individuals by name. She still reinforced the process of learning as one of relationship and group work.

This failed lesson is instructive, given the current debate about the importance of cultural compatibility for effective teaching. We believe that indigenous teachers can construct schools that meet their society's goals and also create literate and competent graduates. In order to do this, we believe educators must focus their questions about compatibility on examining the level at which it is expressed. Compatibility and congruence with the goals and actions of the society must exist at both a macro- and microlevel. Teachers must have the power to structure classroom organization, curricula, and social interaction and the relationships between parents and the school in culturally congruent ways.

The current volume calls on schools to negotiate all levels, including curriculum, content, personnel, leadership, community–school relationships, and classroom organization. To only negotiate one or two levels may allow Native teachers to effect only surface-level changes, in which teachers achieve an interactional level of compatibility as seen in both lessons. However, cultural compatibility must occur at the social, political, curricular, classroom teaching, and management levels. Parker clearly outlined and knew during student teaching the ways learning and teaching took place in her community. With the help of an expert teacher within the school who acknowledged her experiences, she could have used this knowledge to mold herself in a way of teaching compatible with her culture and could also have learned how to integrate the elicitation technique with her own style. Lipka also supervised her and supported her development of voice and confidence in her own way of teaching, but he was an outsider to the school.

Missing in most rural Alaskan schools is any significant realization of the positive potential of Native teachers to construct teaching and learning situations more effective than those typically expected by the school. The optimistic note is that the Odawa example shows that indigenous communities can achieve levels of power that will allow this creation of indigenous schooling to occur.

CONCLUSION

Lipka argued, in his 1991 report to the Alaska Schools Research Fund, that "School research in Native American communities consistently shows that if conflict and control issues predominate then the school performance will be negatively impacted" (p. 2). Parker's and Trudeau's cases show that this simultaneously remains a problem in one area of Alaska, and presents an alternative for Native communities and schools. Beyond their practical insights into the power of changing the norms and culture of the school, the cases have other implications.

No one factor can create school success and cultural compatibility. One must ask whether the school is culturally compatible. To answer this, we must look at multiple dimensions. One must understand congruence in terms of control issues; the locus of control, the culture of leadership, the freedom of teachers to develop culturally compatible methods and curriculum, and the school's ability or willingness to represent the wishes of the community. All factors are relevant. Without one part of the puzzle, the whole is incomplete. The two schools and two teachers vividly show us the importance of both control and the level at which it is exercised. The Odawa school shows us that a community can have a school congruent with its wishes for self-determination, and that self-determination can exist within the leadership and teaching force of the school. The people and the school are then free to design all aspects that constitute their school. If this is not done, then the talents and competence of teachers such as Parker are muted and limited.

This alternative is exciting. As Lipka (1991) said: "By combining expert–apprentice modeling, contextualizing education, connecting literacy to community, excellent possibilities for school improvement exists" (p. 47). Parker's talents would then become free to design and carry out programs congruent with the culture and ethos of the village. The direction of the future for indigenous education lies in directing its efforts toward a total redesign of all aspects of schooling to create 21st century indigenous schools that do not repeat the mistakes of the past century. With significant change in the power relationships between the dominant and indigenous societies, this is possible.

REFERENCES

Brookover, W. B., & Lazotte, L. W. (1979). *Changes in school characteristics coincident with changes in student achievement.* East Lansing: Institute For Research on Teaching. Michigan State University. (ERIC Document Reproduction Service No. ED 181 005).

Chubb, J. E., & Moe, T. (1990). *Politics, markets and America's schools.* Washington DC: The Brooking Institution.

Coleman, J. S., Campbell, E., Jobson, C., McOareland, J., Mood, A., Weingeld, F., & York, R. (1966). *Equality of educational opportunity.* Washington, DC: Government Printing Office.

Darnell, F. (1979). Education among Native peoples of Alaska. *Polar Record,* 19(122), 431–446.

Erickson, F., & Mohatt, G. (1982). Cultural organization of participation structures in two classrooms on Indian students. In G. Spineller (Ed.), *Doing the ethnography of schooling* (pp. 132–174). New York: Holt, Rinehart, & Winston.

Good, T., & Brophy, J. (1986). School effects. In M. C. Wittrock (Ed.), *Handbook of research on training* (pp. 570–602). New York: MacMillian.

Harris, S. (1994). "Soft" and "hard" domain theory for bicultural education in indigenous groups. *Peabody Journal of Education,* 69(2), 140–154.

Lipka, J. (1991). Report to the Alaska Schools Research Fund. Unpublished manuscript, Center for Cross-Cultural Studies, Fairbanks, Alaska.

Mohatt, G., & Erickson, F. (1981). Cultural differences in teaching styles in an Odawa school: A sociolinguistic approach. In H. Trueba, H. Gutherie, & K. Au (Eds.), *Culture and the bilingual classroom* (pp. 105–120). Rowley, MA: Newbury House Publishers, Inc.

Mohatt, G. (1978). *Final report: Study of Odawa and non-Native Teachers. Canada: Government,* Department of Indian and Northern Affairs.

Ogbu, J. (1995). Understanding cultural diversity in learning. In J. C. Banks (Ed.), *The handbook on research of multicultural education* (pp. 582–593). New York: MacMillian.

Ogbu, J. (1987). Variability in minority school performance: A problem in search of an explanation. *Anthropology and Education Quarterly, 18*(4), 312–334.

Sarason, S. (1971). *The culture of the school and the problem of change.* Boston: Allyn & Bacon.

Sarason, S. (1986). *Schooling in America: scapegoat and salvation.* San Francisco: Jossey-Bass.

Stairs, A. (1994). The cultural negotiation of indigenous education: Between microethnography and model-building. *Peabody Journal of Education, 69*(2), 154–172.

Stedman, L. C. (1987, November). It's time we changed the effective school formula. *Phi Delta Kappan,* 214–224.

Steele, C. (1992, April). Race and the schooling of Black Americans. The Atlantic Monthly, 68–76.

Villegas, A. M. (1991). Culturally responsive teaching. In J. Bower (Ed.), *Culturally responsive pedagogy: Praxis series, professional assessments for beginning teachers,* (Vol. 1, pp. 3–11). Princeton, NJ: Educational Testing Services.

4 Don't Act Like a Teacher!: Images of Effective Instruction in a Yup'ik Eskimo Classroom

Sharon Nelson-Barber and Vicki Dull
West Ed

Just before the holidays in a small village classroom in New Stuyahok, a group of fifth graders settled into small groups to begin work on a preassigned project. Excited about their upcoming vacation, the students fidgeted and chattered as their teacher moved among the groups handing out materials. As the teacher paused between desks, she overheard two pupils expressing a dislike for several individuals and one in particular. "I don't like her!" remarked one of the students. "She talks down to me. She acts like a *teacher*."

She acts like a teacher. How is it that teachers act? What exactly did the students dislike? What can be made of such an indictment? Is this the idle chatter of elementary students or do they have a real point? Vicki Dull, the young Yup'ik classroom teacher who overheard this conversation, would argue that indeed these students have a point. For far too many students in today's ethnically diverse classrooms, the images of teaching—the actual language used, the strategies devised to manage interaction, the approaches drawn on to facilitate control, ways of organizing activities, the styles used to display authority, and so on—run contrary to accepted norms or to the taken-for-granted models of "real" teaching in their own communities. Vicki's students' astute observation is supported by a growing body of research, including the chapters in this volume, which specifically elicits the perspectives and experiences of teachers from diverse cultural backgrounds who are highly effective in working with nonmainstream students (Delpit, 1995; Hollins, King, & Hayman, 1994; Lipka, 1991).

91

What Dull has come to realize is that teaching success is tied to a teacher's ability to devise a curriculum that is more personal and more directly linked to their students' cultural experiences, local values, shared communicative norms, and interactional styles. In other words, the teacher's cultural understanding and ability to communicate with and motivate students on the basis of that understanding can be most critical to student learning. For example, "cooperative learning" may not look the same in all cultural settings. Conditions for establishing trust between teacher and students necessarily entail understanding particular cultural values; culturally acceptable communication patterns that allow students to participate in classroom discussion need to be respected if critical thinking is to be tapped and fostered; and finally, linking students' personal experiences with learning activities requires an appreciation for and understanding of those experiences.

Unfortunately, even when presented with those experiences and perspectives, many educators are unwilling to lend them credence if they fall outside the parameters of what is accepted as "good" or "progressive" practice in current educational literature. When, for instance, Delpit (1995) recounted the pedagogical practices of her former Black colleagues, she described their preference for structured learning environments and for teacher-directed methods of instruction, their focus on skills, and their emphasis on correctness. These features, she wrote, were "at the very least," neither consistent with research nor reflective of the current state of educational thinking.

Because few schools of education require their students to demonstrate multicultural knowledge, knowledge of language diversity, or skill in interacting effectively with nonmainstream children, outside teachers are often underprepared to draw on the personal and cultural strengths of these students. In the absence of such cultural knowledge, teachers frequently misinterpret their students' behavior and motives, and, as a consequence, misjudge their abilities and potential. Such classrooms are often characterized by patterns of communicative interaction, which, over time, only reinforce, and even deepen, the lack of understanding between students and teacher (Cazden, 1988; Delpit, 1995; Heath, 1983; Mohatt & Erickson, 1981; Philips, 1983). Knowing little about their students' backgrounds, teachers are unable to make connections between the content knowledge they are attempting to teach and the experience and knowledge their students already possess, nor are they able to forge the kind of relationship with students that motivates them to succeed. Albeit unwillingly, such teachers contribute to academic problems for many students because they lack the kind of knowledge and experience that would enable them to better serve student needs.

In this chapter, Dull offers an account of her personal experiences growing up in the same community in which she has been a teacher, and she examines many of the forces that she believes influence teacher effectiveness. She describes how, as a new classroom teacher, she struggled to find her own way of teaching. Central to this struggle are the discontinuity between her own cultural knowledge and the culture of the school as well as what she considers inadequate preparation, as a teacher, for viewing cultural knowledge as an asset.

Dr. Nelson-Barber has been associated with Dull and the Ciulistet as a researcher concerned with broadening conceptions of what counts as "good" teaching. She has spent several years with the group, sharing her own experiences of work with teachers from diverse communities who also were affected by the clashing cultures of school and community. The authors provide further evidence that the ways in which teachers engage and interact with students can indeed be at the heart of their own success or failure in the classroom.

VICKI DULL:
A COMMUNITY-BASED PERSPECTIVE

After many years as a classroom teacher, I have learned a lot about teaching, and what I believe to be the most effective did not come from textbooks or college classrooms. Most of what I have learned has come from practical experience, from studying videotapes of myself and other Yup'ik teachers in the classroom, and from discussions with those same teachers about why and how we have done things. We are always trying to find effective ways of teaching. By contrast, my formal education to become a teacher mostly involved studying about theory—how children learn, the developmental stages of children—and reading endless pages of research written by researchers. Very little of what I read was written by people in elementary classrooms. My role models as I was learning about teaching were my own teachers and a few with whom I had worked on various practicums, though it would be inaccurate to call these individuals "mentors." Generally a small group of children would be excused from their regular schedule to work with me and I would essentially "do my own thing" with very little, if any, feedback from my so-called "cooperating teacher." So, from the beginning, I had questions about what it meant to be considered a "real teacher."

Real teachers, to me, were those I had in elementary school. These individuals, who often were fresh from the Lower 48 and filled with their own visions, came into the village for 2 years and then were gone. I can remember being in awe of these people who wielded so much power. A set of dirty fingernails got us sent home to be scrubbed until they were presentable. We sat in rows, and to be recognized we were required to raise our hands and wait to be called on. Our days were fragmented; reading with workbooks, spelling, math, science, social studies, health, and art. Each was taught at its appropriate time. Our desks were crammed with textbooks and workbooks. Each subject had its given order: Read first, answer questions, do the workbook—all very traditional to the Western style of teaching. There was no other way to do it.

This was the method of teaching as I entered the field of education. My mentor teacher taught this way. The day was chopped up into bits and pieces, with the clock dictating the subject matter. Those in charge had good intentions, and still do. But, in spite of what they read in research journals on teaching methods and what they asked about community definitions of effective teaching, they still went about things in a fragmented manner. This style just did not fit with how things are accomplished in real (Yup'ik) life.

Berry picking offers a good example. We go out in the fall and pick berries until the freezer is full or it snows. If we picked berries the way teaching is done, there would not be enough to last a month—pick a cup here, pick a cup there. The same with hunting, fishing or any other task. In real life, we start a task and complete it rather than doing it in bits and pieces. In school, a traditional "Western" teacher does just that—teaches what kids view as bits and pieces of unconnected matter. I've kept several quotes that explain this. Although the book is long gone, I wrote them down as I remember them. In his book, *What We Owe Our Children*, Caleb Cattegno (1973) wrote that teachers in traditional schools—the schools we have today—know that what they know and have to teach is unknown to the learner and they believe that they are making the unknown known by imparting their knowledge to their students. The way they do this, as Cattegno put it, is to accumulate props, all to support the weak memory such as … exercises, homework, reviewing, testing, more exercises, more homework, more reviewing, more testing, and on and on to ensure retention of material. This is what most teacher education teaches. We're to go into a classroom and fill these kids up with things they don't know. Although we were Yup'ik people living in a Yup'ik community, we had a very traditional Western school. And for this reason, among others, my first year of teaching was one of the most harrowing experiences I have ever gone through.

I had no role model except for non-Natives who did not share the "real" life system with me. They were taught in the "Western" way and replicated this style of teaching in their own classrooms. The first administration I worked for recommended that we use the step-by-step "clinical teaching" method during all lessons. This method, which was "the thing" at the time, calls for the teacher to stand in front of the classroom with a hand raised to bring the class to attention. As each student notices the teacher waiting, they are to raise their hands to show that they are ready to learn. We were constantly in-serviced on it.

The teacher whose classroom I took over used this method with success. But for me, it was a failure. I felt some of the steps were valid, but doing it for every lesson was outrageous. So much time was wasted waiting for each of the 14 children to come to attention like unwilling little soldiers. As for the master teacher's direction, for each minute I waited, the kids lost a minute of recess. It didn't seem fair to me to punish the class for the mistakes of a few. The students didn't think this was fair either. Eventually they rebelled. Maybe they tried to disrupt things because they knew how unnatural it all seemed to me. Although the kids and I came from the same cultural background, I was out of synch with my students because I was wearing a different hat—that of the Westernized teacher.

The second year was better, but not by much. I was still trying to be an authoritative figure, which went against what I believed in. Children in the village are raised to be self-reliant and have a great deal of responsibility. However, when they come to school, they learn to depend on the teacher. They learn to look upon the teacher as an authority figure who tells them what to do, when to do it, and how to do it. Very seldom have students in rural schools been allowed to think for themselves.

As other chapters note, in Yup'ik culture the "group" is important. There is very little, if any, competition among Yup'ik people. When the Western school system entered the picture, the unity of the group slowly shattered. Children were sent hundreds and often thousands of miles away to be schooled in boarding schools where they were forced to abandon their own language for the foreign English with its accompanying foreign ways. They learned the Western value of competition. They learned to be individuals competing against each other instead of a group working in unity. When the children returned, torn between two cultures—what the new one had to offer and what the old one seemed to lack—each Yup'ik community began to lose its sense of self. The returnees had new expectations that could not be realized at home, and, at the same time, they had lost many of the skills needed to be competent in their home communities. A vicious cycle developed as the returnees went on to become parents—who came to depend on schools to fill the parenting void because they had little sense of even these skills, having lived away from home most of their young lives.

Such dependency traces back to the territorial days and Alaska's early statehood, when the federal and state governments found ways to control the people of rural Alaska. They were told which schools to go to, which teachers they would have, and which classes would be offered. The dependency necessarily carried over into village life. The people began to depend on the government for money and help whenever problems arose. The villages no longer had any say in what their lives would be like. They looked to the governments for money to build their houses, to improve their villages (not to community standards, but to "outside" standards) and to feed and educate their children. Village people were no longer allowed to think for themselves. This dependency has carried over into the schools of today. Teachers and administrators from the Lower 48 mandated what would happen in the schools. The teachers came "knowing" what was best for Native children. They taught the children as though they were little vessels to be filled with information, little vessels that couldn't think for themselves, much the same as the governments treated their parents in the past and still do today. The teachers were, in a sense, foreigners mandated by the government to instill in Native children the values of a culture alien to them, and one of the key values they fostered was competitiveness.

This was striking to me during my first 2 years of teaching. Always the children had been encouraged to compete against one another, and there were seldom, if any, times when they were allowed to help each other, which would have been construed as "cheating." The children were so busy competing and tattling on each other that no real learning was going on. They were also frustrated and unhappy. This atmosphere, along with being an "authority figure," was not my style of teaching, and clearly it wasn't the students' style of learning.

Another problem arose with the fragmented day in which I was expected to teach. In order to cover everything, only small segments of time were spent per subject. The day started with basal readers; two groups, one working with me, one working with the aide. To ensure no hard feelings, we switched groups each day. After oral reading, the children answered questions found at the end of the passage and moved to their reading workbooks. Forty-five minutes were allotted for reading, 30 minutes for a page or two of phonics workbooks, then on to spelling. Children who did not finish the work within the given time had to stay after school to catch up. When an assignment was completed, it was signed off on individual contracts. In the mornings, I did no real teaching, just directed traffic and signed off kids as they completed the tasks.

The afternoons were pure hell for the students. I tried teaching like the master teacher—sitting in a cushioned chair in front of the class, lecturing to third graders. Although the lesson plan was easy to follow, the children were left out in the cold. A week didn't go by when a student or two didn't rebel by throwing tantrums or books and, in a few instances, their desks. Some days either the principal or I had to carry children out of the room. I felt I was being forced to teach in a manner foreign to me. Yet, I was compelled to do so because part of my evaluation was based on clinical teaching. Such a style worked for the master teacher because the children were conditioned to expect outside teachers to act in a certain way. Because I came from their village, they expected something entirely different. I wasn't a "teacher" teacher to them, I was Vicki, who knew each and every one of them personally—more like a relative. It wasn't MY classroom, it was OUR classroom. When I didn't live up to that expectation, the whole show fell apart. I believe my classroom must have been similar to the one described by Nelson-Barber and Meier (1990), in which the teacher found that one style of teaching did not work for all students in the class.

In other years, my class was composed of sixth, seventh, and eighth graders, and I have to say it was a challenge to have all these levels in the same small classroom. But it also was a challenge having a traditional teacher next door, which made me very conscious that what we were doing differed from other classes in the school. For example, to build on my students' prior knowledge of subsistence living, I developed an interdisciplinary theme project on Alaska state hunting and trapping regulations; the project incorporated math, reading, and science. Rather than filling my students' heads with the unknown, I took something familiar to them and built on that background knowledge. Trappers came to the classroom to talk about their experiences—trappers and hunters who were relatives of many of the students. Not only was the content relevant to the students, but the speakers were able to make meaningful connections with them using local and recognizable strategies for transmitting knowledge.

When relating to my students I tried not to "talk like a teacher." I had observed that when children played school, the child who played the teacher would use a high-pitched voice with an exaggerated accent, enunciating carefully and talking down to the other children. "You should ...," "You must ...," "Now you gotta ...." I used different language. If the children didn't do what was required of them, complaining that the work was too hard, I would often use village English to stress the importance of my words. For example, in challenging situations, village speakers often use the phrase "How could?" When something perplexed my students, I would often pose the question, "How could?" and the students knew immediately that they needed to buckle down and work to figure out the problem. At the same time, some of my students would compare these exchanges with teacher–student interactions in their other classes, pointing out that "other teachers don't speak this way."

One finally asked, "How come you don't act like a teacher?"

"How would you like it if I acted like a teacher all the time?" I responded.

"Not!" they quickly replied.

In my room, anyone was invited in at any time. They were more than welcome. For me, the classroom is just an extension of real life occasions when community members come together. In any other context in the community, if another Yup'ik person enters our space, that person is welcome for as long as it takes. Would you chase away someone who came to visit your home? We, as Yup'iks, believe in sharing and working together. However, the school dictates that only children assigned to a particular classroom should enter that classroom. You only have one space. Other children just aren't allowed.

On one occasion, a first-grade aide scolded a first grader who had wandered into my classroom. My students reassured her that it was okay for him to be in my room. On another occasion, our principal stopped by to ask if the student he was accompanying could stay with us briefly while he ran an errand. One of my students placed a chair next to the door for the boy, who quickly took a seat. When he started to leave, my students reminded him that he needed to wait. They felt a responsibility to keep an eye on the boy. My students were playing out their community roles as elder brothers and sisters, keeping watch over siblings and ensuring their well-being.

This kind of "unity" was typical of my classroom in general. To maintain order, my students kept each other in line. There were no bossy kids; they all took care of each other when someone tried to hassle them. They kept on each other to "Work now!" I directed the academic portion of the day; but, because we viewed ourselves as a classroom community, I would always ask their opinions and, at times, their permission. For example, we often played the radio in the classroom as students completed individual work. But we all needed to agree. If anyone objected, the radio remained off. One of the boys always commented, "This reminds me of summer fish camp."

This runs contrary to the Western style of teaching in which good behavior is rewarded and bad behavior is punished. Early in my teaching career, I attempted to use the reward system set in place by the previous teacher, but this was stressful for both me and my students. Bad behavior led to a check mark next to the student's name on the chalkboard. After a certain number of checks, the student was ineligible for participation in any school sponsored extracurricular activity offered the following week. These activities included basketball, volleyball, dances, and even the very popular gym night. In a small and isolated village with limited entertainment resources for young people, one could imagine the meaning of such ineligibility. However, denying students these opportunities did not appear to be a deterrent. After repeated denials, they simply stopped trying to change their behavior. At the same time, nothing much was done to try and keep them off the list. Without alternatives, the cycle continued. I admit that I used this method when I began to teach because this is what was expected of me. I was an authority figure, dispensing punishment to students who broke school rules. But I always felt that this approach was demeaning—that I was there to teach the kids, not police them. Our elders say that if you nag a child, he will soon stop listening to you. We needed a way to hold the children accountable for their actions.

Finally I just ignored this system. (Having a new principal open to new ideas helped.) I decided to do things that were comfortable for the students and for me. I was not going to do things because I was "the teacher." My class was my family. We were a community of learners and in order to be a successful community, we had to throw out all the old ways of discipline and my policeman's cap. I stopped nagging them about lying on the floor during reading or while they were working independently, stopped pestering them to raise their hands to sharpen a pencil or go to the restroom. "You know what you're supposed to do and what not to do. I don't need to remind you all the time," I would tell them. To their surprise, I threw out the old behavior charts, explaining that our class was no longer like other classes.

Still, this did not mean there were no limits. They could be an unruly bunch, and when they needed intervention, I would often give them the responsibility of finding a solution. "Let's try and take care of this ourselves," I would offer, or ask, "What can we do to change things?" Rather than threatening them, we devoted afternoon time to role playing and self-esteem boosting. Together we worked to devise student punishment. After several weeks, minor misbehaviors vanished. To motivate my students, I began to relate to them as I would in real life.

Many of the student confrontations resulted from incidents that occurred outside the school, with the children bringing their hurt to the classroom and taking it out on their classmates. Seeing my students overburdened with personal problems, I made a real effort to do something. Although the children believed that the school was not a place to speak of private matters, our classroom offered some outlets for their frustrations. We began journal writing activities in which students were asked to write on various topics, such as different ways to solve problems or how problems were handled at home. They were eager to recount various events and seemed comfortable sharing their personal feelings, because the journals were for my eyes only. They trusted me, understanding that I would make referrals to a school counselor or family service worker if necessary.

I also made individual appointments with students, usually in the morning before school began. At first, they believed that this arrangement could only mean trouble, but after a few meetings, the students looked forward to these opportunities. Our discussions were informal and, again, confidential, and they usually involved a walk around campus or to the lunchroom. We would discuss anything that might be bothering the student. I assured them they were not "in trouble"—these efforts were to keep trouble from happening. I felt this was important, because the students needed to know that I would stand up for them. Because of these relationships, I've been called "mom" accidentally, and I have been told their mothers have been called "Vicki."

My first principal would have frowned on this, because he felt students demonstrated respect for their teachers by using the titles Mr. or Miss, and so forth. However, for me, a member of the community, this felt pretentious. I would be putting myself above my own people and I would not do that. I was still a member of the community, even though I wore the label of teacher. Eventually, when a student called me "Miss Dull," I would remind them that "Miss" wasn't my first name. They knew that using a title or not when they addressed me had nothing to do with respect. Either I deserved it or I didn't. Perhaps we behaved more like family members, but that did not mean I was going to let up on them.

I have made students cry, I believe, not because I was mean, but by pushing them to do their best and to make an all-out effort to learn. If they cried, I allowed them the tears to release their feelings—to work out the problem. One fifth grader had a difficult time grasping a particular math concept and I could sympathize with her negative feelings toward math, but that did not prevent me from pushing her. She would cry silently but still tackle the problem. I thought I might eventually hear about the matter from her mother, but apparently she never mentioned it. However, her mother did tell me that she was very upset with her very strict teacher of the previous year. Near the end of the year, this girl was helping her classmates with math and reminding some of them to "Work now!" Contrary to the reasoning on which the school defined my authority role, I believe that things improved because my students felt I believed in them and I was worthy of their respect.

Although being a teacher in the village was a position of respect, I felt uncomfortable about some of the expectations that went along with the label. Teachers were supposed to have a "serious demeanor," which wasn't my style. I spent a great deal of time with my students after school just chatting, visiting the video store or attending gym night. My students also visited me at home. Because of this relaxed relationship, it seemed awkward to then switch hats and behave according to expectations about what a teacher should be. Being a teacher immediately set a barrier between me and my students' parents. During parent-teacher conferences, I was now presumed to know more than the parents about their own children. This made me feel as though I was becoming someone I shouldn't—someone who was supposed to know more than the parent. Rather than the pattern of a teacher telling parents about their children, I preferred sharing what we both knew and working out a plan that we could all agree on for helping each student learn.

On the other hand, a few parents and relatives thought that because I was from the village, I should give special preference to the children, irrespective of their behavior. Once, after overhearing me reprimand her nephew in the lunchroom, a kitchen employee growled that I should treat the boy better because his parents were having problems. I held my ground, saying that this did not excuse bad behavior, and was later informed that I had the full support of the principal, but that the family had called to complain about my actions.

Similarly, school staff from the community often complained to me about outside teachers who were often considered nosy if they asked questions about a student's home situation. I spent time explaining that teachers need to know a certain amount about the personal lives of their students in order to provide the best education. Outside teachers needed to better understand the sensitive nature of such questions, but I also sympathized with teachers of students whose parents offered little support. Sometimes in frustration I would ask, "If the nosy teacher doesn't help the children, who will?" Overall, I stressed that all students must be responsible for their own actions, and although this led to some misunderstandings, these cases were less common.

Ultimately, what these children need is consistency. In spite of all the parent–teacher conferences and meetings to better the schools, little is really done. Now and then a teacher can make an impact on one or two children, but there are a lot of students getting lost along the way. Teachers and administrators come and go, each with a new agenda, each with new ideas, but there is no real vision for the school. School boards have their goals and objectives, but still, many children are being lost. Teachers feel the burden of this and, like me, many must give up the fight. Although I had become much more knowledgeable about effective schooling for my students, and I had begun to structure and organize my teaching in ways that were much more meaningful to them, these innovations were virtually ignored beyond my classroom. Adding to this were pressures from community members who worked in the school, requiring me to conform to their perspectives, and conflicting pressures from community members outside the school who wanted me to "fit" their predefined, Western-based teacher mold. I decided to leave teaching at the end of last school year.

ALLOWING FOR CULTURAL DIFFERENCES:
A COMMENTARY BY SHARON NELSON-BARBER

Although the Ciulistet served as a powerful mechanism for teachers to broaden their thinking and to feel supported in their efforts to make schooling culturally responsive for students, this was not enough. Ultimately, too many frustrations led Vicki to leave teaching. As shown by the events documented in earlier chapters, she had worked hard to create learning environments that would best serve her students' needs. Contrary to the stance taken by many in her school, including some Yup'ik educators, she sought to discredit the belief that what works for mainstream students will work for all students. Citing Nelson-Barber and Meier's (1990) example, in which a teacher deemed to be a model of progressive teaching found her strategies to be differentially effective for Anglo and African American students, Dull also felt strongly that many of the widely recognized strategies and behaviors learned in formal teacher training worked to the detriment of her students when she was required to operate in ways that conflicted with her own community values. As Dull and others pointed out, there is irony in the fact that outside models, having become the accepted norms as well as the standards on which indigenous teachers are prepared and judged, also penalize them for the very practices that they believe make them successful with their students.

For instance, a major theme consistently emphasized by Dull and other Ciulistet members was the importance of the teacher's relationship with students, as well as student relationships with one another. Dull contended that what she learned in teacher training seemed to define a good teacher primarily in terms of an ability to impart content knowledge. She, on the other hand, viewed the ability to teach content as dependent on, and inseparable from, the teacher's ability to establish a strong personal relationship with students. She felt that one cannot underestimate the centrality of what the Ciulistet has termed a "kin relationship" in accounting for the academic achievement of her students. Certainly an emphasis on the importance of teaching content does not mean student-teacher relationships are unimportant. Still, it may well be that the relative valuation placed on student-teacher relationships is configured quite differently for mainstream and Yup'ik teachers. The other Yup'ik teachers in this volume concur that an important quality of those who qualify as "real" teachers is that the individuals "care" about their students and "really get to know them."

Teachers who do get to know their Yup'ik students understand that these students have mastered a range of competencies at an early age. For many reasons, including a traditional subsistence lifestyle, it is practical and necessary for village children to have experience with both careful observation and decision making. They must be equipped to make the right choices in what could be life-threatening situations, given their environmentally harsh surroundings. Expectations about such capabilities become skewed, however, when children with such an upbringing enter school. As Dull described, teachers who lack knowledge about local culture appear tyrannical when they attempt to "coerce" student behavior, even in such completely personal contexts as deciding when to use the restroom or the drinking fountain. Given their training, it is understandable that mainstream teachers consider their own approaches "normal"; however, it is not acceptable when inattention to local perspective contributes to students' lack of success and level of comfort in the classroom. Along with some of the notions of discipline favored in many Western classrooms, Native parents equate these methods with the shaping of "robots" or "nonthinkers" and, as a consequence, frequently opt not to support what goes on in the classroom (Delpit, 1995). Non-participation is then construed by educators as "not caring about education," and the cycle goes on.

For mainstream administrators, questions surface about whether Yup'ik teachers spend too much "instructional time" establishing relationships with students. According to Dull, one administrator remarked that one of the teachers seemed "mainly concerned about establishing a comfortable teacher–student relationship" and that "her purpose was not really to teach the students but to make friends with them." Similarly, another teacher was characterized as being a "buddy to her students" rather than a "professional teacher." It appeared to another that the teacher was "not as interested in teaching the students as she was in having them feel comfortable with her teaching style." Such assessments are not malicious or ill intentioned; rather, they are based on particular assumptions about what it takes to get to the business of schooling. In fact, cooperative learning will not look the same in all settings. Conditions for establishing trust between teacher and students necessarily entail understanding of particular cultural values; what counts as culturally acceptable communication patterns that allow students to participate in classroom discussion is variable, and linking students' personal experiences with learning activities requires appreciation for and understanding of those experiences.

Although the kind of relationship building accomplished by Yup'ik teachers in this volume may have been reduced to "chit-chat" by some, they, on the other hand, speak of how such strategies allow them to "synchronize classroom with community" and enable them to "build group harmony." When describing her own teaching, Dull typically spoke of "cooperation" or "each one helping the other learn." As Lipka and Yanez note in the next chapter, like traditional learning in the community, where novices learn through observation and assisted performance and have some control over how they will participate in a task, school children do the same within limits. As a consequence, children frequently move around, help one another, and may not raise their hands to leave their seats for a drink or a trip to the lavatory—which often gets translated as poor classroom management on the part of the teachers. However, they contend that what might be viewed as "poor classroom management" in mainstream classrooms can be excellent management in Yup'ik terms. Although teachers need not share a cultural background with their students, the chapters in this volume strongly suggest that the degree of cultural congruence between teacher and student can be a significant factor in student success.

A DIRECTION FOR NEEDED REFORMS

Educational research in the fields of anthropology and sociolinguistics has focused attention on the degree to which knowledge (what is learned) is negotiated and constructed in the course of classroom interaction. A central contribution of this research is its conception of the classroom as a social context in which participants cooperate (or fail to cooperate) in creating the communicative conditions in which learning can occur. Viewed through this lens, a model that attempts to account for and explain effective teaching must concern itself with an analysis of how such practices actually work in the classroom. This implies that such a model must take into account the student's experience of the classroom, the meanings he or she attaches to the events that occur there, and the extent to which students and teacher are able to make "communicative sense" of one another. Ethnographic accounts of communicative interactions in classrooms where the teacher and students come from different cultural backgrounds suggest that there is often great distance between the teachers' views of what occurs there and the students' interpretations and experiences of those events. It is the Yup'ik teachers' contention that many of the problems their children experience in school are located in the interactional exchanges that occur among participants in the classroom.

Of course differences extend well beyond communicative style. Yup'ik and Western-oriented worldviews differ along varied lines—time–space orientation, kinship relations, child-rearing practices, relationship to the land, individual autonomy and group cohesiveness ... to name a few. According to Lipka (1991), differences in cultural views, values, and communicative behaviors, as well as the schools' lack of attention to social relationships, partially account for the failure of schooling in indigenous communities. In this volume, Dull and other members of the Ciulistet have expanded on these interesting and suggestive observations. However, we want to stress that all of us have come to these understandings following years of collaboration and deliberation. Others interested in similar collaborative work must enter into it not because it might be fascinating research, but because they are committed to long-term learning. This does not happen overnight, and there can be complications.

In our case, the Ciulistet wished to share its ideas about effective teaching with the larger education community and enlisted the help of researchers knowledgeable about conducting and writing research across cultures. Certainly teachers can benefit from the continued support of, and interaction with, researchers and other teachers to clarify issues, to make explicit their implicit understandings and rationales, and to emphasize details they may take for granted. However, an additional layer of understanding is needed between teachers/ researchers and teachers/teachers if the dialogs are to cross cultural boundaries.

Our group represented years of personal and professional experience and expertise, including formal training in a range of disciplines; ethnography, anthropology, sociolinguistics, and education. We expected our many perspectives to offer checks and balances to any issues of fairness arising along the way. However, sitting together as equals, viewing tapes, devising interviews, attempting to discover effectiveness in Yup'ik terms, the group quickly saw the paradox. How could we ensure that the Ciulistet, the group initiating and guiding the research, would maintain control?

We realized immediately that there were a number of issues we would have to face head on. For example, in spite of being personally committed to the *idea* of the Ciulistet guiding the research, when presented with actual teaching behavior or points of view that differed radically from those espoused in the literature, or that fell outside our experience of our team, how would we ensure that they would be categorized and analyzed in Yup'ik terms? Would non-Yup'ik members of our team know enough about the culture-specific features these teachers were attempting to look for? And how would we determine the questions to get at these under-standings? Even though some of us had experience interviewing well-trained teachers who used known methods in mainstream settings with good results, these experiences did not necessarily translate into the kinds of understandings needed to interview teachers whose approaches have been worked out in a process of interactive adaptation to their students, the details of which are often tacit. On reflection, they realized their rationales or discussion are based on their own experience and not necessarily on socially shared ways of talking about them that could be understood by mainstream educators. In other words, common ground could not be assumed.

We also realized that although we were trying to get at a particular perspective, the disciplinary tools available to decipher or explain this perspective are still organized in non-Yup'ik terms. If we asked teachers to be self-reflective, would we inadvertently rely on methodology devised for non-Yup'ik uses? Even if we attempted to present information in Yup'ik terms, would this ultimately be for outsider goals? Although committed to coownership of the project, if these issues were not attended to, inequality could surface in a very concrete way—authorship. In other words, experienced writers who are really outsiders to the community could become the lens through which the information was interpreted. We realized that outsiders could impose their own ideology on the evidence or find contradictions in elements that made perfect sense to community participants. The undesired result would be that abstracted experience written in text becomes a replacement for the actual interaction and participation with real people in a supposed relationship of equality—a phenomenon that has plagued Native communities since initial contact.

Because we in education are now in the process of constructing knowledge about widely diverse settings, we must insure that the ad hoc knowledge developed by individuals within settings such as these gains the security and recognition of public domain knowledge. Doing this successfully requires a willingness to confront difficult issues as well as a willingness to handle interpersonal conflicts that are often inevitable when collaborating across cultures. Questions like the ones noted earlier must be asked and *answered* for the work to truly represent participant perspectives. And, probably most importantly, the report of the work must include teachers' actual words, emotions, and reflections so that these voices are clearly heard along with experienced researcher explanations. Sympathetic study or inter-pretation by outsiders cannot substitute for this direct input.

Such an approach has real implications for teacher education. One of the reasons students of education have so little access to minority perspectives is that there are so few teachers and students of color in schools of education. Teacher educators make valiant attempts to help students develop an increased understanding of cultural differences, or to explore sources of communicative misunderstanding and conflict in the classroom; however, these efforts are undercut by the fact that there are no students or faculty of color with whom to interact over these issues. There also has been an increased emphasis on ethnography as a tool to help education students view classroom events through new eyes, but one must ask how likely it is that new interpretations will arise from such experiences, when in the end, students and faculty are attempting to interpret the meaning of classroom events for subjects whose perspectives they know little or nothing about.

As the chapters in this volume illustrate, participants in the culture must take the lead in conceptualizing, conducting, and interpreting the research. Without the voices of participants, even researchers with the best of intentions will only force Native explanations into existing categories of Western education. As Phyllis Morrow contended (1988), "decontextualization of cultural traits" in the education setting results in "redefining one culture in terms of another (p. 3)." If this is the case, a Pandora's box *will* open, from which will emerge complex problems of definition, comprehension, interpretation, implicit assumptions, and a lack of shared experiences and values.

REFERENCES

Cattegno, C. (1970). *What we owe our children.* New York: Avon Books.
Cazden, C. (1988). *Classroom discourse.* Portsmouth, NH: Heinemann.
Delpit, L. (1995). *Other people's children.* New York: The New Press.
Heath, S. (1983). *Ways with words.* Cambridge, MA: Cambridge University Press.
Hollins, E., King, J., & Hayman, W. (Eds.). (1994). *Teaching diverse populations: Formulating a knowledge base.* Albany: State University of New York Press.
Lipka, J. (1991). Toward a culturally based pedagogy: A case study of one Yup'ik Eskimo teacher. *Anthropology in Education Quarterly, 22*(3), 203–223.
Mohatt, G., & Erickson, F. (1981). Cultural differences in teaching styles in an Odawa school: A sociolinguistic approach. In H. Trueba, G. Guthrie, & K. Au (Eds.), *Culture and the Bilingual Classroom* (pp. 105–119). Rowley, MA: Newbury House.
Morrow, P. (1988). *Yup'ik students of Yup'ik culture: A project-based high school curriculum.* Bethel, AK: Lower Kuskokwim School District.
Nelson-Barber, S., & Meier, T. (1990, Spring). Multicultural context: A key factor in teaching. *Academic Connections.* New York: The College Board.
Philips, S. (1983). *The invisible culture.* New York: Longman.

Part III
Transforming the Culture of Schooling

In Part II of this book, we presented Yup'ik teachers' personal narratives and their struggle to find a place for themselves in schools and classrooms without having to deny their Yup'ik identity. Each of the teachers began to bring their culture and language into the classroom through their teaching and their relationship with the community. Their struggle had its risks and casualties. However, viewed from a long-term perspective, the work of these teachers and the Ciulistet established a pathway that slowly changed schooling. Yup'ik ways of organizing classroom space, conducting lessons, and teaching through the Yup'ik language, and the use of Yup'ik conceptions related to mathematics and science have entered the discourse and practice of school.

The chapters in Part III of this book explore the possibilities for how teachers, elders, and university colleagues working from the margins of schooling can transform mainstream conceptions of what constitutes schooling. Here the Yup'ik culture, ways of transmitting knowledge, and knowledge itself, are no longer viewed from the perspective of struggle and conflict but from the perspective of inclusion. In these chapters, the Yup'ik culture is viewed as a platform upon which contributions to schooling can be made and through these contributions, can change schooling itself.

CLASSROOM DISCOURSE AND ORGANIZATION

The first case differs substantially from those in Part II of this book. Yanez, at the time of this case, was already an experienced classroom teacher with approximately 20 years of teaching as a bilingual aide, a certified bilingual expert, and a certified teacher. Here, we find a teacher no longer struggling to find her place and identity in the school but one who has reached an accommodation with the culture of the school and the culture of the community.

Although this case is about Yup'ik culture, social organization, and classroom discourse routines, it also speaks to more general notions of schooling change: altering classroom routines (see, e.g., Fullan, 1992; Sarason, 1996), developing culturally responsive pedagogy (Hollins, 1996), and of a paradigmatic shift in research (Deyhle & Swisher, 1997). The students are not simply asked known questions by their teacher to which their responses are relegated to an evaluation, but instead, discourse is open and free flowing, facilitating inquiry and explora-tion. A cultural analysis of a lesson not only reveals distinctly Yup'ik ways of organizing speech, but this particular conversational style of classroom interacting also has relevance to notions of school reform on a broader level. Here we see students learning in ways that are culturally related to their life as they explore on their own, and learn in an apprentice–expert type setting. Hollins (1996) called this type of instruction authentic cultural mediation where the connections be-tween the home culture and the school culture are explicitly made. The cases in chapters 5 and 6 go even further, beyond mere one to one correspondence between the home and school culture, in that these are, in fact, cultural negotiations and creations. The school culture and the home culture are evolving realities and the teacher is applying her knowledge of both as she creates a classroom space that simultaneously responds to each.

YUP'IK CULTURE AS CONTENT: EMBEDDED MATHEMATICS AND SCIENCE

Chapter 6 is a case that builds on Yup'ik cultural and linguistic knowledge and ways of organizing space and speech to include content derived from Yup'ik everyday practice that relates to core academic subject matter. Here, the process of transform-ing schooling accelerates, as the group works with elders to interpret that subject matter from an insider frame of reference (that is, understanding Yup'ik conceptions within a Yup'ik framework) and also to interpret this knowledge and rerepresent it in a school domain. This work represents a distinct departure from "traditional" school practices. It was not long ago when Yup'ik conceptions of numeration, geometry, and patterns were nonexistent in this school setting, whereas today they are increasingly embraced by local school districts. Chapter 6 shows how a group created a space to jointly inquire into Yup'ik conceptions of mathematics and science and how we began to interpret that knowledge for a school setting. Crossing cultural boundaries and developing curriculum and pedagogy across such divides is fraught with dilemmas and problems. Despite these potential problems associated with implementing authentic representation (local standards) while simultaneously meeting national standards, this work for our group represents a watershed in pushing the possibilities of schooling in indigenous contexts.

REFERENCES

Dehyle, D., & Swisher, K. (1997). Research in American Indian and Alaska Native education: From assimilation to self-determination. In M. Apple (Ed.), *Review of research in education* (pp. 113–194). Washington, DC: American Educational Research Association.

Fullan, M. (1991). *The meaning of educational change.* New York: Teachers College Press.

Hollins, E. (1996). *Culture in school learning: Revealing the deep meaning.* Mahwah, NJ: Lawrence Erlbaum Associates.

Sarason, S. (1996). *Revisiting "The culture of the school and the problem of change."* New York: Teachers College Press.

5 Identifying and Understanding Cultural Differences: Toward a Culturally Based Pedagogy

Jerry Lipka and Evelyn Yanez
University of Alaska, Fairbanks

The pressure to conform to the culture of the school is very strong, as evidenced by the personal narratives of Vicki Dull, Esther Ilutsik, Fanny Parker, and Nancy Sharp. These teachers each faced their struggle to be an authentic person, as a Yup'ik teacher, in their own unique way. Each struggled to accommodate the pressures of conformity yet still find a way to include their culture in school. Sharp struggled to speak and teach in her first language; Parker struggled against using interactional routines that "put her students off"; Dull sought ways to be "Vicki" both in the classroom and the community; and in this case, Yanez brings to schooling specific Yup'ik cultural knowledge that also relates to Western science, values, and interactional routines.

Although the context of schooling—its curriculum, its culture, and styles of teaching—have not been conducive to a Yup'ik culturally based pedagogy, this chapter argues that a rich Yup'ik cultural heritage exists, and that this heritage opens up curricular and pedagogical possibilities. This case shows that it is possible for a Yup'ik teacher in a Western-oriented school to construct a lesson that reinforces and develops Yup'ik identity, a Yup'ik worldview, and a particular knowledge associated with subsistence living. Furthermore, this case shows how Yanez conducts a lesson in which she uses Yup'ik sociolinguistic routines, makes authentic connections between students' experiences and learning, and relates classroom work to authentic community participation.

This chapter presents background information to the case and a detailed description of a lesson, including transcribed discourse and a detailed description of the social organization of the classroom——how the class is organized into work groups. Second, this chapter offers an analysis on a number of different levels: Mrs. Yanez describes the relationship between her culture and her teaching, and she provides background for understanding her teaching from a Yup'ik cultural base; and I build on Yanez's insights and further develop both a critical and an interpretive analysis, presenting meanings of this lesson for both Yup'ik culture and for Western schooling. More specifically, I analyze this lesson on the microlevel of discourse routines and relate those routines to the social work groups and social organization of the classroom. I also relate students' work and teacher praise to deep Yup'ik cultural values of subsistence, survival, and proper ways of behaving in and out of the classroom. Finally, I discuss a tension that arose for Mrs. Yanez, her reluctance to share this tape with the Ciulistet group because "it was too Yup'ik." Reinforcing the rarity of this lesson is the fact that it occurred during "Yup'ik Cultural Heritage Week," meaning the other weeks of the year are *kass'aq* (Western/White) culture heritage weeks. The rarity of this lesson and her desire to teach in a Yup'ik way show that the school and the classroom are contested space. The struggle is over cultural primacy of schooling—Yup'ik, Western, or some fusion of the two. This struggle speaks to issues in minority education, to educational reform, and to larger theoretical issues concerning ways that schools are failing communities. More positively, this struggle speaks to how indigenous and minority teachers are finding ways to authentically present their cultural background and knowledge within schools and are thereby slowly encouraging a process of inclusion and change.

METHODOLOGY

Yanez, at her convenience, placed a videocamera in a far corner of her classroom on a tripod and it recorded all activity before, during, and immediately following the lesson. Following the procedures identified by Erickson and Mohatt (1982), we selected footage for further analysis. In this particular study, we chose one lesson selected for its unusual style and delivery from a non-Yup'ik viewpoint. The first level of analysis occurred when the Ciulistet, Mohatt, Nelson-Barber, and myself viewed the videotaped lesson in a group setting. Sections of that tape were more carefully examined as we asked simple questions: "Why did you do this? Why didn't you do this?" In addition, during the viewing, we would pause the tape and replay sections of mutual interest and analyze microevents. Further, I conducted ethnographic inteviews with Yanez as we watched specific sections (Erickson & Mohatt, 1982; Trueba, 1989) to gain additional contextual and cultural insights. The lesson was transcribed, and the Yup'ik portions were translated into English and transcribed. We conducted a line-by-line analysis using Jefferson's protocol for communication analysis (Sacks, Schegloff, & Jefferson, 1974). To achieve as accurate a representation as possible with the transcription and analysis, I gave my initial transcription to Jordan Titus, a conversational analysis specialist, to check and fine tune it. After receiving her input, I reedited the transcription and shared it with Nastasha Wahlberg, a Yup'ik translator. I also discussed specific sections with Mrs. Yanez.

In addition, the analysis included lesson phases or lesson transitions, recorded nonverbal behaviors during some of the transitions, and discourse patterns. We achieved a multidimensional analysis by interpreting the lesson from insider and outsider perspectives, using both the tools of conversation analysis (an analysis of the structure of the discourse) and an ethnographic approach. Further, we analyzed the lesson along the dimensions of social organization; how the lesson was started, the types of statements used in beginning, the way the underlying Yup'ik values were brought to light, the relationship of the teacher to the students, the way the content was delivered, and the relationship of the content to its cultural form and meanings. Particularly important was the insider–outsider relationship and different frames of reference. At the time of this analysis, I had been working with Yanez and other members of the Ciulistet for approximately 10 years. Our mutual trust allowed for probing questions that sought to understand the connection between her classroom behavior and Yup'ik culture. This process increased both our understanding of mainstream teaching and Yup'ik pedagogy—casting the familiar in a new light and bringing insiders new understandings.

YUP'IK DISCOURSE PATTERNS: SMELTING

The Lesson

This lesson took place with first graders. These were some of the first students to enter the Togiak School who were not fluent Yup'ik speakers. However, their English was strongly influenced by Yup'ik. It was springtime and the villagers were engaged in smelting. Smelt enter the river that enters Togiak Bay at the village site. Smelt could be seen drying on fish racks throughout the village. The following lesson involved the students in preparing smelt for drying.

The first phase of the lesson consisted of the students and the teacher cutting and cleaning the smelts. The transcription symbols follow those developed by Jefferson (Sacks et al., 1974), and the symbols are listed later. Comments in Yup'ik are italicized and the translations are in brackets. This is an exact transcription. English is the language of instruction with occasional Yup'ik words and phrases interspersed. Wherever possible, students were assigned a subscripted number, otherwise they were indicated by an "S" for student. The analysis that follows explored questions of classroom discourse (the structure of classroom talk—who talks to whom, with what frequency, who gets the floor and how), the relationship of community knowledge and activity to this lesson and school learning, and the possibility of using an apprenticeship or practice model over direct instruction (Lave & Wegner, 1991).

The Classroom Scene

The following describes the students' work and physical movements in the classroom. The teacher was seated around a rectangular table large enough for approximately eight students. At the right-hand side of the table, positioned on the floor, was a bucket of fish. Students took fish out of the bucket and placed the smelt on the table as they were needed. Yanez cut the fish slowly and carefully and remarked to the students on the need to be careful. The cut fish were placed in a neat pile at the other end of the table. A few of the boys at this table cleaned the fish by squeezing them and carefully pulling out the guts. The guts were then placed in a pile on the middle of the table. One girl took the cleaned fish to another work table, where they were stretched, smoothed, and arranged in neat piles. Up to four girls moved from one work station to the other. The four different work roles were not assigned, but students filled them according to the need of the overall task. The following discourse occured as the students engaged in the processes just described.

The following symbols used were developed by Gail Jefferson and reported in several places, including Sacks, Schegloff, and Jefferson (1974, pp. 731–734). This list is presented here to aid the reader in understanding the dialogue.

Transcription Symbols

T	teacher
A	teacher's aide
S	student
[[	utterances starting simultaneously
[	overlapping utterances, at point where overlap begins
]	overlapping utterances, at point where overlap ends
=	latching of utterances (no interval between parts of talk)
(0.0)	timed silent intervals, in tenths of a second
(.)	microintervals, less than two tenths of a second
(words)	items enclosed in single parentheses are ambiguous or uncertain
( )	empty single parentheses indicate that no hearing could be achieved

(( ))	items enclosed in double parentheses are transcriptionist's comments
italics	words in italics are spoken in Yup'ik
{ }	items enclosed in curved parentheses are an English translation of preceding Yup'ik
__	underscoring marks emphasis either pitch or stress
:	colons mark extension of sound
.	periods mark stopping fall in tone
?	question marks are rising inflection
,	commas mark continuing intonation
—	a dash marks a cutoff word
≠	an upward pointing arrow marks a rising shift in intonation, prior to the rise
Ø	a downward pointing arrow marks a falling shift in intonation, prior to the fall

Phase I: Preparing the Smelt

1. S₁   Look, *Al'i*. Clean
2. A   Going down to Galick. Wow.
3. S?   Yuck ( )
4. S?   one
5. S?   two
6. S?   one two two round (and)
7. S?   [two]
8. T   [*qiryungtua*] {I started sweating} ((laughter))
9. T   *Ilakluqu-llu* {included with previous speakers}((several people speaking))
10. S₃   It's a girl kind?
11. S₂   Yeah
12. S?   Under the boy.
13. T   From the intestines, I think.
14. S?   From dis one?
15. S?   ≠Δ Øbo:::y.
16. T   Hmm.
17. S₄   ≠Δ Øbo:::y.

The scene begins with a student requesting the teacher to look at her fish. The teacher is referred to by her nickname "Al'i."

Here the students are examining the fish that they are cleaning. Student S3 is asking if the smelt is female while a number of students state that if you look under the intestines, you can tell if it is male or female.

18.	T	Ryan, I saw your uncles, [*they*]	The teacher interjects and states that she saw Ryan's uncle fishing this weekend at a place called Kulukak Bay. S2 interjects and states that his dad caught a big seal. The teacher continues the conversation.
19.	S₂	[te—] (1.9)	
20.	T	wen [t (.)] fishing wa:::y by [(.) K]*uluqak*	
21.	S₂	[Teacher] [my]	
22.	S₂	my dad [caught a big seal]	
23.	T	[and they said they caught]lots of trout.	
24.	S₂	Teacher, my dad caught a big (.) *seal.*	
25.	S?	(A trout?)	
26.	T	A ≠ seal?	
27.	S?	Boy	
28.	S?	[[My my dad caught]	
29.	T	[[Did you guys make seal oil?] ( ) ((several students talking softly))	
30.	S₁	You want me to (.) could use deeze. (1.9)	
31.	S?	(n') you (3.1)	
32.	S₂	Gad ya are <u>deeze</u>?	
33.	S₄	They're the eggs.	
34.	T	*Muryartulag'gu.* {Go wash it quickly.}	The students continue to explore the smelt, checking for female fish and finding their eggs. The teacher ends this segment by stating, "I need to put [up] more fish." The teacher directs students to get more fish and to clean them.
35.	S₃	They're from the birds of the egg. ((laughter))	
36.	S₄	Ah, not the birds, the fish. ((laughter))	
37.	S?	Right I squeeze this?	
38.	T	I need	
39.	S?	*Eruq* {wash} this fish?	
40.	T	to put more fish.	
41.	S?	Teacher.	

42.	T	Go put these it on the <u>nex</u>—(.) other table *Gali*.
43.	S?	Teacher, wash this?
44.	S?	(w) one
45.	T	Somebody [can clean this.]
46.	S?	[Another one.]
47.	S₅	The::se, Ali?

48.   A   *Uryulngiquk*, Chris-*aaq-llu* . {Chris and this other person are not washing their fish.} (1.4) ((students speaking softly))

Here the teacher notices that some students are not washing their fish. She begins to address the whole class while the students are still working. The students do not stop and look at the teacher. The teacher does not make direct eye contact to the students who are not washing their fish properly; she speaks to the group. She emphasizes important Yup'ik values of doing things properly, of being a hard worker, and having dried fish for the winter. Lines 50–60 are concerned with these values and this part of the "lesson" ends when she says, "you have to learn how to make dried fish."

50.   T   Do you know what will happen if you're *qessanquq* {lazy bone} and don't fish when you're older?

51.   Ss   What?

52.   T   You won't have any (.) ah (0.5) dried smelts.

53.   S₄   We buy it.=

54.   S₃   =*Kita* {Here}Dee.

55.   T   Even in the summer if you don't (1.1) split ah (.) salmon you won't have *neqerrluaq* {dried fish}

56.   S₁   My mom

57.   T   so::≠*you* (.) *have* (.) *to* (.)*learn* (.) Ø*how*

58.   S₁   splits

59.   T   to make dri::[ed fish.]

60.   S₃/₄?   [We're learnin' how.]

In line 60, a student ends that phase of the lesson by stating, "we're learning how [to make dried fish].

61.   S₃   When ((chuckles)) when (.) my dad caught da fish I went like this, how. ((pretending to pull in the net with his arms))

62.   T   ah

63.   S?   When we're (.) ah

64.   A   *Uksuk* {winter} (you)

In lines 63–70, two students are vying for the teacher's attention. The students are trying to get the floor

65.	S₄	[Teacher, you know what?]
66.	S?	[When we are using the ah]
67.	S₄	[Teacher, you know what?]
68.	S?	[( )]
69.	S₃	Teacher.(1.1) Do you know what?
70.	T	*Arah* [Enough]
71.	S₃	We caught sea lions *Teqenaq*. {a person's name and place}
72.	S₄	Teacher. We got mmmm.
73.	S₃	We got lots of sea lions ah ah in the net.
74.	S₄	Teacher. We had, we had
75.	S₄	Teacher.
76.	T	(*Anarupall*) ( ) too much.
77.	S₅	We caught one beaver and
78.	S?	trapped
79.	T	beaver
80.	S₅	on our *kuviaq* {net }with lots of yellow. (.) That kind.
81.	S₅	( ) by house *ayarak* {little house}, by Annette's them's new house.
82.	T	uh huh
83.	S?	Teacher.
84.	T	Where's their house?
85.	S?	Teacher.
86.	S₅	Far.
87.	S?	Teacher.
88.	S₄	Four, nine, one ( ) nine, nine, sav'n, four.
89.	S?	Teacher.
90.	T	[[Don't touch me with your hands.]
91.	S₃	[[*Teacher*. (1.5) We had ten sea ≠; li:Øons.]
92.	S₃	When we were (0.9) far away we net them, we net

and bid for the floor by stating, "Teacher, you know what?" However, the teacher does not respond until line 70 when she says, "Arah [Enough]." This interactional routine continues through the next five lines as these two students continue to bid for the teacher's attention. In line 76, she says, "too much."

Students tell about various subsistence activities that they have been engaged in with their families. One student says that his family caught a beaver in their fishing net, and they also caught some flounders. In line 91, S3 finally picks up from the point that was started back on line 69 "do you know what?" In line 91, the student answers his own query by stating that his dad caught a sea lion. Lines 71–95 show a conversational classroom discourse style between the teacher and between the students. The conversation relates to such subsistence activities as fishing and catching flounder, beaver, and seals. The teacher names places such as Kulukak Bay and the activities that are associated with these places at certain times of the year.

them, my dad caught ten sea
⊁, ll:Øons.

93.   T   I wish I could ah (0.8) bring
my (.) smelts here everyday
after I go fishing so we can
all work on them ((laughter))
like this.

Phase II: Tying the Smelt

The second phase of the lesson began later in the school day. The students just returned from their computer lab class. Previously, all of the smelts were cut and prepared for stringing. Yanez began this phase of the lesson by directing the students to observe her tie the smelt, so that they may learn. She demonstrated the process by tying the smelts. Smelt are tied together so that they may dry properly. In the first part of this lesson, Yanez had her own work to perform, similar to other Yup'ik teachers (see next chapter and reported elsewhere, Lipka, 1991). While she performs this task the students observe her, and are involved in dialogue (see Fig. 5.1).

This phase of the lesson ended when she announced, "Look, this is done." The next phase began shortly thereafter when she asked, "Who's ready to string?" This transition from modeling and demonstrating to having a student who is ready to

FIG. 5.1. Modeling, observing and apprenticeship.

string smelt creates a shift in roles; the student now becomes "a teacher" as responsibility for learning shifts to a more experienced novice who assists less experienced novices by demonstrating. The teacher stepped back from the group and observed the students' work, periodically offering verbal and physical assistance. We join the class again as Yanez continued instructing the students.

FIG. 5.2. Students perform task.

94.	A	((laughter))
95.	T	Fast.
96.	T	Don't make a loop, just tie it.
97.	S	Teacher, look.=
98.	S	=Oh no.=
99.	S	=Anita. (0.9) Look.
100.	S	I found this. It ≠works.
101.	T	*Maurluq*, how are you ≠tying Øit.] ((spoken softly))
102.	S	[( )]
		(3.3)
103.	S	Hey, I found them.

In line 96, the teacher provides direct instruction through an injunction, "don't make a loop." She does this quietly and directly to the student in private. Her voice is not audible to the whole group. In lines 101–119, the teacher steps away from the student and now speaks in a public tone. This instance represents the second time during the lesson of a student not doing something that the teacher deems very important. In those lines she emphasizes the Yup'ik cultural values and the need to "do it right."

104.	S	I, I.
105.	T	You have to do it right.
106.	T	If [you don't do it right]
107.	S:	[( )]
108.	S:	[( )]
109.	T	[they'll] fall down and ah
110.	S	Lo::::ok
111.	T	a *mayrrlussaagaq* {little ole grandma} comes along and (0.8) sees your fish she's gonna lau[gh and she'll say]
112.	S	[It:: wo::rks]
113.	S	Lo:::ok,
114.	S	Over there. ((spoken quickly))
115.	T	that [you guys are, ah]mm
116.	S	[( )]
117.	S	( ) doesn't do it.
118.	S	(no,) [no way.]
119.	T	[not Yup'iks.] (1.8)
120.	S7	Look. (1.8) Te::ach[er:::]
121.	T	[Um hum.]
122.	S	( )
123.	S	How's you one, Tess?
124.	T	*Key-am acantuq.* {It's under the key.}
125.	S	Ohh.
126.	T	Or you could keep tying this (.) piece.
127.	S	Gir:::l.
128.	T	Johnny, look.
129.	S	This looks (like [there's something in there)].
130.	S	[There's somebody in ≠ there.] ((spoken loudly and fast))

She ends her statement by saying that if a grandmother came by and noticed fish like this, she would say that you are "not Yup'ik." Here the cultural value of not wasting, and learning how to prepare and preserve smelt comes directly to the forefront of the lesson. In addition, being and becoming a Yup'ik person and knowing one's identity are clearly expressed in this part of the lesson.

Interestingly, from lines 111–119, even though Mrs. Yanez is stating, from her perspective, a Yup'ik cultural imperative, the students continue to talk aloud while she is making this important statement. She does not sanction the children for talking while she is talking.

131. S: Look.

132. S: No it ain't.

133. T   That's too far.

134. T   Leave these here.

135. T   Untie it and do it over.

136. S₆   I see little one.

137. T   Good, Deanna. You're not
           wasting your string.

138. T   Don't waste your string.

139. S   ( ) good one.

140. S₈   I'm not.

141. T   Um hum.
           (5.9)

142. S₉   [Look at this.]

143. S   [*Kemugtem.*]{dog}

144. S   ( )

145. T   ((sighs))

146. S   Teacher.
           (1.8)

147. T   Ah::

148. S   Look.

149. T   April,

150. S   Teacher.

151. T   maybe you could show Gally
           how to tie (1.3) her [strings.
           She doesn't] know how.

152. S   [We need to change] this
           one too.

153. T   [Or Deanna.] Maybe you
           could show Gally how to tie
           her strings.

154. S   [( ) Gallik.]

155. T   Go show her.

In line 137, "You're not wasting your string," Mrs. Yanez emphasizes publicly for the third time during the lesson another important Yup'ik value of not wasting.

When April displays her tied smelt, the teacher tells her that maybe she could help another student. This can also be interpreted as her reward as April's role changes from a beginning novice to a more advanced status, a helper. Here Mrs. Yanez is conveying and connecting Yup'ik values of work and cooperation. Her classroom connects to the world of the community as she provides a space in which students are performing a task that is continuous with their world.

FIG. 5.3. April displays her smelt.

Three minutes later another student finishes. One student is working by himself because the other students are finished. A student comes by, observes, and takes the string and begins to tie it and then leaves. An aide is giving him instructions. When he is finished, Mrs. Yanez says:

156.   T   Wo:::w.

157.   T   *Aspiaq.*{beautiful}

158.   T   Now you can help your
           grandma.

The entire lesson was completed after the students go outside the school and hang the smelt on a drying rack. The lesson is now finished.

Insider Interpretation of the Lesson

In this section, Yanez analyzes this lesson from the viewpoint of her culture—the values that she learned as a child from her mother and other kin. This establishes a Yup'ik cultural frame of reference for understanding what, how, and why she organizes the social and academic portions of her lesson. Critical connections are made between community norms, behaviors, values, and her classroom teaching during this lesson.

Yup'ik Values

In my community, we have cultural values that are passed down, and we use these values in learning survival skills in our community. For example, we are taught how to work in groups. One of the skills that we do in groups is hunting. It is very unusual for one person to go hunting alone because a lot of things can happen to him. The weather is very unpredictable, and a hunter can be stranded in an isolated place for weeks without any help or food. Whereas if that hunter went with a couple of other men, they would help each other in trying to survive. This is why it is important for the students to work together in the classroom, because outside of the classroom, we work in groups. In reading and math, the students work better in pairs. For example, in my classroom I encourage my fast readers to read to my slow readers because the students learn faster from each other.

During the process of cleaning smelt, I teach my students not to waste any part of the fish because being wasteful in our culture is not allowed. I want them to learn that if we are not wasteful of food that we get off our land, we will keep subsisting off our land in the future because animals and fish will still be plentiful. This example from the lesson shows the importance of not being wasteful.

T: Good Deanna, you're not wasting your string. Don't waste your string.

My mother and my aunt always told me to clean up the area that I used for splitting fish and always to give the guts and the heads of the fish to the dogs. If for any reason I didn't clean up the area, they would be after me to hurry up and clean up. In the classroom, after any activity, I always encourage my students to pick up and clean up the area because they need to learn to respect the land that gives us food and shelter. The value here is that the people believe that by keeping our area clean, we show our respect for the land and for the animals that use it.

Another value that we learn from our parents is we have to do things right the first time. This is probably one of the main reasons why most of our children do not like to make mistakes in the classroom. Out in the tundra when it is very cold, you can't make a mistake or you will freeze to death. Another example is if a woman makes dried fish that do not dry out right, she will end up without food for the winter, so it's very important for these students not to make mistakes, especially when it's part of surviving in our communities.

We look up to our elders as professionals in our villages, and they are the ones who tell us if what we are doing is right or wrong, so I try to motivate my students by using their grandparents in our classroom activities. For example, during the smelts lesson, I told one of the kids to do it right—in working with the smelts—because if they did not, a grandmother would come along and laugh and say that they were not Yup'ik if the smelts were not tied right.

In our culture, we don't time ourselves in finishing the product we are working on. For example, I would never tell my aunt to make *kameksaks* [boots, typically caribou skin] for me and expect her to finish by the next week because a lot of things could happen. This is why I don't expect my students to finish or learn something at the same time because this does not happen outside of our classrooms. I also do not force students to learn something that they are not ready to learn. For example, in the tape, I wasn't forcing the students to work at the same time and finish tying the smelts at 3:00 because they are individuals and they do not finish working at the same time.

My dad, if he knew I wasn't interested in lighting the *maqi* [steambath] stove, he wouldn't teach me how to light it. He taught me this year, when I am almost 40 years old, because I was ready.

All my life, I wasn't ready; I wasn't interested in learning something. A couple of years ago I got interested in learning about different things, and then my mom and aunt were there to teach me. All those years I never asked them to teach me. They would not teach me anything until I was ready. For instance, when I was going to make a parka, my aunt and mother were there if I needed help. Before that, I was never interested. They would talk about other people who knew how. How Yup'ik they were to make things for their culture ... it would be good for other people to make things from their culture. During the winter, if I didn't have dried fish or *agutak* [Eskimo ice cream] she would say, "People who have dried fish don't crave for them." But she didn't say I should learn how. She would say, "Whenever a person is ready there are people around who would make things." If she didn't know she would ask one of the relatives to help.

Note this evidence from the video on smelts:

T: Who's ready to string?

S: April Me!

T: Tie it from this end ... (discourse was edited here)

T: Who else is ready to string? (invitation: Student takes responsibility)

S_1:   Me.

S_2:   Me.

S_3:   Me.

Learning by Observing

We learn by watching and doing. I often encourage my students to watch someone and then try it themselves after they learn it. For example, I wanted to learn how to make fermented heads, so I asked my mother to teach me. After we got the heads and buckets, we went out by the fish racks and my mom went ahead and made fermented heads while I watched. A couple of weeks later, I had to make some when my mother asked me to. I was alone and I was kind of nervous because I did not want to make a mistake and die from botulism, so I had to do it right.

Here is another example from my tape on smelts.

T: Galik you should go watch April.

S: Excuse me.

T: Go watch her so you could learn. Go by her.

S: Excuse me.

T: Who else wants to be a teacher?

S: Me. (choral)

T: Um, maybe you could teach Janet, since she doesn't know how.

T: Now you can help your *Aluk* [relative] tie some.

S: You can have these ones.

S: Chris doesn't know how (inaudible)

S: Can you tie me some?

T: You could help him Deanna. (she initially declined Evelyn's invitation to work)

Praising and Evaluating

Overly praising is also not heard of in my family. My mom and dad both believe that overly praising will ruin a person. We are taught not to think we are better than another person. Sometimes people who think they are better than everyone else are put down and made fun of, just because of the way they act. In my lesson on smelts, once in a while I tell the students "good," but I try not to make a big thing out of it.

T: Good Galik.

Sometimes, my mom would shame me nonverbally, by using different body language, smile, nod, or just say *ii-i* (pronounced like a long "e" sound) [yes], or her use of an example would tell me she approved of it … of her own experience. She could use herself as an example to tell me she approved of what I did. She would not praise me. We do not praise ourselves. If we accidentally did that, she would put us down right away.

I didn't tell the kids that they were doing it wrong; I told them to watch the people who were doing the stringing right. If I told the kids they were doing it wrong, it would turn them off. If somebody said that to me, I would give up and not try.

Instead, teaching the value of help would turn on Yup'ik students. They do things to help extended families.

That's why it's so hard for the kids. It is so different from their homes. The *kass'aq* values conflict with what they learn at home. Maybe that's why we complain about kids who are reserved, who don't like to give speeches. At home, you're not allowed to talk. For instance, there is this loud lady. Everybody talks about her, just because she talks. We are not supposed to ask questions, because that is being nosy. We are comfortable the way we are. It's hard. If the kids learn about the *kass'aq* way, it's good for them. They can get along with other kinds of people. They're not scared; they know how to act.

Outsider Interpretation

The following analysis builds on Yanez's interpretation and provides additional interpretation and analysis, and places her teaching within a theoretical framework. By using conversational analysis, her brief life history, and interviews, this section develops some parameters for understanding how a Yup'ik-based pedagogy can become an effective part of modern schooling. This section shows how she weaves Yup'ik identity into her lesson, how she connects kin and community to the classroom, and how she uses her cultural discourse patterns as an integral part of her classroom discourse procedures. Furthermore, the analysis shows how she uses students' everyday knowledge and makes it part of her classroom, both academically and socially.

Becoming a Yup'ik—Cultural Values and Moral Imperatives—and Science, Too

One way to view this lesson is to see it as a lesson about becoming a Yup'ik, as her behaviors and her commentary show. Yanez accomplishes this through the values of respecting elders, not wasting, being a good hunter and provider, and knowing how and where to subsist. In this lesson, she creates a classroom environment for this group of students to be in a Yup'ik milieu by the way in which she organizes her classroom social discourse: No students are spotlighted, students speak to students, and students are encouraged to take responsibility for getting turns at talk and for the task of preparing smelt. The task itself is organized from start to finish in a Yup'ik manner, that is, from catching the smelt to preparing them to drying them. Students are to engage in the task when they are ready and they are to take responsibility for their own readiness. For example, she uses such phrases as "Who's ready to be a teacher?" "Who's ready to string?" These comments are said to the group. She does not pressure any individual to begin the task. Group work is encouraged because it relates to survival on the tundra—cooperation is still a necessity for the harsh realities of subsistence living. Simultaneously, this lesson engages students in science. The students learn about the anatomy of smelts, about their seasonal migration, habits, and about parasites that attach themselves to smelt. When the students query each other "Is it a boy kind?" they are investigating the smelts' internal organs and identifying male glands and female eggs.

The evening before the lesson, Yanez catches the smelt. The next day, students clean and prepare them for drying by tying the smelt together with string. Finally, they hang the smelt on a drying rack. The importance of this activity is underscored by Yup'ik moral imperatives, which Yanez invokes three times during this lesson.

For example, she states, "Do you know what would happen if you're *aqessanguq* (lazy bone) and don't fish when you're older? …. You won't have any dried smelts …. Even in the summer if you don't split salmon you won't have any. So you have to learn how." One more example is powerful because it goes right to the heart of being a Yup'ik. After observing that one girl is not tying her smelts correctly, Yanez talks to the group: "You have to do it right. If you don't do it right then they'll fall down and a *marrlugaq* (grandmother) comes along and sees your fish she's gonna laugh at you and say that you guys are not Yup'ik." This statement underlines the seriousness of this lesson. Each time Yanez states these Yup'ik cultural values, she does so because she has just observed a student making a mistake in either preparing or tying the smelt for hanging. In both instances, she talks to the class as a whole and therefore does not address the particular student directly. In a sense, the student will, of course, know who she is referring to, but these important lessons are also meant for the entire class. Yanez connects the classroom activity to elders, their values, and quite literally to becoming a Yup'ik through knowing how to subsist properly.

Critical to subsistence hunting and gathering is the ability to be a keen observer (Kawagley, 1990). During this lesson and other analyzed videotapes, the Yup'ik teachers reinforce and emphasize learning by observing. In this tape, Yanez instructs the students to observe her "so that they can learn." Later in the lesson, when students are assisting students, she again evokes the importance of observing, which is directly related to learning. Similarly in Lipka (1991; and in the next chapter), *Capenaq*, a Yup'ik teacher, intentionally does not respond to a number of questions by students because she wants to reinforce independence over dependence. He expects the students to attend to visual demonstration.

Kin and Social Relations

The very first line of the transcription indicates the kinlike relationship between teacher and students when a student says *Al'i*, which is Yanez's Yup'ik nickname (a variation of the word sister). Furthermore, this nickname is like a pet name and was made up by a village youngster years ago. Now many villagers address her by this name, including children in her class. Similarly, in other analyzed classroom videotaped footage, students address their teacher as *Cap*, a Yup'ik dimunitive of *Capenaq* (a Yup'ik name). These familiar forms speak to what William Gumlick-puk called creating a comfort zone for students and the importance of social and kin relations in the classroom.

In addition, Yanez makes at least three references to either seeing or knowing about the students' relatives and their involvement in subsistence living. For example, she states that she saw students' uncles fishing by Kulukak (an old village site east of Togiak), and students fishing. She says a student's grandmother is a "professional" because she spends so much time fishing.

Discourse, Social Relations, and Culture

During this lesson, students are not following typical classroom discourse patterns of teacher initiating, students responding, and teacher evaluating (IRE), or social procedures such as raising a hand to be nominated by the teacher, or adhering to "only one speaker at a time." Yanez's discourse routines are distinct from so-called mainstream IRE (Mehan, 1979), but they also differ from those noted by Boggs (1972) and by Watson-Gegeo and Boggs (1977) on Hawaiian children's use of multiple speakers contributing to a "talkstory," and they differ from those routines reported on by Malcolm (1980) concerning Aboriginal children and the use of "empty-bidding" when multiple speakers vie for the teacher's attention, only to not respond when nominated. Similarly, the discourse routine markedly differs from those reported in chapter 4, when Parker utilized a discourse strategy of nominating and requiring a student to be a respondent. In those instances, she and the children were uncomfortable. During those nominations, Parker continually received either inaudible responses or declined turns at talk—quite similar to Malcolm's research (1980). However, Yanez utilizes a discourse routine that results in a lively discussion between teacher and students.

From the very opening of this transcription, with its kinlike reference to Yanez, to her choice not to "stack" the instruction for the day such as, "today we are going to clean and prepare smelts for drying, which later we will dry ...." Instead, this classroom lesson has a shared context with community activities which, I assume, removes the need to explain the obvious to the students. Yanez's discourse is more conversational, like what Stairs calls "overlaid narrative" (personal communication, November, 1993). For example, in lines 19–29 Yanez talks about seeing Ryan's uncles fishing and simultaneously a student (S2) wants to share that his dad caught a seal. Although S2 is "interrupting" the teacher and she continues with her sentence, she does not sanction S2's remarks. Later in the transcription, and at very important points, when students talk between her statements in lines 50–60 and 101–111, Yanez does not reprimand the students for speaking while she speaks. Furthermore, throughout the discourse there is evidence of multiple speakers talking to Yanez while other conversations are occurring between different students. Yanez does not control the students' turns at talk. Nor does she directly control the topics of talk while they are preparing the smelt for drying. The multiple student speakers can be interpreted as competing for the floor. Student discourse overlaps, begins simultaneously, and finally results in a student telling his or her story. This is quite similar to many of our Ciulistet meetings, when multiple speakers will speak simultaneously until one speaker desists and the other speaker continues.

The structure of this lesson's discourse also diverges from typical mainstream classroom discourse in the relative number and type of "teacher turns" compared with "student turns." Yanez's turns at talk are "informative." For example in line 18: "Ryan, I saw your uncles," (social referencing), engaging in conversation; line 29, "Did you guys make seal oil?" (concerning subsistence living); directives, line

34, *Muryartulag'gu*. [Go wash it quickly] (accomplishing the immediate task); Yup'ik cultural values or morals, lines 50–60, "Even in the summer if you don't split ah salmon you won't have *neqerrluak* [dried fish]; and evaluation and praise, lines 156–158 "Wow! *Aspiaq* [beautiful]. Now you can help your grandma." Similarly, students talk to other students on a relatively frequent basis, as indicated by lines 10–17, where they discuss whether the fish is a "boy" or "girl" smelt.

Turns at Talk.   During a portion of this transcribed discourse, three students are talking to the teacher at the same time (see lines 18–33). Not once does she overtly state who should be the speaker or the order of the student speakers. For example, student 4, who keeps saying "teacher" (in lines 65, 67, 72, 74, and 75), does not get a response, while the student who said "teacher" (in lines 69, 71, and 73) and begins a story gets a response. For example, in line 77, the student says, "We caught one beaver and." The teacher responds "beaver." Then Yanez asks in line 84 "Where's their house?" In the meantime, student 4 has not gotten the floor. In lines 91 and 92 student 3 gains the floor by speaking, even though that student's speech overlapped Yanez's. It appears that the rules governing classroom discourse in this lesson do not include either the teacher giving permission for students to speak or denying permission. The rules for gaining access to the floor appear to be that the student must take responsibility to speak when ready, to speak to the discourse of subsistence hunting or to related "science" themes. Permission to talk and control over talk are not the principles governing this discourse.

Further evidence exists in lines 50–60, where Yanez stresses a very important Yup'ik moral—to be industrious and to be a good provider. While she is making her statement, there are four unsolicited student comments. Similarly, in another section of the tape, she is stating an even more powerful Yup'ik moral imperative—to be a Yup'ik you have "do it right" (meaning know how to properly process and dry fish)—in lines 101–111. While she makes this strong statement, students are making unsolicited comments that are not germane to her point. In neither case does she ask for all students to attend to her, nor does she ask for quiet, nor does she call for "all eyes on me."

Interestingly, in the 158 lines of discourse transcribed and analyzed from this videotaped lesson, there are very few instances where Yanez nominates a student. In each case, the student nomination is not a taken for granted "you will respond," or "you will do ...." Instead, these nominations are invitations to participate, not coercive control strategies. When direct questions are asked, they are posed to the group; there are no instances of a student being "spotlighted" through the entire discourse. Students initiate questions to the teacher as well as to each other. The only exception are directives concerned with accomplishing the task or learning from somebody. In either case, being right is not the object of the directive.

It is clear that turns at talk and control of talk are not solely the responsibility of the teacher. In fact, the student has the responsibility to decide when to talk. This does not mean the teacher abrogated her responsibilities.

Tone, Prosody, and Rhythm. Twice during the lesson, Yanez invokes powerful moral imperatives about subsistence living, and in each case, although she is making an important point, students do not necessarily look at her, and a few students are producing overlapping speech. Yanez uses slight tonal changes to convey the importance of her message. During the statement "you have to learn how" she conveys the importance of the message by subtle shifts in her tone. The tone slightly rises on the word "you" and each succeeding word is stated in almost staccato fashion, producing emphasis. When she reaches "how" her voice begins to descend. This pattern occurs again when she says "you have to do it right." In work with ethnomusicologists and teachers, viewing this and other tapes, the Yup'ik teachers appear to those listeners as speaking slowly and within a narrow range. Upon detailed analysis, this was in fact confirmed. While working with an ethnomusicologist, I shared a number of very brief audiotaped portions of classroom lessons. These audiotaped lessons were from both Ciulistet teachers Nancy Sharp and Vicki Dull, and two outside teachers. The analysis transformed the spoken speech into a musical score where tonal qualities, pitch, rhythm, and overall contour of the speech patterns could be graphically viewed. In addition to the obvious sociolinguistic differences concerning "stacking" instructions at the beginning of a lesson for the outside teachers and Yup'ik teachers beginning more directly, other less obvious differences were noted. For example, the Yup'ik speakers spoke more slowly, their speech was more staccatolike with pauses between words and syllables whereas the outside teachers spoke in a more sing-song manner; rising, then falling, and so on. The range of the Yup'ik teachers was much narrower and emphasis was gained through subtle changes.

Table 5.1 describes typical categories used in analyzing classroom talk (Cazden, 1988). This simplified structural analysis shows the rarity of nominating students for this teacher in this lesson. This deviates from the established structure of classroom talk; initiate, respond, and evaluate. Reprimands are quite infrequent and those counted as reprimands mostly concern Yup'ik cultural values such as "don't waste." In this lesson, students talk more often than the teacher (62% to 38%). Approximately once in every eight lines there is an instance of a student's speech overlapping another student's. Fifteen times student talk is followed by another student's talk. In lines 10 through 17 the talk pattern can be represented by the following, S–S–S–T–S–S–T–S. This pattern is representative of the overall conversational style of interaction between the teacher and her students.

Physical Movement

Similarly, during this discourse the students are moving from one work station to another. In addition, two students appear to be engaged in other activities; one is working at a computer whereas another is writing at her desk. The four girls who move back and forth between where the fish are cleaned to where they are prepared for stringing do so without asking for permission. During the entire videotaped

TABLE 5.1

Summary of Discourse Patterns and Classroom Conversation in the Transcribed 158 Lines

Teacher Nominates	Reprimands	Teacher/student Turns at Talk Ratio	Instances of Overlapped Speech	Student-to-Student Talking
No nominations for a student to speak or to do the task. Two nominations for a student to help another student.	5 reprimands Use of the word "don't" constituted a reprimand.	60/98 teacher talk represents 38% and student talk represents 62% of the talk as a function of the number of lines.	22 (approx. 44 lines of classroom talk)	15 instances of student talk to other students.

lesson, there is no directive from the teacher telling the students that they should take on a particular role.

This analysis suggests that the value of individual autonomy within a cooperative interdependent group is an underlying Yup'ik cultural principle guiding the students' physical movements and turns at talk.

Praise

Yanez stated that overly praising is wrong because it can make one feel better than others and this could be particularly damaging in an interdependent society. In the lesson, praising occurs in the later part of the lesson when the children are completing their stringing of the smelts. When the first student finished her stringing, Yanez said, "Wow April, you can do it now." Four turns later she adds, "now you can help your mom tie smelts at home." Each time a student finishes, Yanez praises him or her for being able to process smelt and says, "Now you can help your *aluk*," or mother or grandmother. Again, praise is situated within the larger cultural task of learning to be a Yup'ik, in this case, learning how to prepare smelt, and it carries an implied expectation: Now the learner can join the family and help.

Work Groups

Yanez emphasizes cooperation and helping one another throughout this lesson. However, she is connecting "cooperation" both to the task at hand, tying smelt, and to the larger Yup'ik culture of helping one another and helping one's family. She accomplishes this adeptly throughout the lesson. When she observes students having difficulty tying smelt she says, "Go watch her so you could learn." Or, "Can you help him tie some?" These statements in the lesson are made in close proximity to her statements about helping one's *aluk* [relative].

These work groups share similarities with fish camp work groups. At fish camp, the mother is the head of the work group and she is in charge of the processes, from gathering to cutting to drying to distributing the harvest for the winter (Schichnes & Chythlook, 1988). In her classroom Yanez is in some ways is playing the role of head of the household.

Geographic Places and Place Names

Throughout the early part of the discourse, Yanez and the students make reference to important places in which subsistence activities occur during specific times of the year. Knowing place names and their specific locations is an important aspect of learning how to orient and how to travel through this country. Yanez is, at the least, reinforcing these local geography skills as well as Yup'ik place names and their locations.

Cognitive Processes and Valuing

Cognition is also situated within the framework of starting a task from the very beginning and taking it to its logical conclusion; drying and eventually eating. The lesson is not broken down into subject matter compartments, nor are skills decontextualized out of the lesson in an unrelated fashion. She is reinforcing and constructing a worldview that connects these Yup'ik children to their environment—economic, ecologic, and cultural—by modeling what *yuut* [people] do and how they act when they harvest food. She contextualizes the activity by engaging in all aspects, from catching through cleaning, processing, and drying.

She defines and categorizes smelt not simply as fish but as a vital part of the environment in which there is a spiritual relationship between humans and animals. Smelts, beavers, and seals are discussed in this lesson not as belonging to various biological categories but as representing Yup'ik cultural categories and meanings. This is engendered in the lesson through brief moral lessons about not wasting food and about people's responsibility to animals. This is conveyed in brief narrative discourse, which Yanez begins with a question: "Do you know what will happen if ...." However, this question is actually the first part of a three-part sequence in which students respond by saying "what," not by answering her "question," thus indicating that they know she will respond. Her response (line 52), "you won't have any dried smelt," connects proper ways of acting, of not wasting food, and of respecting land and animals, to "real people's" (literal translation of the word *Yup'ik*) cyclical relationship to fish and animals (Fienup-Riordan, 1986; Stairs, 1992). She states, "If we are not wasteful of our food that we get off the land, we will keep subsisting ... because animals and fish will still be plentiful." These are all examples of the social construction of knowledge, identity, and ways of being that are still vital to being a Yup'ik.

She also conveys this value through modeling these behaviors with her students. She equates the importance of being a good provider and harvester to "being a person—a Yup'ik" at a number of critical points in the lesson. For example, Yanez presents and reinforces the Yup'ik values of subsistence, implying the low status associated with individuals who are lazy and the high status of those who are *nukialpiaq* [an expert hunter] by valuing expertise in subsistence harvesting.

Expert–Apprentice: Modeling

Yanez uses an expert–apprentice model of learning, in which observational skills are reinforced, respect for elders is practiced, and respect and individual autonomy for her students is the norm. Within an expert–apprentice paradigm, she slowly removes herself from direct modeling and subtly shifts the responsibility of teaching to the students. She guides and directs students to help their classmates, and while she is doing this, she steps back from the group, physically distancing herself from what is now becoming the students' work. As an expert, she has engaged in the work of processing and stringing smelt herself and has shown the students her finished product. This is not busy work. Every aspect of this set of lessons, from cutting the smelts to drying them, is done as group work, but none of it could or should be labeled cooperative school learning, although, of course, there are overlaps. Yanez establishes work groups that are cooperative in nature and that connect directly to community values and work. These work groups are situated in a Yup'ik cultural frame of reference. This work is required to survive and to be a Yup'ik.

SUMMARY

Contextualized Learning

Learning emanates from a shared context that exists within the classroom and within the community. Starting from this common ground, Yanez is able to provide opportunities for extending learning from the familiar into less familiar areas. Within her lesson, as the students are preparing the smelts for drying, they are naturally investigating the anatomy, from the reproductive system to the cardiovascular system. The students compare female and male smelt, observe intestines and stomach, and observe worms that have attached themselves to the smelt.

In sum, the students are engaged in socially constructing knowledge related to their identity and their place in the world, and they are learning specific skills related to cleaning, cutting, and drying smelt. Students learn not only the Yup'ik values related to helping, sharing, subsisting, and respecting both animals and land, but they also learn emotionally their relationship to the natural world and their place within it.

This case shows how one Yup'ik teacher in one lesson connects in-classroom behavior to community and cultural norms. In almost every aspect of her teaching, she reinforces and constructs a Yup'ik worldview. This lesson has implications for mainstream and minority teachers and schools. The adept ways in which this teacher connected school and community had an immediate impact. She was later thanked by community members because their children helped at home with the fish harvest. Also, the students are learning "school" content in an everyday context. Again, she brings to the students' awareness notions of smelt migration, seasonality, anatomy, and place names. This academic content is conveyed in a Yup'ik way. This way, which both represents academic knowledge and occurs within a recognizable Yup'ik context, provides insights into what an emerging Yup'ik pedagogy could be.

Further, part of this potential Yup'ik pedagogy resides in her utilizing nonstandard school discourse routines that result in lively discussions. This is in stark contrast to the discourse routines reported in chapter 4 where nominating and requiring a student to respond to questions that would be evaluated resulted in the almost complete absence of teacher–student dialogue, and no student-student dialogue. Yet, the present case adds to our collective repertoire on ways of conducting classroom talk. Yanez, in the lesson previously analyzed, shows that a teacher can conduct classroom discourse and social organization effectively while using discourse routines that differ widely from the norms of IRE. I believe that Yanez's lesson represents a model for how others can conduct classroom interactions more in line with their own cultural traditions. Although the routines noted in this chapter are clearly culturally specific, the "breaking of the mold" provides alternatives to the three-part discourse structure so often associated with schooling. In this fashion, mainstream classrooms, as well as other groups in which the discourse routines from the community may differ from those used in schooling, can observe from this lesson that there are multiple ways of organizing speech and group interaction within classrooms. More specifically, classroom practices as part of a larger school culture ought to evolve, and I believe that Yanez's class shows some ways in which Yup'ik culture, language, and identity do not have to suffer and that schooling itself can become an evolving culture far more inclusive than has been the experience for many minority and indigenous groups.

Difficulties that minority and indigenous groups may face when using alternatives to school discourse patterns (IRE) are not hard to find when standard classroom management textbooks posit rules for classroom management that directly contradict having multiple speakers, or that would keep talking from being an acceptable strategy for gaining the attention of the teacher and class. For example, Evertson, Emmer, Clements, and Worsham (1994) suggested the following classroom rules: "Students are expected to face the teacher and listen attentively … that students raise their hands, wait to be called on, and remain in their seats. … It is not a good idea to allow students to call out answers" (p. 34). It is also easy to predict that teachers who don't "control" their students' physical movements, and who allow students to talk "out of turn" would not be perceived well by other teachers and administrators from mainstream society. In addition, the flat-sounding tonal qualities her speech has to many Western ears would move supervisors to comment that she should "speak up," putting emphasis in her voice when she says something important, and having students' attention when she speaks. In fact, these comments have all been made.

Caveats and Questions: The Issue of Power

The smelt lessons occurred during "Yup'ik Cultural Awareness Week"—a week that highlights different aspects of Yup'ik culture; Yup'ik dancing, smelting, storytelling, kayak building, and other similar activities. The problem with Yup'ik cultural week is that the rest of the weeks are devoted to *kass'aq* cultural activities. In fact, during my years of observing in this and other classrooms, activities such as smelting have been marginalized, occurring during special events or times, never acknowledged as part of the ongoing curriculum and never part of the philosophy of schooling.

In this and previous chapters, Dull, Parker, Sharp, and Yanez have voiced a fundamental struggle concerning their identities as teachers, as Yup'ik teachers. Each case highlights different struggles related to such fundamental classroom issues as communicating and relating with students, what language one chooses while teaching, and using one's knowledge of the students, their community, and the environment in teaching. Yanez's concern that her video might have been "too Yup'ik" to share with the Ciulistet underscores the dilemma that these teachers each face in their own way. Contrary to other research, particularly Ogbu (1987, 1995), the Ciulistet teachers' struggle is not about "secondary cultural characteristics" (Ogbu, 1987, 1995) or oppositional behavior or resistance, but active attempts to bring the Yup'ik culture and language into both the classroom and the school. Ciulistet teachers' struggles concern issues of power, culture, and identity. The primary struggle concerns the culture of the school. The Ciulistet teachers in these cases have each shared fundamental ways in which they are making their culture visible, adapting schooling to their culture, and/or accommodating to the culture of the school. Historically, the school has attempted to alter the community, influencing it toward Western culture and the English language. Now, the Ciulistet teachers have become increasingly aware of this force.

Concluding Remarks

The marginalized place of the Yup'ik culture and language within this and many other school systems further jeopardizes the very skills, knowledge, and values celebrated in this case. Yanez's adept teaching represents her growing awareness of herself and of her ability to create and transform this school, at least during this time period, into a much more accommodating environment. This learning environment allows students to explore smelts, learning many of their anatomical features, learning about human and fish life cycles, and learning their place in the world.

The next chapter explores ways of using Yup'ik patterns of communication, social organization, and knowledge of the natural world as core parts of schooling. Here we identify ways in which Yup'ik ways of enculturating can be combined with everday knowledge, particularly in mathematics and science. This raises the possibility of transforming the culture of the schooling by including local knowledge.

REFERENCES

Boggs, S. (1972). The meaning of questions and narratives to Hawaiian children. In C. Cazden, V. John, & D. Hymes (Eds.), *Functions of language in the classroom* (pp. 299–327). New York: Teachers College Press.

Cazden, C. (1988). *Classroom discourse: The language of teaching and learning.* Portsmouth, NH: Heinemann.

Erickson, E., & Mohatt, G. (1982). Cultural organization of participation structures in two classrooms of Indian students. In G. Spindler (Ed.), *Doing the ethnography of schooling: Educational anthropology in action* (pp. 132–175). Prospects Heights, IL: Waveland.

Evertson, C., Emmer, E., Clements, B., & Worsham, M. (1994). *Classroom management for Elementary Teachers.* Boston: Allyn & Bacon.

Fienup-Riordan, A. (1986). The real people: The concept of personhood among the Yup'ik Eskimo of western Alaska. *Inuit Studies, 10*(1–2), 261–270.

Kawagley, O. (1990). Yup'ik ways of knowing. *Canadian Journal of Native Education, 17*(2).

Lave, J., & Wegner, E. (1991). *Situated learning: Legitimate peripheral participation.* New York: Cambridge University Press.

Lipka, J. (1991). Toward a culturally based pedagogy: A case study of one Yup'ik Eskimo teacher. *Anthropology and Education Quarterly, 22*(3), 203–223.

Malcolm, I. (1980). *Classroom communication and the Aboriginal child: A socio-linguistic investigation in Western Australian primary schools.* Unpublished doctoral dissertation, University of Western Australia, Perth.

Mehan, H. (1979). *Learning lessons: Social organization in the classroom.* Cambridge, MA: Harvard University Press.

Ogbu, J. (1987). Variability in minority school performance: A problem in search of an explanation. *Anthropology and Education Quarterly, 18*(4), 312–334.

Ogbu, J. (1995). Understanding cultural diversity in learning. In J. Banks & C. Banks (Eds.), *The handbook on research on multicultural education* (pp. 582-593). New York: MacMillan.

Sacks, H., Schegloff, E., & Jefferson, G. (1974). A simplest systematics for the organization of turn-taking for conversation. *Language, 50,* 696–735.

Schichnes, J., & Chythlook, M. (1988). Use of fish and wildlife in Manokotak, Alaska. Dillingham, AK: Alaska Department of Fish and Game.

Stairs, A. (1992). Self-image, world-image: Speculations on identity from experiences with Inuit. *Ethos, 20*(4), 116–127.

Watson-Gegeo, K., & Boggs, S. (1977). From verbal play to talk story: The role of routine speech events among Hawaiian children. In S. Ervin-Trip & C. Mitchell-Kernan (Eds.), *Child discourse.* New York: Academic Press.

6

Expanding Curricular and Pedagogical Possibilities: Yup'ik-Based Mathematics, Science, and Literacy

Jerry Lipka
University of Alaska, Fairbanks

Throughout this book, we have presented the teachers' struggles, perseverance, and ways they use their cultural knowledge as a strength. These analyses and discussions illustrate Yup'ik ways of organizing speech, social interactions, and guided practice. In this chapter, we describe in detail a process of inquiring into Yup'ik knowledge that builds a substantive foundation for reshaping the culture of the school. This process was initiated 8 years ago, almost serendipitously when Esther Ilutsik suggested that we examine fish camps (a summer residence organized for the catching, preserving, and distribution of salmon for the winter). Fortuitously for the Ciulistet group, this idea and the inclusion of elders began a process that accelerated the group's understanding of Yup'ik knowledge. This knowledge, intricately related and situated in subsistence living in a subarctic environment, forms the basis for this chapter.

In the previous chapter, we analyzed one lesson taught by Evelyn Yanez and demonstrated some of the ways she organized her classroom around Yup'ik values, speech conventions, and everyday knowledge. Her lesson and the other cases documented in this book begin to present an outline of what a Yup'ik-based pedagogy could be. Furthermore, the connections Yanez made between a community and its practices and how schooling can include guided practice are highly suggestive of how the culture of the school and the culture of the community can coevolve (Lave & Wenger, 1991). These teachers stress the connections between community practice, knowledge, and schooling. However,

139

an even larger possibility for transforming the culture of schooling exists if the Yup'ik teachers have a larger Yup'ik knowledge base to draw on, especially if this knowledge base relates to core academic content. This is in fact what the Ciulistet has been engaged in for the last few years, interpreting and translating Yup'ik everyday practice, culture, and language into school-based mathematics and science. This chapter describes in detail both processes and products as we work with Yup'ik elders, communities, Yup'ik teachers, school districts, and university consultants.

This chapter first presents a theoretical background related particularly to ethnomathematics. Next we explore the relationship of everyday knowledge and practice (ethnopedagogy) to the teaching of school mathematics. The chapter also explores the process of interpreting Yup'ik knowledge and translating it to schooling. Here we address the null curriculum (Hollins, 1996) by making it possible to include curricular areas once totally excluded. This chapter describes in detail Yup'ik-based mathematics—numerating, geometry, and measuring—and how these conceptions differ from Western conceptions. Our approach to developing ethnomathematics is twofold; interpreting and adapting Yup'ik knowledge to schooling and more systematically understanding Yup'ik conceptions of mathematics.

Since about 1992, the group has included elders in its meetings. At that time, we had an intuitive sense that everyday existence and traditional Yup'ik knowledge could benefit the teaching of core academic subjects. In 1994, we obtained a U.S. Information Agency grant to hold educational exchanges with indigenous peoples of the Russian Far East—Sakha, Even, and Evenk—who were already developing ethnomathematics and ethnoscience. This relationship proved to be very positive. From their knowledge and our work with elders, we began connecting everyday knowledge to mathematics, literacy, and science. Further, the Sakha educators introduced us to both their "national culture conception" (ethnopedagogy) and specific ways of connecting the local culture to schooling. Foremost among their ethnopedagogical technology is a simple and elegant game called *sonor*, which features elements from their traditional games and oral stories. This chapter also provides a description of how we adapted a Yup'ik story to a *sonor* board game.

In addition to mathematics, this chapter also shows how Yup'ik knowledge of the environment has direct application to the teaching of science. In particular, Yup'ik elders have stressed the importance of knowing how to predict weather, and this chapter includes several examples of the relationship of traditional knowledge to school science.

The chapter concludes with a discussion of the implications for collaborative, community-based work in educational reform by emphasizing the processes used in coconstructing curriculum and pedagogy. We believe the coconstruction of curriculum and pedagogy with elders is one critical step in transforming the context of schooling, which slowly alters asymmetrical power relations. In this sense, this chapter responds directly to the various calls issued to transform schooling in indigenous contexts of North America, responding to the dilemma of being both an authentic indigenous person and an accepted teacher, as noted in the autobio graphical accounts in this book and elsewhere (Annahatak, 1994; Ilutsik, 1994; LaFrance, 1994; Sharp; 1994). The future prospects of this work and the challenges facing Yup'ik communities, Ciulistet, and local school districts are also discussed.

THEORETICAL BACKGROUND

If we could combine the Yup'ik enculturation—social discourse routines, values, social organization, and instruction as guided practice—with the teaching of core academic subjects informed by Yup'ik knowledge, then we might be able to more inclusively and effectively coevolve schooling and community.

In particular, the field of ethnomathematics has provided insights into how a local group such as Yup'ik Eskimos may use their knowledge in math education. For example, Bishop (1988) wrote that the following six activities are the foundations for the development of mathematics across cultures; counting, locating, measuring, designing, playing, and explaining. Different cultural groups meet these universals in different ways and have their own worldviews and ways of thinking mathematically (Moore, 1994). Over the past 20 years, anthropologists, educators, psychologists, and mathematicians (Bishop, 1988; Bockarie, 1993; Cole & Scribner, 1973; Harris, 1989; Saxe, 1991; Zaslavsky, 1973) have described the variety of ways in which different groups numerate, locate, measure, and design. Educators Denny (1986), Harris (1989), Lipka (1994), and Moore (1994) have been working with such diverse groups as the Inuit, Australian Aborigines, Yup'ik Eskimos, and Navajos to develop mathematics curricula and pedagogy that respond to the culturally specific ways each group embeds mathematics within their cultural activities. Nelson-Barber and Estrin (1995) have reviewed problems faced by Native American students in math and science and strongly recommend the inclusion of culturally based concepts, sociolinguistics procedures for communicating and solving problems, informal and inductive learning, and teaching and learning situated in the context of the local culture.

In addition, *context* (learning in and out of school and the transfer between the two) is also problematic (Boaler, 1993). The importance of connecting underlying contextual circumstances (transfer) to underlying principles of mathematics holds promise for transferring learning from one context to another. Open-ended, constructivist approaches to mathematics that encourage student exploration and explanation also hold promise.

One possible way to bridge the context of community and school is to use some of the concrete and more experientially connected Yup'ik conceptions of math and science as a means of teaching in school. For example, the human body and its relationship to the world becomes a central point of convergence for mathematical and scientific conceptions. The human heartbeat, first heard in the womb and later recognized as an underlying rhythm of time, is associated in Yup'ik culture with the drumbeat. The drum, of course, keeps time. The shape of the drum, an oval, is also associated with the *qas'giq* [traditional men's house], which is also in the shape of an oval or circle. According to Yup'ik elders, the *qas'giq* symbolically represents the human life cycle—the entryway represents the birth canal and the skylight is the passageway into the next world. Further, Yup'ik numeration is base 20, a number achieved by forming one whole person [*yuk*]. (This is discussed more thoroughly in the math section of this chapter.) From numeration to the heartbeat and drumbeat to the *qas'giq*, life is adapted to daily, seasonal, yearly, and life cycle events. The body, therefore, provides the first insights into temporal and spatial dimensions. More concretely, the first "clocks" are the drum and heartbeat; the first measures are body standards, and numeration is directly associated with the body. For purposes of schooling, the body provides young students with a means of understanding space and time. Body proportionality and their experiences with moving through space give students their first concrete ideas about estimating distances and judging time (Piaget, 1929).

THE CIULISTET AND EVERYDAY KNOWLEDGE

During the summer of 1991, Esther Ilutsik first suggested that the group study fish camps (seasonal summer residences where villagers catch, process, and store fish for the winter) as cultural work in which everyday activities may translate into mathematics and science. From that time, elders have increasingly become active members of the Ciulistet. They have realized that their culture is threatened, and finding a group of Yup'ik teachers and their associates willing and eager to learn has caused them to willingly share, and to our surprise, interpret this knowledge into school-based knowledge.

What educational possibilities can make a positive difference when teachers collaborate with community in coconstructing curriculum and pedagogy? We show how traditional cultural knowledge can form a basis for math curriculum and pedagogy while simultaneously meeting standards such as those established by the National Council for Teachers of Mathematics (1989).

This exploration begins with Yup'ik numeration and geometric patterns (those used on clothing and cultural artifacts) as central components of a Yup'ik-based mathematics. In addition, the ancient meanings of these patterns (symbols) connect and reinforce Yup'ik oral literacy while simultaneously teaching math. Students can appreciate the Yup'ik designs, the geometry, and symmetry. This approach to teaching mathematics is additive; it can supplement traditional math instruction or it can be a basis for teaching certain parts of the math curriculum. This approach can move Yup'ik knowledge from the margins of schooling toward the center; math is always a core academic subject. Also, this approach can be made equally accessible to Yup'ik and non-Yup'ik speaking teachers and students.

The Possibilities for Yup'ik Culture Contributing to School Math and Science

Yup'ik culture is highly interrelated with the natural environment. Within this environment and the subsistence activities that occur, Yup'ik people have their own way of conceptualizing knowledge, categorizing, and performing everyday tasks. For example, a recent study (Fall, Chythlook, Schichnes, & Morris, 1989) described a system of categorizing types of Dolly Varden (troutlike fish) by their fat content; Dolly Varden are also categorized by use and function related to subsistence living and not by a scientific abstraction such as the number of gills. Further, Yup'ik have a number system that is based on the human body (base 20). The culture and linguistic system relate to a specific environment; thus cognition and the making of meaning are socially constructed in unique ways, yet share attributes with many other societies. This is similar to Mayan mothers making rugs in Guatemala and to tailoring in Liberia (see Rogoff, 1990, p. 111). For example, expert-apprentice modeling has been effectively used in Yup'ik classrooms by Yup'ik teachers (Lipka, 1990, 1991). Fish camps abound with everyday uses of mathematics, from estimating the number of dried fish needed for an extended family for a year—fish racks and fish houses being units of measure—to solving packing problems in order to efficiently fill storage space so that the fish lie on top of one another. The tails lie on top of the heads in alternating rows so that the fish are tessellating (fitting the surface so that fish fit together like a puzzle, thereby reducing gaps and overlays). (See Fig 6.1 for an example of fish processing and storage.) Everyday cognition (Lave, 1988) provides an opportunity for developing pedagogy and content that is based within and from Yup'ik culture.

Approach to the Study—Methodology

For the past 8 years, we have been working on using Yup'ik knowledge of the environment as a basis for mathematics and science education. In addition to the approximately 14 members of the teachers' group, we have been joined at each of our meetings by at least four and sometimes as many as 20 elders.

The research topic of investigating the science and mathematics embedded in everyday fish camp experiences was generated by the group 8 years ago. The initial research method of videotaping, generated by the group, was used to capture fish camp work groups and the enculturation process. We chose fish camp because there, work groups are still organized in traditional ways. The group analyzed these tapes, which show an expert–apprentice modeling of the tasks surrounding fish processing. The youngest members of the family cut their fish independently with an *ulu* [Eskimo knife] after observing elders and older siblings perform the task.

The next phase used ethnographic research methods such as participant observation, formal and informal interviewing, and linguistic analysis, as we were directly instructed by the elders in a variety of Yup'ik cultural activities. During

FIG. 6.1. Evelyn preparing salmon.

these meetings, elders demonstrated and described various activities, such as how they tailored parkas, built fish-drying racks, made traps, and navigated in extremely limited visibility. We analyzed tasks and activities as a means of elucidating cultural principles that might help transform this knowledge into school lessons. In particular, when similar ways of solving everyday problems arose across disparate settings, we took these "natural experiments" and analyzed underlying features as a way of getting at cultural principles. On occasion, we would intentionally change variables to understand the way elders, for example, perceived shapes. Gathering Yup'ik knowledge and having elders respond to questions, tell stories, bring in cultural artifacts, and take us on "field trips" to forecast weather are representative events of this phase. All meetings were video or audiotaped and catalogued and significant portions were translated and transcribed. However, it must be noted that this work progresses *very slowly*. As we interviewed elders individually and in a group setting about a whole host of topics, such as the construction of the Yup'ik numeration system, these interviews took multiple iterations over many meetings to arrive at a consensus. Elders were as interested as we were in getting it right, and they continue to say that they are learning at these meetings.

The meetings are increasingly conducted in Yup'ik and translated into English for nonspeakers. There is a high degree of kinship within the group—some Yup'ik teachers attend these meetings with their parents, spouses, and children. Group members themselves are well known to each other or are distantly related. Within this kinlike context, elders have presented their knowledge in gender-specific ways;

men presenting information on hunting and trapping and other subsistence activities and women presenting information on patterns, measurements, tailoring, crafts (such as parka making) and their meaning, and storyknifing. The elders have shared in leading the "seminars." Increasingly, a few elders are becoming the leaders of the group.

Ethnomathematics

Principles and Problem-Solving

From the elders it has become increasingly clear that Yup'ik "mathematics and science" or ethnomathematics originate from the knowledge required to survive and to live a long life in the harsh and unforgiving subarctic. Under these circumstances, elders have passed along a tradition in which empirical observation of minute changes in the physical and biological environment can mean the difference between life and death. If, for example, you picture yourself out on the vast tundra viewing a mountain that is nearby, approximately 3 miles away, what is important is not the distance but the conditions—light, temperature, wind, snow or ice, and their interaction. Under some of these conditions, travel could be treacherous. The mountain could look closer or farther away with blowing snow or increasing humidity. The elders shared their way of seeing the world, which provides us with another set of tools to understand the world around us.

To solve problems encountered while living and traveling on the tundra or on the water, elders have passed on a tradition of "bottom-up" problem solving. In solving a problem, knowledge of the environment, problem-solving ability (including patience), and the use of local resources available at a particular time all play a role. For example, during one of our workshops, elders and teachers fashioned a drying rack. To build the drying rack, we measured off land and cut some limbs from birch trees. The elders established standards for measuring distance based on their body and the task at hand. This approach ensured that the height of the drying rack would be in proportion to the user's body size. The drying racks are custom made, as are *qaspet* [summer dresses], *mukluk* [footwear], and kayaks. In addition, kayaks are individually designed for balance between user and boat. The human body is instrumental in empirical observations, in creating standards for tasks, and for navigating in inclement weather. For example, navigating in inclement weather depends on the traveler knowing his or her relative position to the home village and the numerous signs located in the tundra grass and patterns in the snow (see Carpenter, 1973 for a similar discussion). Furthermore, although the Yup'ik words for the cardinal directions are the same in different regions, the meaning of these directions varies according to prevailing wind and weather patterns (Boas reported on this in his work with the Inuit, 1964, p. 235; Fortescue, 1988). A key to knowing where you are is one's relative position. The body at once gives an individual a sense of time, space, and place (Fienup-Riordan, 1994; Kawagley, 1995). Kawagley

(1995) also identified the body as a "sensing" instrument. Therefore, Yup'ik ethnomathematics and ethnoscience begin with the body as an instrument and source for spatial/temporal relations, numeration, measurement, orientation, geometry, and symmetry.

Yup'ik math and science gain an added meaning in the modern world, since one pathway to this knowledge is the human body—used as a direct sensing and experiencing instrument that provides the modern person with access to senses not often used in today's world. First and foremost, this allows students to learn from their bodies, from concrete experience and observations, and then to move on toward abstractions and generalizations. This embodiment of knowledge stands between the world "out there" and the world "in here"—between physical and biological phenomena, math and science, and between knowing *about* and knowing *how*. Our bodies provide us with our original sense of space and time.

The human body also provides us with orientation, because it can be viewed as an axis—top/bottom and left/right. Further, the body gives us our original sense of time through our heartbeat. Our initial sense of space is learned from our movements in the world—learning to visualize, estimate, and approximate. Many peoples, of course, used such body measures as spans, cubits, and feet (Zaslavsky, 1973). The Yup'ik, in fact, use the body in similar ways, creating the possibilities of grounded knowledge for students, providing insights into the evolution of mathematics and science. It is from the body, the meaning of Yup'ik words, and the doings associated with subsistence living that basic topics in mathematics and science can be derived.

Examples of Yup'ik Mathematics

Numbers are an obvious and basic place to investigate linguistic and cultural ways of representing mathematical ideas. Yup'ik language and culture relate the cardinal numbers to the human body in the same way as do the Inuit (Denny, 1986). Yup'ik cardinal numbers illustrate number patterns in the base 20 subbase 5 counting system, and the literal meaning of some numbers adds to our understanding of Yup'ik numeration. The numbers linguistically indicate (Jacobson, 1984) four sets of five, and elders organize counting in a similar manner. The literal meanings (in parentheses) are noted next to some numbers in Table 6.1.

Again, counting beyond 20 shows how base 20 is included within the language; 30 *yuinaq qula* [a whole person plus "above"—20 plus 10], 40 *yuinaak malruk* (two wholes or 2 times 20). Yup'ik counting from one through five begins on the right hand with the pinky and ending with the thumb, and then crosses over to the other hand repeating this process. Counting takes place in groups of five—the first five is represented by *talliman* [the arm] and the second five begins with *arvinlegen* ["the cross over" or "the other side"]. Numbers five through eight are constructed by adding "two plus this side," (as noted in Fig. 6.2) "three plus this side." The pattern switches at nine, for which the literal meaning is "not quite 10" or "almost

TABLE 6.1

Yup'ik Numeration

Cardinal Numbers

Counting on One Hand	Counting on the Other Hand
1 *atauciq*	6 *arvinlegen* (crossed over)
2 *malruk*	7 *malrunlegen*
3 *pingayun*	8 *pingayunlegen*
4 *cetaman*	9 *qulngunritaraan* (not quite 10)
5 *talliman* (one arm)	10 *qula*

Counting Below on One Side	Counting Below on the Other Side
11 *qula atauciq*	16 *akimiaq atuaciq* (one on the other side)
12 *qula malruk*	17 *akimiaq malruk*
13 *qula pingayun*	18 *akimiaq pingayun*
14 *akmiarunritaraan*	19 *yuinaunritaraan* (not quite 20)
15 *akimiaq* (finished going across and reaching 15)	20 *yuinaq* (the whole person)

above." Ten is achieved by two hands (the literal meaning of *qula* is "above"). The system follows this way of counting up to 20, which represents a whole person [*yuniaq*].

Also, elders at the workshop represented counting materials, such as sticks, in bundles of 20s. This knowledge of numbers is readily accessible to Yup'ik speakers, and for non-Yup'ik speakers it is cultural heritage. Further, the literal meaning behind the numbers, accessible to Yup'ik speakers, adds meaning to numbers and counting, giving students a sense of how numbers were originally derived. It offers students a comparison between base 20 and base 10 and it shows how the body was originally connected to counting in many different cultures (for example, the use of the word "digit").

Problems of Developing and Designing a Yup'ik Mathematics

Numeration

While reviewing Yup'ik counting, we encountered a problem in the use of two words, both used to signify 11 [*qula atauciq*—ten plus one, and *atkhaktok*—descending]. The former represents a modern Yup'ik way of counting 11 whereas the latter may represent a precontact method (Closs, 1986; Nelson, 1899). Also, some Yup'ik elders did not know the literal meaning behind words such as *qula* [10], just as we would not expect an English speaker to necessarily know the meaning behind the words for 11 or 12. However, we wondered what *qula* [above] represented in the counting system, and asked the question: Above what? To find an answer we turned to the ethnographic record. Nelson's (1899) description of counting, recorded almost 100 years ago, differs from modern-day counting. Nelson described:

FIG. 6.2. Charlie Chocknok demonstrating counting.

> As ten is said the two hands, thumbs near together and fingers all outstretched, palms down, are extended a little from the body. Then the right foot is advanced a little and the right forefinger points at the little toe of that foot as the counter says *at-khakh-tok*. This word ordinarily means "it goes down," and is used here both to indicate the descent in counting from hands to feet … [acquiring] this connection to eleven. (p. 237)

In this case, the ethnographic record (Denny, 1986; Nelson, 1899) and personal correspondence (Caulfield, 1995 on Greenlandic Eskimo) also supported the notion of "it goes down," which makes sense logically, linguistically, and mathematically. Other ethnomathematicians indicate that Eskimo and other groups probably used their feet in counting (Barrow, 1992; Closs, 1986; Denny, 1986; Zaslavsky, 1973). This differs from contemporary understandings—*qula atauciq* [10 plus one, or 11, without a reference to using the feet]. The question remains open as to whether precontact Yup'ik used their feet in counting. However, these musings and others became points of inquiry for the group; not only were elders interested in reconstructing parts of their own system, but they became increasingly interested in how other cultures constructed their knowledge.

Representing traditional knowledge even as supposedly straightforward and concrete as counting shows that translating basic Yup'ik knowledge into school knowledge is a difficult and nonlinear process. Furthermore, taking a concrete contextualized counting system into the classroom, formalizing its operations, then making it abstract, changes the nature of the indigenous activity. Furthermore, the systematic Yup'ik worldview and knowledge—part of an aboriginal context—no longer exist in that old form. Instead, knowledge is becoming increasingly fragmented from its context and its cultural bearers. This makes it all the more important to capture this knowledge before it is lost forever. Knowledge is not written but remembered differently by different people. This requires a very careful approach to interpreting Yup'ik knowledge and applying it to a modern context, schooling. Because we work together—elders, teachers, aides, and university faculty—we have built-in checks against inauthentic interpretations.

Interpretive Ethnographic Approach to Place Values

The problem of deriving Yup'ik-based mathematics is further complicated by the fact that the ethnographic record (Nelson, 1899) and interviews with Yup'ik elders during our meetings show that Yup'ik did not have written numerals for their number systems. This became another area of inquiry.

Working as a group, first with two faculty members and two Yup'ik research assistants, we began analyzing the counting system as a way to work through the problem of representing numbers, particularly regarding the meaning of "11." Using the body to represent the counting system suggests a division of the body into four quadrants with a vertical and horizontal axis. To assist us in visualizing the system, we placed and traced our hands on one-by-one-centimeter graph paper to represent 1 through 10. We placed our hands facing down, forming two sets of hands, and traced them. Both hands placed above [*qula*] represented 10, and the "below" hands or feet represented 10 more. This procedure was also in alignment with the way Yup'ik numbers are ordered linguistically, as noted earlier. Next we traced the outline of the hands and this formed four arcs, representing 20 [*yuniaq*] or "the whole person." We then used Cuisenaire rods instead of hands and formed four sets of five (each set represented subbase 5). In addition, we decided to place the oval on a grid to further represent the sub-base 5. We noticed that the pattern formed by the Cuisenaire rods in descending order from a five length to a one unit's length created a pattern often used in Yup'ik baskets. Finding this familiar pattern could have been purely coincidental, or it could indicate that the Yup'ik used body symmetry in creating their "mathematical" system. Furthermore, Yup'ik counting to 20, following the linguistic and physical way in which counting occurs, suggested a top/bottom and left/right axis (see Fig. 6.3). A physical representation of a circle surrounding the top/bottom—left/right axis is significant because this conception of numeration implies other concepts; orientation and directionality, part-to-whole relationships (fractions), circles, arcs and degrees, coordinate geometry, and symmetry.

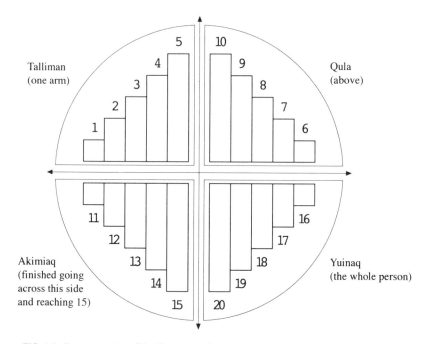

FIG. 6.3. Representation of Yup'ik counting from one to twenty.

In addition, Noelting (as cited in Denny, 1986) suggested that Inuit counting starts with the left hand and then switches to the right hand, which links left–right to east–west and thereby to the rising and setting of the sun—left is thus a beginning and right an end point. The use of a circle on an axis is an excellent mnemonic device for counting. Furthermore, by slightly altering Fig. 6.3, a person [*a yuk*] can be drawn within the circle, further concretizing the notion of 20 as a base. Associating subbase 5 to the corresponding body parts makes the teaching of base 20 and subbase 5 very accessible. One of the Yup'ik research assistants stated, "I would have learned to count in Yup'ik a long time ago if I learned this in school."

To create place–value symbols, we consulted the Mayan and Egyptian systems as a frame of reference (Closs, 1986). Because the Mayan system is similar to Yup'ik (base 20 and subbase 5) it was chosen to model the symbolic representation and place value system. We also referred to Yup'ik cultural artifacts and Yup'ik ways of orienting in selecting symbols for numbers. We decided on an oval because it is represented in Yup'ik material culture as a drum, in masks, in the form of the *qas'giq* and appears to have a similar meaning to *yuniaq* [a whole person]. For the place values, we simply used tick marks for units, one circle on an axis for 20 and two circles on an axis for 400 (400 being the highest precontact number that is noted in the ethnographic record—see Nelson, 1899, and Denny, 1986). See Fig. 6.4 for this symbolic representation.

Approval of the Elders

During a week-long workshop, we introduced elders to the interpreted symbols and their representation. The elders began debating the acceptability of this symbol and counting in Yup'ik. Also debated were dialectal differences from one subregion to another and possible mistakes in the Yup'ik dictionary (Jacobson, 1984). They engaged in long discussions as to the Russian influence on their numbers and the variety of ways of constructing numbers past 400. For example, one elder stated, "It seems that counting up to 1,000 can be reached using exclusively base 20 rather than *tiisitsaaq* [Russian loan word] 1,000." After some further discussion this elder asked another, "[Can you] count using base 20, it's 500? How would you say half of a thousand without using the word *tiisic* (1,000)?" After awhile the elder replied, "half of a thousand, *tiisicaam avaga*, is included in Yup'ik counting system." However, other elders persisted in counting by using Yup'ik constructions. This discussion indicates that Yup'ik counting today is "pure" between 1 and 400, and beyond 400 it is strongly influenced by the Russian language. Yup'ik counting is base 20 up to 400 and is a combination of base 20 and base 10 past 400. Past 400 it uses a modified base 10 system, using a 1,000 as a unit, hence 500 is obtained by halving 1,000. Further complicating Yup'ik counting is the English influence. Many people today find it easier to count using the shorter English words than the longer Yup'ik words. Despite these difficulties, the elders strongly indicated that

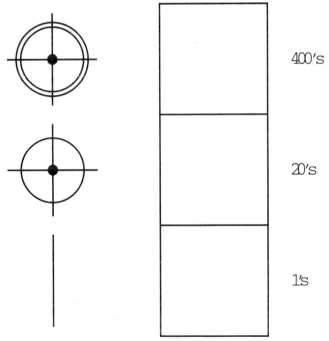

FIG. 6.4. Base 20 Place Value System.

they wanted to "get it right" and practice using the Yup'ik numeration system.

Later in this workshop and in subsequent ones, the elders tried out the place–value system and used the symbols that we suggested. To accomplish this, we teamed elders with the Ciulistet teachers and gave each pair 1, 20, and 400 place–value markers. Everyone sat on the floor in a large circle as another Ciulistet member used a Yup'ik drum with different beats to differentiate the different place values. According to the beats, the elders and the teachers formed the number. After the activity, one elder stated that he "felt that he could learn this system," meaning that it made sense to him. There was a tacit acceptance evident in the fact that different elders worked with the symbols and the place–value system during the course of the week. Fig. 6.5 shows the elders and teachers working together.

The group agreed to continue to develop Yup'ik-based math. This development was motivated, beyond the elders' desires, by the teachers, after a small group meeting of only Ciulistet teachers and university consultants. We discussed a variety of ways that mathematics is used unconsciously at fish camp during the process of storing fish for the winter. For example, participants discussed how their mothers estimate the amount of fish needed for the winter, enough to fill a smokehouse, and the amount to be divided among the different family units of the extended family. Furthermore, the way fish are stored is an example of tessellation. Each family seems to cut fish in their own distinct manner, indicating an individual "signature," and these cuts form distinct patterns.

FIG. 6. 5. Drumming and numeration.

A Yup'ik Math Tool Kit

Patterns

During a small group Ciulistet meeting, the teachers and I realized that Yup'ik symbols could easily supplement such approaches to mathematics as "Math Their Way," a hands-on manipulative approach to teaching elementary school mathematics (Baratta-Lorton, 1976). We realized that we could develop a curriculum and pedagogy that could be termed "Math Our Way." Presently, we are developing this approach from traditional symbols as a geometric set of manipulatives. (Other ethnomathematicians are developing mathematical approaches based on indigenous culture; see Anderson & Stein, 1992; Bradley, 1993; Denny, 1986). Diverse cultural objects such as hair nets, baskets, and storyknives provide excellent examples of rotation (e.g., an object looks the same when it is rotated), reflection (when a mirror is placed at the line of symmetry the object appears symmetrical in the mirror), magnification (the object is made proportionally larger or smaller), and sliding symmetry (the object appears the same from left to right). Students can create Yup'ik patterns, learn the meaning of the patterns, learn the stories that accompany these patterns, and create novel designs. These tool kits can assist in teaching fractions, factors, simple algebra, and tessellations (puzzlelike designs in which all the space is filled without overlapping). Based on this work and on subsequent meetings with Ciulistet teachers, we began to visualize how Yup'ik symbols or patterns could form a basis for developing a "Yup'ik Math Tool Kit." In our preliminary development work, this tool kit took advantage of Yup'ik symbols (see Fig. 6.6).

Some women form the basic building blocks for parka border patterns by laying together two strips of material, typically long thin rectangular strips approximately 1 inch by 10 inches (depending on the particular task), at right angles to form a small square.

From this square other shapes are constructed such as rectangles and right triangles. Lines, circles, and dots are constructed in other ways. Fig. 6.7 represents a set of Yup'ik border patterns. The following patterns are derived similarly to those shown above.

We designed the Yup'ik pattern blocks similar to the way some women create border patterns. Some women, when sewing fur, would initially cut a long strip and a second strip of the same width. They would overlap the strips as shown in Fig. 6.6. They would cut out the resulting square from the two overlapping strips of fur. (Wahlberg, personal communication, December 2, 1997). We began by using a square, and from that square we derived all the pieces necessary to make Yup'ik border patterns, as shown in Fig.6.8. See Fig. 6.8, which shows how we made the individual pieces for the Yup'ik pattern blocks.

The wooden Yup'ik pattern blocks are not numbered because the relationship between pieces is critical: Each shape fits every other shape. Because they are

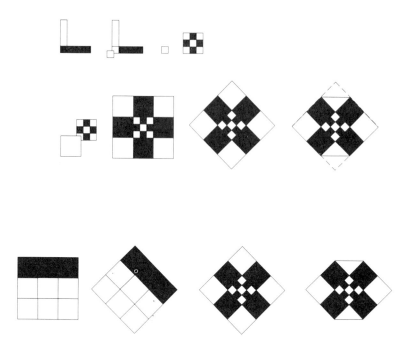

FIG. 6.6. Creating a standard for Yup'ik patterns.

constructed from the same base (the square), there is a good fit among the pieces. Yup'ik women manipulate similar geometric shapes to make their border pattern. This math tool will allow teachers and students to manipulate shapes to make geometric patterns. The very process of creating the elemental pieces from the whole is an activity that students should engage in. The students will visualize, create, and transform a raw material into a design, and this process would be lost if students just used the blocks. By adding colors, the power of the tool increases as the attributes increase. Because the Yup'ik design is inherently flexible, the number of attributes—color (2), shape (5), size (3)—that can be manipulated is 30. By adding an additional color, it could be as high as 45. Also, teachers and students may experiment with the size of the base square. In addition, this tool will be used for teaching numeration as the "base" or the "unit" of measure. Again, this increases the power of this tool, because it is not only used for geometry but it also has use in numeration, measuring, fractions, and estimating. As our work progresses, other items will be added to the Yup'ik pattern block and tool kit.

Furthermore, these black and white geometric shapes correspond with traditional Yup'ik colors; they are included in the kit in 3- and 9-cm sizes. Also included in our developing math tool kit are beads (white, black, red, and blue), a Yup'ik drum (preferably one from the community), mirrors for use in symmetry, 1-cm interlocking cubes, Yup'ik puzzles (following tangrams), graph paper in 3- and 9-cm sizes (as full pages for use in designing and making border patterns), and materials for making sonor games (felt board material and geometric shapes).

These symbols and objects can be used to teach a wide array of mathematical topics, including estimation, factors, fractions, geometry, prealgebra, problem solving, symmetry, and tangrams. These topics conform to the standards established by the National Council of Teachers of Mathematics. Further, this approach to teaching mathematics simultaneously reinforces the indigenous culture and its knowledge while building knowledge of Western mathematics and science.

These symbols and others can also be used in the Yup'ik Math Tool Kit to connect literacy to mathematics. For example, traditional parkas are walking stories; the symbols tell of a legendary person, identify a region, and identify particular families (Meade, 1990; Wahlberg, 1997). These shapes alone—and in conjunction with others—tell a story. The literal meaning for *ingriruaq* is [false] mountains—"false" indicates that these are symbols, not the real mountain. Other patterns include

FIG. 6.7. Yup'ik border patterns. The symbols in the center were collected, documented, and translated by Mary George and Marie Napoka, associated with the Ciulistet, they are from the Kuskokwim region. The principal investigator with the Ciulistet group and May George adapted these traditional shapes for mathematics instruction. The Yup'ik terms have the word "fake" within the meaning to differentiate between real life and the replica.

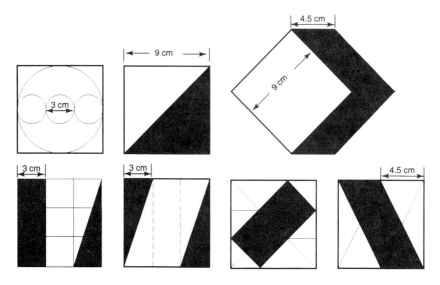

FIG. 6.8. Geometric shapes for creating Yup'ik patterns.

kuiguaq [a river], *cen'a* [a shore or border], and *ikamram tumelini* [sled tracks]. Some of the symbols have multiple meanings, depending on the story depicted.

Orientation

More recently, while working with elders and Yup'ik teachers, we were reviewing the Yup'ik border patterns. When we showed a shape to elders and rotated that shape 90 degrees, the elder gave a different name for the shape. After we observed this, we reviewed the pattern symbols that Mary George and Marie Napoka documented and noticed that some shapes when transformed from a triangle into a square retain their original name. Furthermore, dividing a square or a rectangle in half results in the new shape called an *inglu* [separate a whole into a half as well as two parts separating and no longer in harmony]. The same symbol may have multiple meanings depending on its orientation and its relationship to the action. Similarly Harris (1989) reported that Pitjantjatjara and other desert Aborigines, when shown a square, circle, rectangle, and triangle named it flat or smooth, round, long, and having sides respectively. Harris pointed out the importance of cultural background and its relevance to the teaching of mathematics.

Ascher (1991) suggested that Inuit and Yup'ik localizers, words that deal with space, make more distinctions than in English. These localizers or demonstratives describe actions taken from the perspective of a person. From a Yup'ik perspective, it appears that the orientation of an object, the action taken, and the relationship of the original object to the changed object all are critical in understanding what the object is. These insights from a traditional Yup'ik perspective have implications for mathematics and science. Ascher (1991) speculated that habitual use of this

> system of localizers clearly reinforces precision in observing and transmitting information about location … We can also see how time and motion, as well as configuration, become a part of the clear specification of place … More important, there is no presumption that perspective is fixed or shared; location is always relative, that is, a point of reference is clearly established … Motion is intrinsic to Inuit space-time … Shape and size within it are transient. Reference points for location have to be continually established since reference points themselves are not presumed to be fixed (pp. 135–140).

Furthermore, Evelyn Yanez suggested that the names of objects are often related to features in the social and natural environment. Here we have a direct example of differences in Western and Yup'ik conventions and cultural rules concerning orientation, space, and geometry. Carpenter (1973) observed rather distinct differences in the way perspective was handled by Inuit and Westerners:

> I ran an experiment with a number of Eskimo. I sketched on paper some twenty figures, each oriented in a different direction. Then I asked each individual to point to the seal, the walrus, the bear. Without hesitation, all located the correct figures. But though I had made the drawings, I found it necessary to turn the paper each time to ascertain the accuracy of their selections.… Igloo walls are often covered with magazine pictures obtained from the trader. These reduce dripping.… Some—but little—effort is made at vertical rendering, and the over-all result is haphazard. When children wanted to imitate me, a sure way to provoke delighted laughter was to mimic my twisting and turning as I tried to look at the LIFE pictures.
>
> With multiple perspectives, the moving eye of the observer glances here, there, over here, until the observer himself is drawn unconsciously into the scene. (pp. 134–137)

Speculating on the example just discussed, Ascher contrasted it with Western conventions and stated:

> The entire picture could only show what a viewer could see from a single fixed place in a single fixed instant; one could not show simultaneously what could be seen from above, below, behind, and inside as well as outside. (pp. 136)

Clearly the Inuit do not share our conventions. For them, time and space remain unified and the contents of the picture are not confined to what can be seen from a single fixed position in space–time. Particularly important to the development of mathematics from a Yup'ik perspective is the notion of multiple perspective (Carpenter, 1973), orientation, movement, and the relationship of these attributes. These examples and analysis point out the continued need to not only translate and adapt Yup'ik everyday knowledge and cultural artifacts but to understand them in their own right. Work with the elders is a continuing process as we need to go back and forth from theorizing to grounding our assumptions in concrete experience.

Measuring

The elders also showed us a system of informal or body measurements and proportions. Some of these measures are indicated in Fig. 6.9. They are *ikusegneq* [elbow], *angvaneq* [sternum], *taluyaneq* [a measurement for fish trap length], *yagneq* [distance between one's arms extended in opposite directions]. By working with these body proportions—for instance, from elbow to fingertips equals approximately one fourth of a person's length and elbow to spine equals another fourth—we can begin to move away from abstract conceptions to concrete conceptions of spatial awareness and skills for estimating. In activities concerning estimating, creating, and constructing, the body measures can be applied where the relationship between the object and the person is important. In this, way students can learn about body measures that were traditionally used (and continue to be used by many people today) in estimating, proportionality, and the concept of "fit."

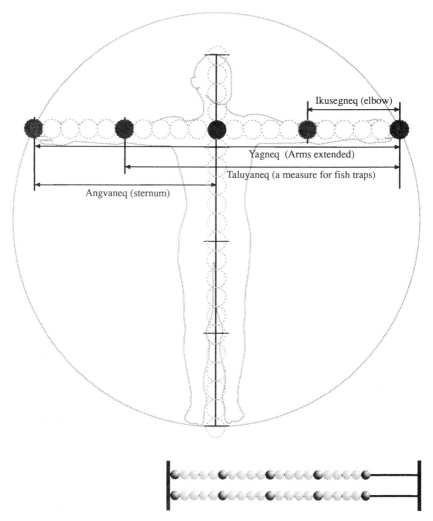

FIG. 6.9. Body measures.

In a Yup'ik math workshop, an elder, Lily Pauk demonstrated tailoring and Yup'ik ways of measuring. Pauk asked one of the Ciulistet members to stand, and in less than a minute, she visually "measured" the person. She then made a paper parka, using scissors, no ruler or pencil. She made a paper hat to accompany it. Both were accomplished in a few minutes. During this brief exercise, Pauk never used a standard measure or touched the volunteer. From discussions and some practice, we hypothesized that she took a mental picture of the volunteer and "measured" this person against a norm, then made adjustments from the norm. Also, it appears that the symmetry of the body is used in measuring a person, as well as body parts that are asymmetrical, such as the chest and the back. From these different data sources, the tailor makes the garment. This learned process of visualization has implications for the teaching of geometrical patterns, symmetry, and visual representations.

From this exercise and other demonstrations, a system of informal body measures was demonstrated to the group. These measures were contextualized with particular tasks such as making a parka and constructing a fish trap. See Fig. 6.10 for an example of contextualized measuring.

Jacobson (personal communication, May, 1993) shared with the Ciulistet a system of Yup'ik body measures [*cuqtaarityaraq*]. Further, Kawagley (1995) noted that Yup'ik elders defined mathematics by the word *cuqtaarityaraq* —the process of measuring—and estimating in time and space. However, Kawagley stated that "in ancient times, it was not important to measure things precisely" (p. 57). From

FIG. 6.10. Henry Alakayak demonstrating with a snare.

our work, it appears that Yup'ik measuring is not based on an agreed-upon standard measure such as a 12-inch ruler, but it is based on a task and a standard derived for this task as well as a set of agreed-on body measures. Within this context, the object and its user are a unit, one in proportion to the other, and exactness is required to achieve balance. (For a similar discussion of "anthropometric measurements" see Birket-Smith, 1953, p. 47–48; and for a similar description of the relationship of kayak builder and fit see Zimmerly, 1986, p. 40). For example, a kayak would be tailor-made made so that the owner's body fit in proportion to the kayak. So, one size kayak for one person and another size kayak for another person. An elder recently described a body measure for the width of a kayak. He explained that it is a "standard" measure, meaning this measure is used by most kayak builders. Here we have a social task (building a kayak) with a socially agreed-on set of procedures (specific body measures for different aspects of the kayak) resulting in balance between the builder and the kayak. Body measures are typically noted in the literature as informal or nonstandard; however, our work suggests standard body measures are individually applied. This is the opposite from Western society in which manufactured clothing, for example, is standardized for mass production and not for perfect fits between user and clothing.

The key variables are individuality, tailor-made crafts, local resources, and the establishment of a standard for a task. Measurement is a process of achieving balance based on visualizing, local materials, and specific tasks. This makes sense for a society that depends on custom-made tools. (See Denny, 1986, for similar discussion). From this discussion it appears that in Yup'ik mathematics, and later as is discussed in Yup'ik science, the guiding cultural principle is task; the relationship of the person to the environment or object and the creation of tools (measuring) in proportion to function and user. This principle was also interpreted from our work and experiences with the elders: We built a fish rack and created a standard measure that "fit" the end user. We also dried fish using what was locally available (birch trees and an ax). This principle is also shown in evidence from the ethnographic record, particularly Denny (1986). Furthermore, the Yup'ik names for months of the year are organized differently in different villages, depending on local environmental factors such as coldness. These examples underline important Yup'ik cultural rules used in organizing their world.

Also, the concept of body measures can be connected to numeration. For example, if we have a person stretch out his arms parallel to the ground, this distance approximates a person's height. If we take a piece of string that measures from one finger tip to another, tie a knot at each elbow and a knot at the spinal column, then we could bead the string, using the Yup'ik colors, to create an abacus related to body measures and proportions. Initially designed by Susan Royer, a math professor at the University of Alaska Fairbanks, such an abacus follows the symmetry of the Yup'ik numeration system; four sets of five each. Royer placed beads on a metal wire in groups of five, using Yup'ik colors to denote the number pattern. She used black for the first four in each set, white for the fifth bead in the first, third, and fourth sets, and red for the second set (to separate top from bottom). The second frame of the abacus follows the same pattern (see Fig 6 9)

Classroom Implementation
of Yup'ik-Based Mathematics

Pattern identification is an important part of beginning geometry. A number of ethnomathematicians and math educators (Harris, 1989; Presmeg, 1989; Zaslavsky, 1973, 1985) interested in multicultural education and the importance of everyday cognitive experience suggest that basing and building from local patterns is one excellent way to develop mathematical understandings.

Two Ciulistet teachers, Ina White and Esther Ilutsik, began a unit on patterns. White introduced the unit by connecting the human heartbeat to patterns and the Yup'ik drum. She had students listen to their heartbeats through a stethoscope. After listening carefully, the students began to beat out the rhythm they heard. The drum's beat, elders have said, is a reflection of the human heartbeat. Further connections were made to mathematics, using the drum and Yup'ik patterns. White also had the students make headdresses for Yup'ik dancing. While the students beaded their headdresses, White asked them to pay attention to their beading patterns. The students created simple patterns such as red, red, black, black, white, white. Also, these colors and patterns have meaning and as Ciulistet member Wahlberg (in press) noted in the *Shaman Story*, white represents snow, red, the people's death, and black represents the fly (others have suggested different meanings).

White's students drummed out the patterns they made—a specific beat for each color, so that the students could distinguish the patterns aurally and visually. For example, a color pattern could be represented as AA, BB, CC, with the pattern repeating, or it could be ABC, ABC, ABC, and so on. In these ways, students began viewing their symbols in both traditional ways and in new ways that brought out the mathematics of beading.

Recurring patterns in parka borders are right triangles, rectangles (rotated and straight), the plus sign, and circles. Often, these shapes are embedded within each other, and sets of shapes can be viewed on multiple planes. Math educators suggest that pattern recognition assists students in problem solving, particularly as related to geometry (Baratta-Lorton, 1976; Bradley, 1993; Harris, 1989; Zaslavsky, 1973).

As students make headdresses and parkas by copying traditional ones, they are also learning traditional stories. The geometrical patterns used throughout a parka connect literacy to mathematics. The patterns themselves are stories, and exact placement is required for the story to be accurate.

The Yup'ik Calendar Dance

Ilutsik devised a calendar dance after a workshop in which elders discussed the importance of dancing and drumming. The elders shared with us the process of creating dances according to traditional methods taught to them in the *qas'qig* [the traditional men's house]. They told us that first, elders shared stories, then the initiates picked out the words, chants, and movements; the drumbeat was the last to be created. The students in K–8 class used this method to create a dance. Each Yup'ik month is based on seasonal activities, and their names designate important activities that take place at that time of the year. The literal meanings for the Yup'ik names of the months provide more insight into science topics. The Yup'ik calendar, for example, corresponds to seasonal happenings—*Iralull'er* [the Western equivalent to January] literally means "the bad month" and *Tengmiirvik* [the Western equivalent to April] literally means "geese come." *Tengun* [August] is represented by birds flying south for the winter. The children learned the meaning behind the name of each month, and with the help of Virginia Andrew (a bilingual aide and Ilutsik's sister), they created the movements and the drumbeats. For example, for *Tengun*, the students repeated the word *piyuci* [good-bye] with their hands outstretched like birds. The dance was performed this past winter. Now the children remember all the movements of the dance for each month. According to Ilutsik, "it is wonderful to see the children get a deeper appreciation for the meaning of the months—how they relate to seasons and our yearly cycles. Using this method we have created five dances at Aleknagik; before we had none." The Yup'ik calendar clearly marks the seasons and the seasonal rounds of activity. Other Ciulistet teachers continue to use both traditional Yup'ik songs and dances and to create modern ones.

Yup'ik Adaptation of "Sonor": A Yakutian Pursuit Game

During 1994, we enjoyed a series of educational exchanges with educators from the Sakha Republic (an autonomous region in the Siberian part of Russia). It was during these exchanges that the Ciulistet teachers became familiar with "*sonor*". This pursuit game is directly adapted from traditional Sakha games and hunting (sonor means "pursuit" in Russian). Sonor was developed by Professor Tomski of Yakutsk State University (YSU) and brought to our attention by Elizabeth Barakhsanova, an ethnomathematician and teacher educator at YSU.

The beauty of sonor is that each game represents one legend or story, and the pieces, board design, and board illustrations reflect that story. Sonor is what Barakhsanova calls an intellectual game—one of several games of the mind in the tradition of checkers and chess. The Ciulistet group decided to adapt this game because of its visual appeal, ease of play, and most importantly, because it is a vehicle for transmitting traditional stories. Playing it, Yup'ik students can learn their legends and their designs while learning logical thinking. The board serves as a mnemonic device while the symbols and the drawings help students memorize their traditional stories. Barakhsanova demonstrated the game at a Ciulistet meeting. She showed the group handcrafted pieces representing a particular story and suggested that a teacher using sonor tell the story first to the students before playing. Next they might act out the story. Here, she and Anecia Lomack, a teacher at Manokotak, in Russian and in Yup'ik picked up their respective pieces and engaged in an animated discussion. One discussed how she could catch her opponent, whereas the other talked of her attributes and abilities to escape the fox or the raven (or other pursuers, depending on the particular story told).

In sonor, two people play at any given time. Five pieces are played on one side and one player is "in pursuit" on the other side of a playing field. The object of the game is to advance the five pieces as far as possible and accumulate the highest point total. After one round, the players change sides. The player with the most points at the end wins.

The playing field is approximately 42 by 30 cms. Three lines mark the playing field at 2, 11, 20, and 40 cms. Each line represents points—1, 2, and 3 respectively. The pursuer captures the opponent when the playing piece touches an opponent's piece. The pursued gets no point if it is captured before the first line. The pursued moves first. An additional piece is used to measure the moves for both the pursued and pursuer. Pieces move by having the mover piece touch the piece to be moved. A player can move in any direction, and a pursued can move all five pieces before the pursuer takes a turn. The pursuer gets one move. The players sit on circular pieces that vary in size from 3 mm to 7 mm, depending on the age of the players and the size of the playing field. The pursuer is approximately twice the circumference of the pursued.

After the initial exchanges, we held a few workshops devoted to adapting sonor to a Yup'ik context. Ciulistet teachers, with the help of elders, chose stories, created board game designs based on the story and Yup'ik symbols, and made the playing fields out of cloth and plywood. Cline (a bilingual coordinator and a Ciulistet member) made a particularly beautiful playing field for a story called, "The Pike and the Bullhead." (See Fig. 6.11 for the playing field.)

The Pike and the Bullhead

It was a beautiful summer day. The grass along the banks of the Nushagak River swayed in the gentle breeze much as a lady's dance fans would sway to the rhythm of the beating drums. The Bullhead was paddling upriver in his kayak to check on his traps. As he was traveling, paddling, he noticed the fluffy clouds in the sky, the sun shining, butterflies fluttering about the banks of the river, the greenness of the willows, and the loftiness of the spruce trees. The Bullhead was lighthearted and in the mood for doing something more than paddling along the river. As he was approaching the bend, he heard the sound of the Yup'ik drum.

He was elated. He thought he finally would have a chance to get a break from monotonous paddling and dance with adults. As he paddled around the bend of the river, he noticed little pike dancing and drumming. He felt so deflated, he parked his kayak and immediately devoured the pike. After eating the pike, he felt sad and wondered why he had done such a thing and thought, "Oh, well, I'll paddle up the river to check on my traps."

The beautiful day, the sun shining, the gentle swaying of the grass, the butterflies fluttering no longer made him feel elated. He just continued the monotony of paddling his kayak and he didn't notice a kayak go past him down river. He didn't know that in the passing kayak was the mother of the baby pike.

Mrs. Pike approached the area where she had left her children and wondered where they were. She thought they were playing hide and seek, so she called for her children. "Come on down now, I'm here, quit playing hide and seek." She waited, but no one came down. An otter watched what she was doing and called to her and said, "Hey, Mrs. Pike, you know what? The old Bullhead you passed ate your little pike." Mama Pike became enraged. She swung her kayak toward the river and followed the Bullhead. She soon caught up to him. The Bullhead realized he was being pursued, so he thought, "Oh, good, here's an eddy to help me." [An eddy is like a whirlpool in the water.] The Bullhead turned and faced the pike and knew he was being attacked, so he bit the pike right on the nose as hard as he could. Finally, the pike slithered out and became doubly enraged, and went right through the eddy and bit the Bullhead so deep, all that was sticking out was the head. Finally, the Bullhead slithered out and looked at the pike and started to laugh. The pike had a questioning look, so the Bullhead said, "You look so funny, look at your nose—it's so flat!"

The pike didn't want to be outdone and noticed what she had done to the Bullhead so she said, "If you think I look bad, you should see yourself—your head has become bloated, your body is now skinny—you look downright ugly!" The pike laughed and laughed. The Bullhead was so embarrassed and afraid other fish might notice him, so he slithered to the bottom of the river and hid behind a rock. To this day, the Yup'ik Eskimos say that is why the bullheads behave the way they do—hide behind rocks and stay on lake and riverbeds—and why the pikes have flat noses.

This delightful story shows why the pike and bullhead look and behave as they do. Our colleagues from Yakutsk provided us with a simple and elegant vehicle, sonor, for transmitting oral stories enhanced by art and mnemonic clues. In this fashion, the game, through its flexible design, can incorporate numerous stories that tell how, morals, and fun stories. By the end of our workshops on sonor, we had approximately 10 different game board designs and stories, each representing different aspects of Yup'ik culture and life. Through this simple technique, stories, Yup'ik patterns, and symbols typically not used in school can find a place within the curriculum. In addition, some of the teachers have incorporated their family symbols into the board's design (see Lipka & Ilutsik, 1997).

The simple uses of Sakha culture impressed the Ciulistet with how they might use Yup'ik culture in games, in classroom decoration, in toys, in stories, and other cultural symbols. Further, through stories and sonor, as the players plot moves and strategy, they learn logical thinking, simple mathematics, folklore, and science.

Sonor connects literacy to mathematics and to science. The game encourages students to use their math skills to estimate moves to avoid capture and to score points, add points, to understand the relationship between angles and movement, and to encourage logical thinking. It connects to science because the Yup'ik stories are embedded with "how" and "whys" of animal appearances, behavior, habitats, and niches. We have extended these connections by having teachers develop storyboards as another means of recounting stories (in addition to more traditional ways of recounting through dance and storyknifing). These storyboards incorporate the Yup'ik border symbols, representations of environmental features such as

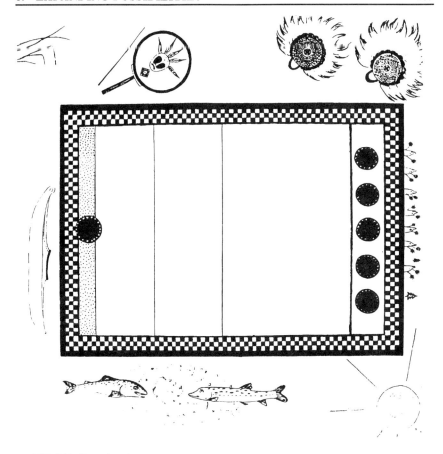

FIG. 6.11. Sonor board game.

mountains, lakes, rivers, and resident animals of southwest Alaska. In this fashion, teachers have the necessary tools to retell most traditional stories and relate them in ways that teach literacy, science skills, and knowledge.

YUP'IK-BASED SCIENCE

Many Yup'ik stories tell about the natural environment; these stories and Yup'ik science have their basis in subsistence hunting and gathering through elders' intimate knowledge of the environment gathered from repeated observations of animals, habitats, and physical phenomena. These experiences provide the opportunity for students and their teachers to learn about the environment from elders. Also, elders' knowledge emerges from the wisdom of past generations. The following example impressed the Yup'ik teachers, as well as the university faculty, because the elders' knowledge of kayaks included "physics." Specifically, the elders talked about the use of visors that trapped air when a kayak flipped over. As one Yup'ik teacher translated:

> They would figure exactly what kind of curve this visor cap made out of wood was
> ...and when they went down in the water, this curve would trap the air, just like
> when you put a cup in the water (upside down). They figured exactly what curve
> to use.... They put it [visor] over their *kuspuk* [clothing] and they tied it right there
> really tight so that thing would not come off and move around, (Alakayak, Ivan,
> Pauk, and Phillip, personal communication at Ciulistet and Math Science Meeting,
> July 1992, Fairbanks, Alaska)

Presented in this section are two major science topics; navigation and weather prediction. From a Yup'ik perspective, skills common to both are observing your surroundings and noting recurring patterns that relate directly to living off the land.

The human body, being a finely tuned sensing instrument, is critical to understanding the natural world. The Yup'ik use it to interpret minute changes in the environment. As Joshua Phillip (personal communication, November 12, 1993) told the Ciulistet, "All the bad weathers have scents that smell different. The snow has its own scent, the strong wind has unique smell, and the calm weather its own smell." Based on empirical observations, ordered and interpreted, this knowledge correlates to recurring biological and physical phenomena. The elders hope that transmitting this knowledge to the Ciulistet and their colleagues will ensure that their culture and its ancient wisdom will be passed on to the next generation. The following sections provide examples of elders' knowledge and how this knowledge may be translated to a school context.

Navigating on the Water

Navigating on water in inclement weather provides examples of the rich pedagogical possibilities for basing part of school science on Yup'ik culture. Navigation has been presented by the elders on a number of different occasions. The first example pertains to traveling on the ocean (or large bodies of water) during very poor visibility. The elders have reported two types of wave patterns. The first is a short wave, which is said to be caused by local conditions such as local winds. This wave is unreliable for travel, as local wind conditions may cause waves or ripples to travel in any direction. The second type is a long wave, measured from the apex of one wave to the apex of another. This type of wave is relied on for navigation. It always tends to go to shore, so travelers follow this wave in inclement weather (Henry Alakayak, interview, September, 1992).

In addition, the elders have explained that if the weather is very foggy, to the point where the sun is blocked and visibility is measured in a few feet, then very carefully have your boat make a circle. While doing so, observe the fog crystals. As soon as you observe the crystals sparkling, a rainbow, or a shadow, stop. At this point, the sun lies directly behind you (typically to the south) and the land lies ahead of you (typically due north on the southwest coast of Alaska depending on the time of day).

In a recent meeting, another elder reported on how other "signs" exist for the traveler. He said that you can use a wooden paddle, dip it down into the water, and place your ear on the paddle. You will be able to learn to "hear" an approaching storm. Plausibly, the energy in the form of sound waves from the approaching storm gets transmitted into the water and travels at a faster rate than in the air, thereby warning the observant traveler of the impending storm.

Navigating on Land—Memorizing and Patterns

The elders have also talked about navigating on land during inclement weather when the stars and the moon are not visible. Under these conditions, it is critical for travelers to know their surroundings and have memorized specific features of the landscape. Stories are told of a person's traveling from one location to another even though that person had never seen this land before. Place names and specific visual "road maps" are passed from one generation to the next. Further, there are also specific land features that give the traveler clues to reading the patterns that wind and snow make, dependable clues that lead one in a specific direction. For example, when the snow falls early in the season and then melts, it eventually freezes the grass in the direction that the wind is blowing. The grass stays frozen in that direction for the duration of the winter. Knowing this, the traveler can dig through the snow to the grass, which acts like a street sign, pointing the way. Also, the north wind forms the snow drifts into a specific pattern, shaping another dependable pattern that the knowledgeable traveler can follow back to a village. Joshua Phillip (November 12, 1993, Ciulistet meeting) stated:

> Snow conditions that were formed by the north wind are rough and curved. North wind is the only wind direction that develops this type of snow formation … Our ancestors used these land and snow formations as a compass when they traveled. They never got lost. The sharp-edged snow formations facing toward north are landmarks used for leading the traveler home … even though they cannot … see what's ahead of them.

Recently, while traveling by air to a Bristol Bay village, I observed a distinct snow pattern on the tundra. This particular pattern, approximating a semicircle, pointed due south mile after mile. However, once the plane passed over a forested area, the distinct snow pattern was no longer visible from the air. Yet the experienced traveler is not without clues.

Sun and Trees

Trees are another reliable source for navigating. The elders carefully showed us that tiny fungus grows on the north side of trees. In addition, the elders pointed out that the branches on the south-facing side grow much longer, and in a sense, point toward south. The elders stressed knowing the relationship between the south-facing branches, the sun, and your home village as a means of orienting in inclement weather. Using the tree and its north/south axis, then orienting the body on a left/right or east/west axis provides more valuable information for navigating. Further, directionality was implied in Yup'ik counting by starting with the left hand and then switching to the right hand and this linked left/right to east/west axis. Fienup-Riordan (1994) provided further support for this: "Inuit people all across the Arctic practiced the act of circling in the direction of the universe (with the sun from east to west)" (p. 358). Elders (women) in our workshop in May, 1993 added a semicirclelike design to their *kuspuks* [dresses], which they said symbolized the rising and setting sun, reinforcing the importance of orientation in everyday artifacts and of east–west orientation.

Another way to determine south and north in inclement weather is to remember that when the shadow is cast, it faces north. Phillip (May, 1993, Ciulistet meeting) suggested that if you face the sun in the morning, "that's east, the back is west, the right side south, and the left side north." The trees, tundra grass, snow patterns, sun, and North Star all provide multiple reference points for traveling. These natural empirical phenomena clearly point to ways of teaching science in school.

Space and Time, Place, and Identity

During these conferences, the relationship of the Yup'ik drumbeat was often equated with the human heartbeat and, hence with time. In Western terms, the heartbeat approximates seconds. In navigating and orienting, the Yup'ik elders use the North Star and the Big Dipper as time guides. The Big Dipper starts in the sky with the "cup" facing upwards, and by daybreak, it empties its cup. The Big Dipper forecasts daybreak, and its relative positions in the night sky can be used to tell time.

In addition, stars, sun, and moon are observed for navigation, for predicting weather, and for knowing the time of the year and the time of night. This intimate knowledge of the land has led one person to say, after being in the *kass'aq* [White] world for a considerable length of time, "I begin to get uneasy. During those times I would sometimes step out at night and look at the moon to find out where I am." These relationships of place and space relate directly to Yup'ik identity. These relationships may also relate to a Yup'ik geometry, resulting in a culturally organized sense of space and of the relationships of objects and persons.

Weather Prediction

Weather prediction, as noted earlier, is a critical area of traditional knowledge. For example, Henry Alakayak (a Yup'ik elder) noted:

> Our ancestors who traveled by walking [reported] how important weather observation was to them. At dawn, when skies turn very red, the storm will arrive before the day is over, even if the weather seems fair. At sundown, the sun rays flash over the sky and its sides turn red. This predicts fine weather for several days.

This reminds us of one of the Western sailors' saying: "Red sky at night, sailors delight. Red sky at morning, sailors go mourning." Another elder states that if "a cloud, several thousand feet or more (9,000 to 30,000) above, appears on a very clear day and it suddenly disappears, then after 3 or 4 days rain and wind will come."

An account almost 100 years ago provides an example of the importance of listening to nature and predicting weather. At that time, John Kilbuck, a Moravian missionary in the Kuskokwim region, was traveling in the Bristol Bay region during a very cold spell. Anxious to return home, Kilbuck (as cited in Feinup-Riordan, 1994) pressed his Yup'ik guide, set out on the journey:

> One morning, in spite of the bitter cold I started early expecting to reach a village 3 days' distant from home. It was so cold that the snow was like sand and the iron would hardly slide over it. We had been on the road about an hour, when my guide advised me to turn back, saying that a blizzard was approaching, and that our only chance for life was to reach the village whence we had started, as I could not reach shelter in time by going on. I was loathe to return, and thinking that probably he did not wish to travel on such a cold day, I said we would push on at any rate. As far as I could see, there was no sign of a storm; on the contrary, it was almost calm, and the sun was shining brightly. My guide remained firm in his prediction of a storm. He, however, prepared to go on, saying, at the same time that he for one was sure of being frozen. I then asked him for his signs of a storm. He directed my attention to a hazy streak along the horizon, and said that I should watch, for it was rising towards the zenith, and that soon we would see it turn black. He then told me to look at the sun. I did so, and I could see far up in the air bright particles flying almost in a straight line. I looked at the horizon again, and there, sure enough, was a dark cloud rising higher and higher very rapidly. Without delay we turned back ... [back at the village] the men calling me "good" because I had listened to the guide .... For almost 2 days the storm raged terrifically. No one ventured 20 paces outside. (p. 161)

This example illustrates why elders have identified weather prediction as an extremely important topic and it underscores the resistance that outsiders have toward Yup'ik knowledge. Obviously, predicting the weather is critical for its survival value during hunting trips, yet it has relevance for the modern world and schooling. Phillip reported:

> When I was a young boy, my father used to ask me to go outside around 5:30 a.m. to 6 a.m. in the morning to observe the weather before the sun came up. My first reaction when I came in was "it is good," when there was no visible bad weather. My father would then ask me, "What is the wind direction?" Since I did not notice the direction of the wind, I would respond, "I don't know." My father would say "Do not drag your life, be aware of everything around you. Next time you go out to check the weather, make sure that you notice which direction the wind is blowing from. If you tell me it is coming from this direction, I would tell you it is *keluklimiluku, wallu waken, calaarniluku, wallu ungalamek wall kanauamek* [they say it is coming from behind us or that it is coming from the east to him or coming from the south direction or west direction]. These are the most important things to be aware for the young men who are learning to hunt. (Joshua Phillip, November 12, 1993 interviews)

Elders have reported on the empirical processes that they use to predict weather and they, especially Phillip, have taken us out to observe sunrises and sunsets. These empirical processes—observing sunrises and sunsets, cloud formations, wind direction, and color of the clouds—provide important data that elders use as a basis of knowledge for weather predicting. Phillip (May 27, 1993 interviews) also said:

> At this time of the year when the sun looks like this with bright ring around it, it means that tomorrow it will snow. Or, it will be foggy …. Then if the ring around the sun is large with faint darkness inside it, the wind will begin to blow in four days. Since the ring around the sun is large it will snow in 4 days. But if the ring size is smaller then the wind would blow for 1 or 2 days.

He also said, "When the moon has orange color around it and its inside is dark, it predicts rainy stormy weather for 4 days." Phillip and other elders at a meeting in September, 1993 noted other observable phenomena that indicate changes in weather. Observing animals provides clues; when they return to their dens bad weather is approaching. Snipes (small shore birds that nest on the tundra) flying up and down during their mating rituals indicate good weather. When birds fly high, warm weather is coming, and when they fly lower, cold weather is approaching. Yet there are other signs that signify weather for an entire season.

Cardinal Directions and Wind

The cardinal directions (north, south, east, and west) are closely associated with weather prediction and traveling. From various meetings with the elders, we learned that the cardinal directions indicate both direction and prevailing winds (personal communication with Steven Jacobson, 1995). For example, *neggeqvaq*, "the cold wind," also means "north," and *ungalaq* means "bad, stormy, and windy" as well as "south" (See Fig. 6.12). Furthermore, Fortescue (1988) described both local and larger area Eskimo orientation systems. He described "two axes intersecting at right-angles … "upriver/downriver" … and the *negeq-ungalaq* "prevailing wind" "one pointing north and south" (p. 18). It appears that the elders have a system of orientation based on multiple factors such as minute details of local conditions, landmarks, basic physics, and mental grids formed from knowing their relative position to key geographical features such as upriver/downriver, to the coast and away from the coast, and a north/south axis (Ascher, 1991; Carpenter, 1973; Fortescue, 1988). This orientation system is a complex problem-solving solution to the difficult task of navigating a land where conditions change dramatically from day to day and sometimes over much shorter intervals. This information for navigating and weather predicting is highly related to specific areas.

Also, the literal meanings of Yup'ik words associated with clouds provide insight into weather prediction. For example, *quunenqatan* [literally—the "no more wind clouds"] would be quite descriptive for a Yup'ik speaker compared to the Latin expression "altocumulus" that English speakers use. Interestingly, the literal Latin translation for altocumulus is middle-height "heap" or "puffy" (see Fig. 6.13).

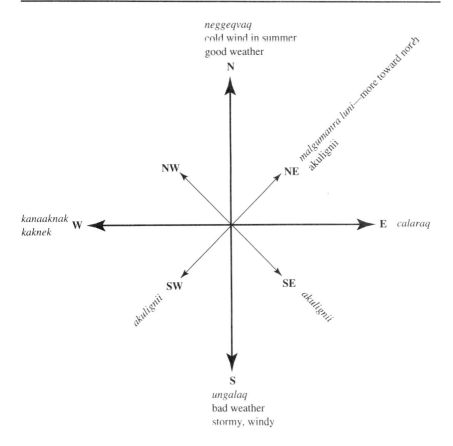

FIG. 6.12. Directions, wind, and weather.

This sampling is only a small portion of our research with Yup'ik elders, but it indicates some of the possible connections between Yup'ik observations of natural phenomena and Western science. Many Western-trained scientists engage in similar complementary empirical and analytical processes (Kawagley, 1990, 1995). We hope to capitalize on these two systems of knowledge, particularly in identifying foundation elements for each system of knowledge. Recently, the elders have asked Ilutsik and me to organize a spring camp where scientists will be in residence along with elders, teachers, and students. Spring is an ideal time for observing and engaging in subsistence activities as the southwest coast undergoes an incredible influx of life. Herring by the millions enter the bays, followed by all forms of sea creatures and birds. During this explosion of life, teachers will work with scientists and elders, each learning how the other observes and interprets natural phenomena such as weather signals and changes in the marine environment. We anticipate project teachers developing homemade weather stations, including barometers,

cagnianateng (means puffy)
angalleggluteng

cumulus

nengqeggluteng (means stretched)

cirrus

cagnigengqeggluteng (means tight)

jet-stream

quunengqataar (the no more wind clouds)

altocumulus

FIG. 6.13. Clouds and their literal meaning in Yup'ik.

anemometers, and thermometers. Teachers will also download weather maps from satellites, record data, analyze and correlate changes in weather, and through this instrumentation, connect their data to the elders' weather predictions. Furthermore, scientists at University of Alaska, Fairbanks will provide background knowledge that may explain the observable phenomena reported by elders. For example, what does the color of light at sunrise and sunset have to do with weather prediction? This collaborative approach is also inquiry based.

A HOLISTIC APPROACH: MATH AND SCIENCE, SPIRITUALITY AND SCIENCE

Yup'ik "science" is not only based on empirical phenomena but also on metaphysical concepts. At a few meetings, elders have told us there was once a time when animals and humans could communicate directly. Today, however, "people and animals no longer talk to each other. That is why now people eat with caution and with care, for [animal] spirits are watching. Hunger will not come when honoring the animal spirits that are watching over" (Annie Blue, personal communication, April, 1995, Togiak). A story told by Chuna McIntyre (1994), "The Blackfish Story," highlights the relationship between people and animals.

The Blackfish Story

A long time ago, there was a fish swimming up a beautiful river looking for a fish trap to be caught in. He closed his eyes and sang up the river … [the song has not been included].

When he opened his eyes, in front of him there was this fish trap. This fish trap was not very tidy and not very kept up. There were even holes in the trap where he could escape even if he did get caught.

Just in case, he said, "I'm going to check who this trap belongs to."

So he got out of the river, stood on a little stump and looked at a little house. There was smoke coming out of the house. It wasn't very tidy around the house. The dogs were tied up in every which way. Then a woman came out with a pot of stew which was once fish stew. Then she simply spilt the stew onto the ground where the dogs were, and the dogs fought for the bones.

Then the fish thought to himself, "I don't want my bones to be fought over. I don't think I want to be caught in this fish trap."

So he went back into the river, closed his eyes, and started going up the river again. The fish started to sing up the river.

When he woke up, right in front of him was this fish trap glistening and gleaming in the water, freshly made with new wood and very well kept.

"Now this is a fish trap that I would like to be caught in," he thought, "but, just in case, I'm going to see who it belongs to."

So he got out of the river, climbed on top of a little knoll and looked down at the house. There was smoke coming out of the house, and it was neat and tidy around the house. The dogs were tied up in nice neat rows. Someone came out of the house with a pot of fish stew with fish bones in it and ladled it out for each dog, food and fish bones.

The blackfish thought, "Now, this is the trap that I want to be caught in."

This story indicates that the blackfish *chooses* the trap and its owner; the trapper does not trap it, but the skill and care of the hunter show that he is worthy of receiving the blackfish. Fienup-Riordan (1994) and Kawagley (1995) pointed out the cyclical and spiritual relationship between animals and people. This story further intimates that the fish bones must be cared for properly, and, for the Yup'ik, this means that the bones of some animals (such as the beaver) must be placed back in the streams so that they may continue to come (Fienup-Riordan, 1994; Kawagley, 1995; Yanez, this volume).

Fred George and Sam Ivan (Akiachak meeting, November 12 & 13, 1993) explained the steps required to build a proper fish trap. They described in detail the type of spruce tree needed, the proper way of quartering the tree, how to measure the opening, and where to place the trap. They said to use those areas passed on by the elders, and "the foxes and the ravens will find the streams for you." Also, in this meeting George and Phillip described a life history of a particular spruce tree; they brought a cross section of this spruce to our meeting. They interpreted the life history of this tree as any good botanist would, by examining the growth patterns, irregularities, hardness, and softness of this cross section.

The knowledge of how to make a fish trap, how to set, how to observe, and "doing it right" not only teaches students in a holistic manner—integrating math and science skills like accurate measuring techniques and learning biological life histories—but also teaches students core Yup'ik values, including their appropriate relationship to the world (in this case to the blackfish). In other examples, Phillip and others kept telling the group "not to drag your awareness," but to be an astute observer of the natural world. The natural world will then "tell" about weather changes and other information vital to life. Furthermore, the elders in these meetings have instilled the importance of learning how to observe, and this relates to the value of a Yup'ik epistemology—the value of knowing how and why from one's own experience (Fienup-Riordan, 1994). Even the Yup'ik names for patterns contain a suffix indicating that this representation is "fake"—not the real thing—thus reinforcing the value placed on knowing from your experience.

To bring this to a school context, then, it is critical for students to experience—observe, do, and analyze—prior to discussing or "discovering." In this way, the culture of the school and community come together, making science part of the living Yup'ik culture and central to the school culture. These "field experiences" form the first phase of introducing students to such subjects as biology, meteorology, and physics.

Elders are steadfast in differentiating learning by personal experience from talking about knowledge that has not been experienced (Fienup-Riordan, 1994). A program that develops science and math curriculum based on Yup'ik knowledge needs to consider Yup'ik ways of constructing that knowledge so that it is authentically transmitted. Similarly, Yup'ik elders stress the importance of a person being aware of one's surroundings—such awareness is tantamount to survival. The astute observer "hears" from the world (*ella*—awareness, weather, consciousness) what the weather will be. Phillip and other elders have repeatedly told us that one senses the environment not only with one's eyes, but with other senses. This emphasis extends to almost every part of Yup'ik culture right down to the circle and dot motif used to decorate storyknives; it symbolizes "the eye of awareness."

DISCUSSION

The previous chapters describe the struggles of becoming a teacher. In the Lipka and Yanez chapter, Yanez demonstrated some of the ways in which she could use her knowledge of the environment, the culture, the community, and the children. Further, in Ciulistet meetings, we analyzed videotapes of teachers and gained a sense of what a Yup'ik pedagogy could be. But partially missing from this discussion was the substance or content that needs to be related to that pedagogy. In this chapter, we began a process of identifying and adapting local knowledge to schooling (and in its own right) by including elders in our deliberations. We deepened our discussions by shifting the agenda from the teachers to the elders as we collaboratively explored everyday practice and Yup'ik culture. At the time we began this work with elders, in approximately 1992, the local school districts' curricula and pedagogical practices did not include Yup'ik knowledge related to numeration, measuring, geometry, or science. However, at the time of this writing, local school districts are increasingly asking elders and Yup'ik teachers to present workshops. They are also including Yup'ik knowledge and Yup'ik competencies within their curriculum. Beyond the specifics that this chapter presents, the process of collaborating with elders, teachers, university researchers, and school district administrators has resulted in the work of the Ciulistet moving from the periphery to the center. Knowledge that was once unknown to local school districts is now becoming valued. This is a major step in transforming schooling. Now it is possible to coconstruct curricula that represent both the school and the community. Our collaborative, community-based efforts with elders has allowed the Ciulistet and local school systems, and other community members to record, learn, and make accessible ancient Yup'ik knowledge for a modern educational context. Furthermore, the Ciulistet continues to evolve its agenda as the curricular and pedagogical possibilities unfold through this collaborative work and reflective dialogue. Elders are increasingly bringing to light knowledge once subdued. The elders' knowledge of the relationship of people to people (proper relations) and people to animals, particularly their knowledge about the environment and how to live in it, adds significantly to our earlier sociolinguistic work. Now it seems possible to reconstruct classroom learning, social organization, and school community relationships in ways that correspond to community and school knowledge and values. The tools outlined in this chapter, along with the working relationship between the Ciulistet teachers and elders holds promise for further evolution of the context of schooling.

Developing Culturally Based Mathematics and Science

By connecting local knowledge with school knowledge and the enculturation process (informal or "natural" learning) with formal schooling, it is now possible to craft a pedagogical and curricular approach that effectively relates and coevolves Yup'ik and Western ways. The instructional strategy of guided practice, meaningfully connected to local cultural norms and locally based knowledge in mathematics and science that can meet national standards, becomes a way to strengthen teacher and student performance. In addition, the possibility of constructing authentic problems based on the complex problem-solving strategies associated with navigating and orienting hold promise for the teaching and learning of mathematics and science. Designing mathematical tools that correspond with cultural and linguistic rules, teaching in ways that relate to Yup'ik sociolinguistic conventions, and assessing this work more authentically all hold promise. The premises behind developing Yup'ik mathematics and science include: (1) to show students that all knowledge is socially constructed; (2) to engage students in a process of constructing a system of mathematics and science that begins with their culturally based knowledge; and (3) to connect students' knowledge of "their" mathematics and science, through comparisons and bridges, to other aboriginal and Western systems. Important connections between an aboriginal system of numbers and measurements and the hunting and gathering context from which it was derived can be used as a bridge to the decontextualized abstract system often used in teaching mathematics and science, and it can demystify how mathematics and science are derived. By beginning within Yup'ik language and culture, students will see that mathematical systems and science have evolved from the concrete to the abstract, are based on familiar patterns and ways of ordering, and relate to concrete and cultural symbols.

Furthermore, this coconstruction of pedagogy, ranging from a specific Yup'ik cultural content to Western mathematics concepts grounded in everyday experience, language, and culture, offers a third alternative to the either/or proposition of "traditional" Western schooling or "traditional" indigenous culture. This third way, most importantly, changes the context of schooling by valuing Yup'ik language and knowledge and by providing an opportunity for elders and the school community to visualize the possible ways in which everyday tasks and knowledge can be a basis for learning in formal schooling.

More specifically, our work illustrates some of the ways in which math and science can be accomplished in the classroom. The possibilities of using the culturally practiced behavior of visualizing and observing in mathematics is particularly promising in the area of geometry. One simple means of translating some of this knowledge into schooling is making base 20 and subbase 5 blocks, developing the number system into a formalized system of counting with implied multiplication, having placeholders vertically organized, and comparing this number system to other extant systems and other ancient systems. Yup'ik ways of measuring and estimating can show students how Western systems of measurement also came from the human body, such as an inch, a foot, a yard, a cubit, and so on. These approaches can make math more easily accessible to students and at the same time, validate Yup'ik knowledge.

Involvement of Elders and Community Members

In the curriculum and pedagogical development stage of these meetings, teachers interpreted and applied the elders' knowledge to a school context. Applications of elders' knowledge ranged from mathematics to science to art to literacy. The teachers invited the elders to participate in the reinterpreted knowledge designed for school. In this manner, elders still retained some control over their knowledge, and they had a chance to further influence the process of curriculum and pedagogy development. This process makes the link between elders' knowledge and schooling direct, thus demonstrating to community members who attend the meetings that their knowledge counts. We believe that the elders' continuing presence at these meetings indicates their support and the growing sense of cultural renewal emanating from this project. At the conclusion of one such workshop, the elders and teachers were asked to evaluate the meeting we and encouraged to write a response in Yup'ik—either in its older or modern form. Of the 25 elders in attendance, several stated similar conclusions: "We learned mutually together with one mind. Right now we are thankful here. This is all there is for now." Another stated, "Very good, we learned lots—let's go forward with what we're doing." Finally, one teacher commented on the importance of elders: "I enjoyed the interaction between the elders and the younger generation. The elders are overflowing with knowledge. I was so overwhelmed and I can see where I can readily have elders help my class and me."

Future Plans

Although we have made substantial progress in learning about Yup'ik conceptions of numeration, measuring, and geometry, additional care and attention needs to occur because it is easy to substitute Western conceptions for the elders' teaching. We need to continue our naturalistic work, using observation and a series of situated activities. Ensuring mutual understanding requires us to conduct "miniempirical experiments" as we clarify particular concepts such as left/right axis, the relationship between absolute and relative, and the agreed-on conventions for navigating.

Despite the progress documented here, the difficult process of negotiating these ideas with the general community and the school district remains. Although this approach makes logical sense and is supported by elders and the Ciulistet, the low priority attached to Yup'ik culture and language has affected community members and school administrators, who often view Yup'ik as irrelevant or even harmful to Western schooling and knowledge. One promising strategy is to show the community and the school district positive evidence for these approaches. To this end, we presented workshops to schools in southwest Alaska, at the Alaska statewide Bilingual/Multicultural Conference, and more recently, to mostly indigenous teachers' conferences in two regions. According to Esther Ilutsik, school board members (some of whom were originally opposed to Yup'ik-based curriculum and pedagogy) who attended some of these meetings were amazed at the potential of basing instruction on Yup'ik ways.

Evelyn Yanez and other teachers from Togiak continue to adapt Yup'ik stories for use in schools. Through their work they are incorporating drama, Yup'ik dance, role playing, and Yup'ik and English literacy. Their approach, particularly the use of Yup'ik dancing, was well received, even though the Moravian church had banned dancing from the village. The elders accepted and appreciated their efforts. It appears that our work is beginning to receive acceptance beyond our group to the wider Yup'ik and school community. This is one of the most dramatic changes in this long-term project—watching Yup'ik culture go from being invisible to being prized by others. The seeds of change are sown. Now elders and teachers are being invited to school district in-services. One local school district is starting to adopt "Yup'ik competencies" as a part of its curriculum. Only time will tell if these evolving forms of curriculum and pedagogy formed by elders, community members, Yup'ik teachers, and their associates will grow and take root. However, the changes occurring in this context are not trivial. The group's work has advanced a long way from the days when we first asked "What is Yup'ik about a Yup'ik teacher?"

CONCLUSION

These events and the persistence of the group have had a profound effect on the curricular and pedagogical possibilities. The superficiality of Yup'ik "cultural heritage week" is giving way to the possibility of basing core academic subjects on Yup'ik knowledge, Yup'ik ways of perceiving the world, and traditional Yup'ik approaches to teaching such as storytelling and dance.

The Ciulistet group has taken the first steps to becoming the "keepers and protectors of the treasure." By fundamentally involving elders as instructors and as active members in curricular and pedagogical development, the group has engaged in an inclusive process of schooling. In this way, attitudes are beginning to shift so that Yup'ik is perceived as a strength, not a barrier. The knowledge base of Yup'ik teachers has increased. This is a direct result of elders' involvement. The confidence of the Yup'ik teachers has increased accordingly. This, we believe, has allowed us to include non-Yup'ik teachers in our meetings and to create a space of collaboration and confidence for both.

Yet Yup'ik teachers still face difficult dilemmas. Schooling for many was an alienating and self-denying experience (Lipka, 1994; Sharp, 1994). Now schools have the potential to be sites of cultural transformation, and despite the contradic-tions implied, groups such as the Ciulistet must take the lead. However, this requires a major shift in attitudes by both schools and communities. Each must see this point of contact as a place of constructive development that reinforces what each perceives as the purpose of schooling. In the past, that very purpose of schooling too often conflicted at the most fundamental levels; to build community and culture or to lead indigenous people away from them and into the Western world. Yet this is exactly what the Ciulistet is beginning to accomplish.

The Ciulistet has squarely faced this thorny and persistent dilemma by rejecting either/or thinking and replacing it with a both/and approach. By showing connec-tions between traditional Yup'ik culture and language, literacy, math, and science, they benefit both the indigenous culture and the school. In this way, school districts and teachers (Yup'ik and others) can see the relevance of traditional cultural knowledge. But whether the Ciulistet can sustain change beyond its current members, elders, and community members remains to be seen. The risk of sharing and using a culture that has previously been denied access to schooling and even ridiculed is great. On the other hand, for school districts to transform the culture of school would be a radical departure from the present reality. School districts too face the risk of having students not perform as well on standardized tests, a measure of the effectiveness of districts on a local and national level. Whether or not changes in curriculum and pedagogy that include Yup'ik culture and involve the community in fundamental ways will produce positive school-based results for students is an empirical question, and we must all risk observing its results.

However, more is at stake than scores on standardized tests. The loss of "song," the growing cultural void, and the very nature of the relationship between any school and any community is at stake. The problematic role between school and community—historically, an arm of colonialism—now must become a site of creative cultural evolution. Today's educational context differs from that of the recent past due to the increased number of indigenous teachers and to the formation of groups such as the Ciulistet. The work of such groups is enabled by funding, tenacity, administrative support, and increased involvement with local school boards. If, as cultural brokers and as keepers of the treasure, groups such as Ciulistet continue to take risks, face the void, and involve communities and schools, then the conception of schooling may change to one far more inclusive than presently exists.

The processes and products of our approach to negotiating the culture of the school have ramifications far beyond southwest Alaska. Involving the commu-nity—in this case Yup'ik elders, teachers, bilingual aides, students, school board members, and faculty—created a rich working environment in which both insider and outsider knowledge was valued. The long-term collaborative efforts of each group are slowly changing the context of schooling. The workshops themselves modeled the importance of Yup'ik language by establishing it as the medium for instruction and discourse. We also valued Yup'ik culture by using it as a base for curriculum content, and we prized Yup'ik social processes by deriving social interactions and teaching methodologies from those processes.

These long-term collaborative efforts by universities and schools can change some of the fundamental dynamics surrounding schooling and the relationship between context and content. What is incorporated in schooling as content, as processes, and as values can become more inclusive and can reflect diverse interests. Deriving mathematics from Yup'ik language, culture, and everyday experience holds promise for teaching mathematics as well as for reinforcing Yup'ik culture. Creating an atmosphere in which the very essences of schooling are analyzed and worked through with community members, teachers, and administrators can reconstitute schooling in ways that make sense for a people being both modern and indigenous. Now the possibility of deriving school practice based on Yup'ik knowledge and practice is moving beyond the possible and into practice. Yup'ik teachers such as Nancy Sharp now incorporate Yup'ik patterns into their classroom; Evelyn Yanez as the bilingual coordinator is instructing bilingual aides on the uses of Yup'ik-based approaches to math and science; and Esther Ilutsik is increasingly being invited to instruct others in both the products and processes of our work.

REFERENCES

Anderson, L., & Stein, W. (1992). The American Indians in mathematics project (AIM). *Journal Of Rural and Small Schools, 5*(2), 24–31.

Annahatak, B. (1994). Quality education for Inuit today? Cultural strengths, new things, and working out the unknowns: A story by an Inuk. *Peabody Journal of Education, 69*(2), 12–18.

Ascher, M. (1991). *Ethnomathematics: A multicultural view of mathematical ideas.* Pacific Grove, CA: Brooks/Cole.

Boas, F. (1964). *The Central Eskimo.* Lincoln, NE: University of Nebraska Press.

Baratta-Lorton, M. (1976). *Mathematics their way.* Menlo Park, CA: Addison-Wesley.

Barrow, J. (1992). *Pi in the sky: Counting and thinking and being.* Boston: Little, Brown.

Birket-Smith, K. (1953). *The Chugach Eskimo.* Copenhagen: Nationalmuseets Publikationsfond.

Bishop, A. (1988). Mathematical enculturation: A cultural perspective on mathematics education. Dordrecht, Netherlands: Kluwer Academic Publishers.

Boaler, J. (1993). Encouraging the transfer of "school" mathematics to the "real world" through the integration of process and content, context and culture. *Educational Studies in Mathematics, 13*(2), 12–17.

Bockarie, A. (1993). Mathematics in the Mende culture: Its general implication for mathematics teaching. *School Science and Mathematics, 93*(4), 208–211.

Bradley, C. (1993). Making a Navajo blanket design with Logo. *Arithmetic teacher, 40*(9), 520–523.

Carpenter, E. (1973). *Eskimo realities.* NY: Holt, Rinehart, & Winston.

Closs, M. (1986). The mathematical notation of the ancient Maya. In M. Closs (Ed.), *Native American Mathematics* (pp. 291–370). Austin, TX: University of Texas Press.

Cole, M., & Scribner, S. (1973). *Culture and thought.* New York: Wiley.

Denny, J. P. (1986). Cultural ecology of mathematics: Ojibway and Inuit hunters. In M. Closs (Ed.), *Native American Mathematics* (pp. 129–180). Austin, TX: University of Texas Press.

Fall, J., Chythlook, M., Schichnes, J., & Morris, J. (1989). *An overview of the harvest and use of freshwater fish by the communities of the Bristol Bay region, Southwest Alaska.* Juneau, AK: Alaska Department of Fish and Game, Division of Subsistence, [Technical Paper No. #166] (Draft on file in the Anchorage office).

Fienup-Riordan, A. (1994). *Boundaries and passages: Rule and ritual in Yup'ik Eskimo oral tradition.* Norman, Oklahoma: University of Oklahoma Press.

Fortescue, M. (1988). Eskimo orientation systems. *Meddelelser Óm Gronland* [Man & Society], 11.

Harris, P. (1989). Teaching the space strand in Aboriginal schools. *Mathematics in Aboriginal Schools Project Series 4.* Darwin: Northern Territory Department of Education.

Hollins, E. R. (Ed.). (1996). *Transforming curriculum for a culturally diverse society.* Mahwah, NJ: Lawrence Erlbaum Associates.

Ilutsik, E. (1994). The founding of the Ciulistet: One teacher's journey. *Journal of American Indian Education, 33*(3), 6–13.

Jacobson, S. (1984). *Yup'ik Eskimo dictionary.* Fairbanks, AK: Alaska Native Language Native Center.

Kawagley, O. (1990). Yup'ik ways of knowing. *Canadian Journal of Native Education, 17*(2), 5–32.

Kawagley, O. (1995). *A Yupiaq worldview: A pathway to an ecology and spirit.* Prospect Heights, IL: Waveland Press.

LaFrance, B. (1994). Empowering ourselves: Making education and schooling one. *Peabody Journal of Education, 69*(2), 140-153.

Lave, J. (1988). *Cognition in practice: Mind, mathematics and culture in everyday life.* Cambridge, England: Cambridge University Press.

Lave, J., & Wenger, E. (1991). *Situated learning: Legitimate peripheral participation.* Cambridge, England: Cambridge University Press.

Lipka, J. (1990). Integrating cultural form and content in one Yup'ik Eskimo teacher. *Canadian Journal of Education, 17*(2), 18–32.

Lipka, J. (1991). Toward a culturally based pedagogy: A case study of one Yup'ik Eskimo teacher. *Anthropology and Education Quarterly, (22)*3, 203–223.

Lipka, J. (1994). Culturally negotiated schooling: Towards a Yup'ik mathematics. *Journal of American Indian Education, 33*(3), 14–30.

Lipka, J., & Ilutsik, E. (1997) Ciulistet and the curriculum of the possible. *Indigenous literacies in the Americas: Language planning from the bottom up.* In N. H. Hornberger (Ed.). The Hague: Mouton Press.

McIntyre, C. (1994). The blackfish story. *Waqaa 2*(2), 5.

Meade, M. (1990). Sewing to maintain the past, present, and future. *Inuit Studies, 14*(1–2), 229–239.

Moore, C. (1994). Research in Native American mathematics education. *For the Learning of Mathematics, 14*(2), 9–14.

National Council of Teachers of Mathematics (1989). *Curriculum and evaluation standards for school mathematics.* Reston, VA: Author.

Nelson, E. (1899). *Eskimos about the Bering Strait.* Washington, DC: Smithsonian.

Nelson-Barber, S., & Estirin, E. (1995). *Culturally responsive mathematics and science education for Native students.* San Francisco: Far West Laboratory for Educational Research and Development.

Piaget, J. (1929). *The child's conception of the world.* London: Routledge & Kegan Paul.

Presmeg, N. (1989). Visualization in multicultural mathematics classrooms. Focus on Learning *Problems in Mathematics, 11*(1) 17–24.

Rogoff, B. (1990). *Apprenticeship in thinking: Cognitive development in social context.* Oxford, England: Oxford University Press.

Saxe, G. (1991). *Culture and cognitive development: Studies in mathematical understanding.* Mahwah, NJ: Lawrence Erlbaum Associates.

Sharp, N. (1994). Caknernarqutet. *Peabody Journal of Education, 69*(2), 6–11.

Wahlberg, N. (1997). *Teaching and preserving Yup'ik traditional literacy. Indigenous literacies in the Americas,* In N. H. Hornberger (Ed.), Language from the bottom up. The Hague: Mouton Press.

Zaslavsky, C. (1973). *Africa counts: Number and pattern in African culture.* Boston: PWS.

Zaslavsky, C. (1985). Bringing the world into the math class. *Curriculum Review, 24*(3), 62–65.

Zimmerly, D. (1986). *Qajaq: Kayaks of Siberia and Alaska.* Juneau, AK: Alaska State Museum.

Part IV

7 Transforming Schooling: From Possibilities to Actuality?

Jerry Lipka
University of Alaska, Fairbanks

Throughout this book, the individual narratives of Vicki Dull, Esther Ilutsik, Fanny Parker, Nancy Sharp, and Evelyn Yanez speak clearly and strongly about their struggles in becoming and being Yup'ik teachers. Some experienced the shame of not being able to use their own language in their classrooms (Lipka, 1994) even when their district's bilingual plan mandated it. Others experienced the shame of a prolonged apprenticeship before being hired. These experiences highlight the concept of schooling as alien and contested space. Unfortunately, and far too often, this space represented one body of knowledge and one way of teaching.

Along with the support of a local school superintendent, these struggles galvanized individual teachers into a group, the Ciulistet. Furthermore, the group's formation created a zone of safety where teachers were finally able to speak openly about what they thought were "personal" experiences and to find that others shared these experiences. The group created a context in which reflective dialogue, the venting of emotions, individual concerns and doubts, were transformed into a collective understanding of the larger issues of which they were a part. Slowly, over the course of more than a decade, the Ciulistet began to function as a zone of proximal development where Yup'ik knowledge was translated and adapted for school pedagogy. This has begun a slow process of transforming the culture of school by including their language, culture, and everyday experience as part of their teaching and now as part of schooling. Critical to the group's evolution and development was the inclusion of a group of elders who provided knowledge, inspiration, and, in a sense, moral strength for the teachers to begin to develop pedagogical strategies and methods that support both Western academics and traditional Yup'ik knowledge and values.

Because the work reported in this book is long term, it is able show a complex relationship between community and school. The adoption of Yup'ik knowledge and pedagogy by one local school district particularly demonstrates some of the ways in which schooling has been transformed.

This chapter includes a traditional Yup'ik tale that is interpreted to show some of the cooperative work of the Ciulistet—elders, teachers, and university faculty coconstructing knowledge and pedagogy. This leads to a complicated question: Have we changed the context of schooling? The response, based on the cases documented in this book, is not a simple yes or no, or good guys (Natives/community) versus bad (Whites/school). The question is answered first through this story and its interpreted meaning. Then Henry Alakayak (elder/leader) reflects on the story and the work we have been doing. After the narrative, we present a more formal response to the question. This book highlights five distinct ways in which the school and community have been transformed; (1) access to the teaching profession by an increasing number of Yup'ik teachers and the formation of the Ciulistet; (2) the use of classroom interactions in a way that alters typical student-to-teacher dialogue; (3) involvement of the elders in the Ciulistet and school community relations; (4) the embedded mathematics contained within Yup'ik everyday experience and language; and (5) changing attitudes toward Yup'ik knowledge, language, and teachers.

Foremost in this change process is the Cross-Cultural Education Development Program (X-CED). This teacher training program increased the number of Yup'ik teachers in southwest Alaska. This established the ground for forming Ciulistet. Furthermore, the teachers' dialogue and action research, the inclusion of elders, and support from the university as well as other indigenous groups encouraged the change process. The role of the community, particularly the elders, has been instrumental in this change and this role in particular provides possible guidelines for how other communities might benefit from our work. Similarly, although the pedagogical and curriculum possibilities emanating from our work are culturally specific, many of the underlying structures are adaptable to other settings and other cultures. Although our work focuses on a particular group, we believe that there are theoretical lessons to be drawn, and this chapter highlights them. Finally, the chapter concludes with what the future might hold for the Ciulistet.

We started this book with a personal narrative, and it seems fitting to end this book with a traditional story because stories are so important to the Yup'ik culture. Recently, Annie Blue and Henry Alakayak (two elders who have worked with the Ciulistet) collaborated in telling the following story about the porcupine and the beaver.

The Porcupine and the Beaver

Once upon a time this porcupine liked these certain trees but they are on the other side of the river and porcupines do not know how to swim. He looked across the river and looked at the certain trees that he could not reach. By and by a muskrat came by. The porcupine yelled at him and asked if he could take him across the river. But the muskrat told him he had chores, but that when he was done he would come back and get him. [Annie Blue's addition]. Instead of just calling the character, the porcupine also said that it would use the tail—"Hey, you with that long tail that looks like a drying rack pole. I wish I could use your tail for a drying rack pole." That is the point when that character's feelings were hurt. The porcupine would put down all the other animals.

The porcupine starts to cry a song:

Ikani, ikani ngaiii, turutek ikaiii, [some kind of a wood?]

[Across, across the river]

aiyarrr,

Asgi, asgii rrai

The porcupine waited for him but the muskrat did not come back. A mink came swimming down and again, the porcupine asked if he could take him back across the river. The porcupine called out to the mink, "Hey you, hey you, with the tail like a ladle, the part you use to stir, why don't you take me across the river?" The mink was highly insulted.

The animal answers and says that he has some chores and will come back later to take him across the river. The mink did not come back, and in his mind he thought that he might try going across the river. The porcupine thought he might drift down, so he said that he better stay on dry land.

The otter came by and he asked the otter if he could take him across. The porcupine called out to the otter, "Hey you, hey you, with the tail like the squirrel skin stretcher/cutting board." The otter's feelings were hurt and he promised to come back again later on.

The otter replied that he had things to do down the river but that he might take him across the river at a later time. The porcupine waited and waited and waited for the otter to come back. He became hungrier and hungrier as he watched the trees across the river. His stomach started to growl as he watched the trees because if you watch food that you cannot reach you become hungrier and hungrier. As the porcupine was hungrily waiting, a beaver came swimming down. A beaver and the porcupine are about the same size. The porcupine yelled out that he needed a ride across the river. The porcupine called out to the beaver, "Hey you, hey you with the tail like the cutting board, take me across the river, I'm going to starve." Instead of the beaver being insulted, he turned to the porcupine and said sarcastically, "So are you starving there porcupine?" Those others came by and did not come back. The beaver also said that he had chores to do down river and that he would come back later. The porcupine sat and waited and to his amazement the beaver came back as he said, "Come and hold onto my back." He held on and the beaver swam across the river. The porcupine was very happy. The beaver went on his way down river. The place where the porcupine was sitting on the beaver has no fat till this day. And the place where the porcupine touched the beaver, he does not have any fat till this day.

The beaver had the porcupine get on his back and brought him across. Where the contact was between the porcupine's belly and the beaver's back, there is no fat on these animals. And so, good luck will be with you as you go forward, meaning, so be it in good fortune with you.

This story highlights the values of persistence, risk taking, cooperation, and interdependence. The porcupine needed assistance to cross the river to reach those tasty trees, but was unable to ask properly and was unable to achieve its goals. Not until beaver understood porcupine's need, despite the rude behavior, did porcupine come to a deeper realization. Then beaver assisted porcupine, carrying it to the other side. As the end of the story indicates, the porcupine's belly and the beaver's back were altered by this experience, possibly indicating the interconnectedness of living things and how each was changed by this encounter.

Furthermore, this story illustrates the evolution of the Ciulistet, persisting and moving away from insults and silence to more cooperative and productive working relationships with each other, with school children, and with the larger school community. As in the story, with the possibility of the porcupine crossing the abyss, the Ciulistet teachers experienced insults and silenced voices, then slowly an awakening, a realization that they were different. Their differences need not be hidden. No longer were barriers of discriminations impenetrable. Through assistance and cooperation instead of antagonism and retreat, the Ciulistet was able to go forward. The real and the psychological barriers, having been crossed, made for the realization of achieving their potential as Yup'ik teachers. Now as the Ciulistet, elders, and university consultants work together, the idea of successfully facing the dilemma in which we began this work—how to be both modern and traditional—is being actualized. Because we are working together, ancient Yup'ik learnings are finding a place within a modern context, and this evolves the context of schooling. As the elders have repeatedly told us, if we work with one mind, we can accomplish anything. By being harmonious, we begin to resolve the question of how to use both Yup'ik and Western knowledge in an additive, dynamic, and effective manner so that both cultural traditions are respected.

When Henry Alakayak and Annie Blue told the beaver and the porcupine story, the story and the meeting affected the group. What follows shows some of the issues that this old story raised, and how these issues recall the larger issues of basing and modernizing traditional lessons so that they can have a place within modern schools. Earlier in the meeting, Esther Ilutsik and Ina White (a Ciulistet member and a teacher) demonstrated to the group a variety of ways of working with Yup'ik patterns. Evelyn Yanez, Fanny Parker, Linda Brown, and Annie Blue adapted a raven story, rendering it with Yup'ik drumming and dancing to accompany parts of the story. Lipka demonstrated elements of the Yup'ik Math Tool Kit and a more recent innovation on how to use Yup'ik oral stories. These tools allow teachers to work easily with folktales, develop literacy skills, connect the stories to science, and incorporate mathematics. Henry Alakayak, impressed by these developments, spoke to the group:

> I understand now that through the traditional stories which we told in the past that you as educators are bringing in all of these materials so that they [the students] can better understand ... we need to give each other ideas and help each other as a whole group so that we can disperse this information better, and use these as tools to give the information to the children and that in their way of thinking now. We need to make those tracks a little easier for them because of the different educational system that we have been through.

Later on, Alakayak, thinking about the significance of these stories, stated:

> The porcupine's ridiculing of each animal's tail, the particular tail, therefore that particular animal, did not bring the porcupine across the river. Even as I listened to this story, [I know] that people even as we get older, will continue to think about these stories as different listeners each time they hear the story. My lesson is that I am not going to ridicule someone because I am Henry Alakayak. I am not going to make fun of other people like the porcupine did. Even as people, we can transfer these animals into people; nowadays a person will not listen to someone who ridicules them. These animal moral stories are like life. I was thinking about these stories in new ways, the last time I heard the story it taught me this and now it is teaching me something else. These stories are an important teaching tool. These stories need to be passed on so that every time the listeners are listening to the storyteller they get something out of it .... As you live your life, you remember parts of the story, they come back to you as you live your life, that story and its moral. The stories serve as certain reminders of the past. Certain reminders of a moral.

> The way for us as a group, or even children, to understand the language in whatever we are teaching or learning, if we are English speakers then we translate it to Yup'ik; if we are understanding in Yup'ik then we translate it into English. Therefore we have a circle of understanding amongst everybody. If we translate something and we forget to say it, somebody helping will make us better understand and vice versa; it works both ways. We need to help each other.

Alakayak's and Blue's collaborative telling of the porcupine story illustrated how each made it better. Also, Alakayak's comments reflected Ciulistet's progress—Yup'ik and *kass'aq* [White], elders and teachers working together. Repeatedly at these meetings, and in Alakayak's comments, working together provided for group solidarity. Furthermore, the story, in its collaborative telling and in our constructing possible modern meanings for it, in fact, are analogous to the group's creating new possibilities. It demonstrates the possibilities and synergy emanating from a conception that Yup'ik language, culture, and everyday experience are valid. New uses of the oral tradition for teaching and learning relate to the progress that we have made and to the transformations taking place within the context of education. The porcupine needed the beaver to cross a chasm; this was made possible by cooperation, and cooperation has transformative powers.

To accomplish this has meant that each teacher must risk facing some combination of anger grown out of denial and ambivalence toward Western schooling, and at the same time create new possibilities that allow schools to become much more inclusive. Some had to face their own lack of cultural knowledge, as Esther Ilutsik alluded to in the preface, by allowing elders to play a vital role in being leaders/teachers of the group.

HAVE WE CHANGED THE CONTEXT OF SCHOOLING?

Access–Increasing the Number of Indigenous Teachers

When the Cross-Cultural Education Development Program (X-CED) began in Bristol Bay, there were virtually no Yup'ik certified teachers. Today, 26 years later,

Yup'ik teachers represent approximately 20% of the teaching staff in one local school district, and the number of Yup'ik teachers is steadily increasing. This, of course, made possible the formation of the Ciulistet. Because the group has reached a critical mass, has a stable membership, and new members have reinforced its ranks, the group is able to evolve and thrive.

The Ciulistet: Indigenous Teacher Support

Now, the Ciulistet members, their university associates, increasing numbers of community members, elders, and school district teachers and administrators recognize the contributions that Yup'ik culture and language may have for schooling. Originally, when the Ciulistet first met in 1986, the research agenda concerned what, if any, contributions Yup'ik teachers were making for their people and communities. Today, after so many years of struggle, most of us are fatigued from this effort but encouraged by the positive response our work receives from other indigenous teacher groups and school districts. We remain hopeful that schools can become sites of constructive change and development. We are beginning to see evidence that the context of schooling is changing from a deficit assimilative model to one that can be called additive. School is becoming a place in which Parker, Sharp, and Yanez need no longer say that they are teaching against their will; it is becoming a place that Dull and others will not find so toxic because of the overwhelming conflict associated with the teaching role; it is becoming a place where Gumlickpuk (a former Ciulistet member and teacher) will no longer have to believe that the very idea of a Yup'ik teacher is an oxymoron. As we work together, these transformations include more positive professional identities for Yup'ik teachers, new curricular and pedagogical possibilities, and new sets of relationships between school and community. Today, our research agenda has shifted dramatically to working collaboratively with insiders and outsiders on developing curriculum and pedagogy that respect and build on both Western and Yup'ik traditions. As our work became more concrete, moving away from the isolated sociocultural and sociolinguistic differences of Yup'ik teachers to how Yup'ik culture can be a tool in developing math and science concepts, there appears to be increased receptivity on the part of school administrators and teachers to incorporate Yup'ik knowledge in schooling. At the time of this writing, Alakayak, Ilutsik, and I have conducted workshops for an Athabaskan teacher's group, presently establishing their educational agenda. We are being called on by a large rural systemic National Science Foundation initiative in Alaska to consult with other school districts, communities, and teacher groups. School districts in other Yup'ik areas of the state are inviting Ciulistet teachers to present our work at their in-service meetings, and other Alaska Native groups and school districts have also begun discussing similar opportunities in their regions. Recently, at the statewide bilingual meeting in Anchorage, an audience of approximately 200 greatly appreciated the presentations of the Ciulistet. The work of the group emphasized four distinct ways of basing instruction on Yup'ik culture; (1) a literacy-based model that uses oral Yup'ik tales in a number of traditional and creative modalities such as drumming, drama, sonor, and story-boarding as a means of teaching; (2) a math approach that uses Yup'ik patterns and symbols as a basis for teaching mathematics; (3) the use of modern games in which oral literacy, symbolic manipulations, math, and science are integrated; and (4) a science approach that uses elders as leaders and "field experiences." These steps (and they exist in varying degrees of completeness) represent major and significant changes from our earlier work, when Yanez stated that she thought that her teaching was "too Yup'ik" to share with the Ciulistet. Now Yanez and others in Togiak are expanding their repertoire of teaching by including their language, oral folktales, dance, and drumming.

Working With Elders

A core group of approximately 15 elders attends most of our meetings, and as many as 200 community members attended one. Esther Ilutsik, surprised by the strength of her mother's interest, said that her mother waited 2 days in Dillingham for the weather to clear so that she might be able to fly to Manokotak for our meeting. After each meeting, the Ciulistet teachers are encouraged by and appreciative of the willingness the elders show to come to the school and to share "what was once hidden." The elders themselves are learning from each other. Their encouragement, their sharing, and their continued interest suggests that they want the teachers to share this knowledge with the next generation.

In our last meeting, the elders continued to reveal their intimate knowledge of the natural world as they described a variety of survival techniques. They explained how it would be possible to find fresh water while out at sea, how they had a mental map of the bays and the relative position of underwater springs and how to identify these springs by using a paddle to mix the water—stirring causes salt water to foam whereas fresh water will not. Another elder demonstrated how to use an oar as a "listening" device to "hear" an approaching storm. Yet another shared how he observed Yup'ik dance in the *qasg'iq* [men's house] in a village that had abandoned this custom because of conflict between the church and traditional ways. The elder's nephew, a Ciulistet teacher, remarked that he did not know his uncle knew this type of information. The importance of these sharings goes well beyond the specific knowledge to the courage and the support that they provide the Ciulistet. These acts signify changes in the contextual circumstances surrounding schooling. It certainly appears that the elders are increasingly cognizant that their knowledge, that Yup'ik language and culture, are threatened, no longer automatically transmitted from one generation to another. Previously, the elders and the community at large had "given over" to the school the responsibility for educating their children. Now, as Henry Alakayak states, by working together, things become possible. The elders have been instrumental in this.

Widening the Circle Increasing the Discourse

Our discourse has not been confined to the "safety" of the group. We have met with indigenous educators from Australia, Canada, Greenland, New Zealand, Russia, Finland, Norway, and from the Lower 48. This discourse has joined us with others who are facing the central dilemma of evolving both a modern and a traditional identity. This discourse, both between and within the group, has made it clear that the issues faced in small rural Alaska villages are quite similar to others throughout the world. As each group discussed and presented information pertaining to the unique ways in which they developed "language nests," indigenous math programs, or developed their tertiary institution, each gained from the other. Particularly important to the Ciulistet was the realization that bilingualism could be considered a "normal" way of living. Interestingly, through all these meetings one group or another would remark on how another group was doing something better than they were. I interpreted this to mean that each group was in the process of reconstructing education, reforming it in fundamental ways, yet each group struggled against their particular colonial past, still not completely beyond that experience.

Embedded Mathematics

The work of the group in unlocking the embedded mathematics within everyday Yup'ik experience, culture, and language represents a concrete way to transform curriculum and pedagogy. Our collaborative research in Yup'ik mathematics brings to light Yup'ik conceptions of numeration, measuring, geometry, and problem solving. Some of these differences from Western mathematics are not trivial: For example, the numeration system is base 20 and subbase 5. Both it and the measuring system are linked to the body. Furthermore, the measuring system is more appropriately referred to as standardized body measures individually applied than as "nonformal or informal" measures. There is nothing informal about this system. The use of measuring is almost always related to problem solving. The solution of problems represents a dynamic relationship between task, person, and resources in the creation of standards and adapting tools to the task. Similarly, we find the process of creating border patterns (geometrical designs) to involve the establishment of a standard unit from which other subunits are created. The resulting shapes are all related to the initial standard. The rules for defining shapes differs from Western conventions: The orientation and relationship of a shape (such as a square) to its transformed state (to a triangle for example), not it's geometrical shape, are defining characteristics. Carpenter (1973) referred to this process as "multiple perspectives" and a lack of "verticality" in orienting, and Harris (1989) described a similar system of cultural rules among Australian Aborigines as they describe geometric shapes. The implication of all of this is that a Yup'ik-based mathematics would include "rules" that differ from Western mathematics. Because of these distinct cultural rules, to develop authentically based cultural tools for schooling requires a process of curriculum and pedagogical development that goes beyond a naive one-to-one translation of knowledge across cultural and linguistic domains. The work reported herein begins to accomplish, at least in a cursory way, an understanding of some of the rules that need to be applied in the process of curriculum and pedagogical development. In fact, as this book readies for press, we have just been awarded a 4-year project funded by the National Science Foundation to develop Yup'ik-based curriculum, to field test it, to train teachers, and to develop authentic assessment procedures.

Yup'ik Literacy and Science

One significant way our meetings and community workshops impacted the Ciulistet teachers was by interpreting traditional knowledge in ways that relate to school-based knowledge. The oral tradition recognized by the Ciulistet as a central feature of Yup'ik knowledge and cultural transmission has led to development in literacy, mathematics, and science. The oral tradition, rich in its explanation of the relationships among people and between people and the environment, offers teachers numerous possibilities for developing oral and written literacy. The traditional genres of story telling—storyknifing, dance, and drumming—all are part of this tradition. The elders' demonstrations and encouragement concerning various methods of transmitting knowledge such as using *sugat* [Yup'ik dolls] has opened the way for other innovative and traditional methods. The use of story boards, symbols, and geometric figures based on Yup'ik patterns and border designs, the rich knowledge of the environment and animal behaviors contained within the oral tradition open up curricular and pedagogical possibilities that simply didn't exist for the Ciulistet a decade ago. Furthermore, interpreting and concretizing the embedded mathematics contained within the Yup'ik language has become another avenue ripe with curricular and pedagogical possibilities. These stories connect Yup'ik metaphysics and science, providing a constructive way to work with both domains. The slow creation of pedagogical tools to teach this knowledge has been extremely beneficial to the group members. From the numeration system, base 20 subbase 5, to the symmetry involved in the base 20 system, to connections to body measurements and on to geometry, pattern designs, and tessellations, the possibilities for teaching mathematics that can simultaneously teach Yup'ik cultural lessons are happening. As we value elders' and Yup'ik teachers' knowledge, respect Western and Yup'ik knowledge, we recreate schooling by providing new ways of teaching core academic subjects. The boundaries of this potential are still expanding.

The Ciulistet teachers have adapted both serious and fun stories. Stories about the beaver and the porcupine, the pike and the bullhead, for example, contain ecological and biological information pertaining to behaviors and physiology. The game itself reinforces the stories and their morals.

Sharing sonor with the elders encouraged them to share more traditional means of cultural transmission with the group. The elders demonstrated *sugat* [dolls], a wonderful vehicle for developing oral language, Yup'ik values, ways of being and acting, and stories (see Lipka & Ilutsik, 1995, for further details). The elders' demonstration of *sugat* showed proper ways of interacting, and the setting was lighthearted, accompanied by teasing, laughter, and joking. This added greatly to the literary uses of "playing dolls." The backdrop was a modern-day problem concerning leaving home and changing—losing one's culture.

Storyknifing, another genre of story telling, combines elements of oral narration, symbolic representations, and manipulating symbols. At a number of our meetings, elders demonstrated storyknifing, and sometimes the children of the Ciulistet teachers were seen imitating the elders and drawing figures in the mud. Ilutsik's adaptation of storyknife symbols in the preface provides an example of how these symbols can be used in new ways. Similarly, it is possible to use storyknife symbols and storyknifing after students hear elders tell a tale. Further, storyknifing could also be adapted in conjunction with sonor. In all, sonor, *sugat,* and storyknifing include symbolic representations and the creative use of language. These particular Yup'ik genres have many valid classroom uses as a way of developing students' literacy skills and knowledge. Heretofore, they were only used during "special" times, such as Yup'ik cultural heritage week.

Changing Attitude

All of the above possibilities also represent a distinct change in attitude toward Yup'ik language and culture. The change from the culture being alternately invisible, a barrier, or punishable (some of the Yup'ik teachers as students were punished for speaking Yup'ik in school) to the creation of a Yup'ik immersion program and the adoption of Yup'ik competencies by a school district represent appreciable changes. Changes in attitude are difficult to attribute. It may be that the work of the group in developing Yup'ik mathematics provided a concrete way for others to see how the culture could be applied to schooling. Further, individuals in leadership roles in small systems like those in southwest Alaska can be affected by a single person. A teacher, principal, or a superintendent can affect school community relations. In the district, a superintendent established the Ciulistet whereas another is adopting its knowledge to schooling. Central staff in a school district have become increasingly supportive, and all of this seems to affect attitude and status of Yup'ik language and culture.

The Group as Change

The group itself stands out as a positive change from the historically rooted colonial aspects of schooling. Researchers such as Ogbu (1987, 1995) offer powerful explanations of historically rooted minority school failure. However, explanations of failure do not necessarily suggest acts that will reverse it and create possibilities. We believe that the following are essential to transform the context of schooling in indigenous and minority communities; (1) increasing the number of indigenous (or minority) teachers; (2) forming indigenous teacher support, research, and action groups; (3) involving elders (and other community members) directly and fundamentally with the teacher groups; and (4) establishing both ties to others who are similarly involved and ties to mainstream teachers and the school district, once the core group has established a clear agenda. For this combination to be effective, the teacher group must establish trust between its members, the action research must have discernible effects, and the group must achieve collective understandings that situate their own struggle within the larger sociopolitical context. Teacher groups then can be in a position to change community attitudes from ambiguity and resistance to hopefulness and possibility.

IMPLICATIONS OF THIS WORK

Where Do We Go From Here?

The answer to this question requires the school to be responsive and the community to see opportunities for its culture, language, experience, and future within the school. There are signs that local communities are increasingly taking the initiative concerning schooling, language, and culture. These initiatives are developing between some of the Ciulistet teachers and their local communities. If this trend can continue and increase, then the prospects for a negotiated school become brighter. A negotiated pedagogy would also alter sets of relationships between dominant and subordinate groups. As Stairs (1988) noted, outsiders in the leadership role must constantly step back as local people fill the roles, once the exclusive domain of southerners. This is one of the thornier problems facing groups like the Ciulistet. As Nelson-Barber and Dull noted in chapter 4, the danger always exists that outside researchers and writers may transform and interpret what is told to them from their own cultural frame of reference, mitigating the power of local voices. Central to changing the context of education is moving out and away from neo-colonialism and its inherent cycle of dependency. Have we as outside educators, who often take leadership roles, who sometimes set agendas for research and meetings, and who coordinate and organize meetings, simply transformed old colonial relationships to new ones? Our role, that of the outside consultants, is both part of the old problem and a step out into new possibilities. Slowly, with the increasing activity of elders in the group, leadership has shifted more and more to people like Henry Alakayak and to founding member Esther Ilutsik. Together we are planning a spring subsistence and science camp as a way to take advantage of and to transmit elders' cultural knowledge and simultaneously to work with Western scientists to understand the "science" behind elders' knowledge of the environment. These changes in the projected uses of Yup'ik knowledge and the increasing leadership of elders represent distinct contextual changes.

The future remains unpredictable and there is no way to know if the changes reported in this book will strengthen or if they will simply wither away. However, it is clear that a crossroads has been reached: On one side, communities and groups like the Ciulistet are realizing that time in which to pass on the wisdom of the elders is getting shorter and with each elder who dies goes a piece of the treasure. Today, a number of Ciulistet and other Alaska Native teachers have children attending the University of Alaska as well as other universities. The question is what path will exist for the next generation of Native students and teachers: Will the gains of the Ciulistet, the lessons learned from the experiences of Dull, Ilutsik, Parker, Sharp, and Yanez get translated into teacher training, into new norms for school culture, or will teaching practices at the preservice and in-service level continue to represent Western practice to the exclusion of Yup'ik culture? At this time, the University of Alaska Fairbanks has dismantled the X-CED program, cutting off the program that graduated the most Native teachers. Within this often contradictory and ambiguous educational environment, the opportunity to evolve the culture of the school and the community remains viable. In the near future, this road may be much more difficult to traverse.

THEORETICAL AND METHODOLOGICAL CONCLUSION

When Mohatt and Erickson (1981) began their work in the mid–1970s, the theoretical paradigm at the time was the deficit model. The experiences of these "disadvantaged" children, at best, were not equal to those of middle and upper class children in terms of language competence, social interaction, and worldly experiences that prepare children for schooling. In a sense, the communities in which these children lived were inadequate to the task of schooling. Hence, remediation was directed to these "children of poverty" through enrichment programs and tutoring. The problem of school failure was placed on the "disadvantaged." However, the work of Philips (1972), Boggs (1985), and Mohatt and Erickson (1981) changed the paradigm from deficit to culture differences. This work on social linguistics clearly noted how differences in communicative competence at home and at school produced conflict and "silence" in the classroom. The past 20 years of research, including the work presented in this book, has produced another paradigmatic shift, one that includes issues of power and culture and one that seeks solutions through insiders changing the circumstances that affect their lives (Begay et al., 1995; Kawagley, 1995; Deyhle & Swisher, 1997). The immediate school environment and the cultural differences between large and small traditions are one part of a larger historically rooted problem and relationship. The existence of cultural differences and negative stereotyping and evaluating are also issues of power. Our work suggests that cultural differences can be an asset, a cornerstone in developing pedagogy and curriculum, and a point of intense discourse concerning the purposes of schooling. Too often the school has used the culture of the "other" solely in the service of assimilation, a one-way process (Deyhle & Swisher, 1997; Harris, 1990; Watson-Gegeo, 1994). We believe that we have shown it is possible, albeit through intense and difficult struggle, to alter this and create circumstances in which a two-way, more mutual exchange occurs.

Throughout the work reported on in this book, the concept of culturally negotiated schooling was stated as a means of negotiating the relationship and the meaning of schooling between the school and the community. Theoretically this is important because too often, simple cultural inclusion of "traditional culture and language" has been uncritically viewed as a strategy and outcome for schooling (Cummins, 1986). However, the modern world is extremely complex, and different indigenous groups are defining themselves in different ways. To assume that more traditional "culture" is what people want is presumptuous. We believe that the long-term struggle of the Ciulistet and the inclusion of the elders shows that many elders are very interested in their traditional knowledge being transmitted, but they also realize quite strongly how the world has changed and the need for the Ciulistet teachers to find modern applications and uses for this knowledge. In this sense, schooling becomes a site of cultural construction and evolution. Our particular circumstances clearly show that the Ciulistet and elders working with the group are struggling over what the culture of school and community will be in the future.

The Ciulistet, in Ogbu's (1987) terms, would be a "subordinate and involuntary group" that should behave in an oppositional, or at least in an ambiguous way toward the dominant group. However, we believe that the life histories, personal school narratives, interviews, and continuing work of the elders point to quite a different conclusion. In fact, all of Ogbu's categories are in play; oppositional, ambiguous, and nonoppositional to mainstream society and schooling. A hundred or so years of contact and colonialism still represent a transition between the aboriginal culture and the modern-day Yup'ik. However, the struggle to use one's language and one's culture are struggles over which culture will dominate or how cultures in contact may evolve into a third reality. This is the struggle that we have presented and have experienced.

This struggle is theoretically important because it suggests that Ogbu's typologies (1987, 1995) are too restrictive and do not represent the complex reality of certain indigenous peoples. The use of the term "nonoppositional" creates logical problems when one considers that if one is not against mainstream society or is ambiguous toward it, then one is not in opposition (see Ogbu, 1995, pp. 586–587). The problem here is that positive alternatives are lumped together into a "non" category. Furthermore, this long transition period between colonialism and modernism shows signs of oppositional identity, maintaining barriers for purposes of not wanting to be like the *kass'aq* [White people], and simultaneously for maintaining the essence of being a Yup'ik. Fienup-Riordan (1994) broached this subject stating:

> Just as Euro-Americans have alternatively viewed Eskimos as an idealized or diminished image of themselves, many Yupiit construct their identity in opposition to a generalized nonnative .... At the same time, many Yupiit actively seek recognition as different—possessing sovereign rights to their land, a special subsistence economy, their own language, a unique view of the world. For contemporary Yupiit, their relationship with animals is still central, although differently defined. Harvesting retains important cultural and economic functions, and the desire to retain control over their lands and waterways is the focus of political action and debate. (p. 366)

Clearly, Ogbu (1987, 1995) and his colleagues (Fordham & Ogbu, 1986; Ogbu & Matute-Bianchi (1986) identified the importance of comparative and cross-cultural research, the shortcomings of ahistorical research—of studying schools in a decontextualized manner—and the importance of community forces, including their folk theories. The importance that oppositional behavior, those secondary cultural characteristics arising out of a colonial situation—White's persistent unequal treatment toward Yup'ik and other Alaska Natives—plays in school failure is not lost on us. The desire to maintain cultural boundaries in opposition to the *kass'aq* is a reality. However, these secondary or oppositional patterns of behavior and identity are ascribed far too much weight when considering the evidence brought forth in this book. Yanez's classroom discourse and her explanations of those behaviors within a Yup'ik cultural framework, Sharp's struggle to teach in her language (1994), and the elders' persistence in wanting to have their culture and language transmitted, point to substantive issues, not stylistic ones as Ogbu claimed (Ogbu, 1992). Further, Ogbu (1992) stated "oppositional or ambivalent cultural frames of reference [occur] ... after a group has become a minority ... such as after Blacks were brought to America as slaves, or after an American Indian tribe was conquered, moved, and placed on a reservation" (p. 289). This sweeping generalization far exceeds its reach. The Yup'ik have never been conquered or put on a reservation. Henry Alakayak and other elders from our group refuse to accept domination and actively seek positive cooperative alternatives. The work that this book represents raises the possibility and increases the probability that both schools and communities can evolve new sets of relationships.

DIALOGUE AND ACTION

Possibly the most important gift that the Ciulistet has to offer to others is the courage to engage in an open dialogue with community, school, and university. This discourse can become fertile ground upon which cultural work takes place. Slowly, through teacher groups, school and community can create innovative ways that can heal. Through an emerging sense of trust, new possibilities in curriculum and pedagogy will emerge. This may involve risk, distrust, and setbacks. However, it is this very process that we believe is applicable to others in Alaska as well as in other minority and mainstream communities. Why mainstream communities, when so much of our work only concerns indigenous people? First, the Ciulistet shows that teachers are a part of the community and the school, because they live in both worlds; teacher groups are an important ingredient for making educational reform. The purpose of educational and teacher reform concerns, in large part, increasing teacher autonomy and decision making (Sarason, 1996). The processes outlined in this book show quite distinctly how such groups can begin processes that challenge internal (psychological) and external (social) forces. Furthermore, by bringing together diverse and sometimes adversarial groups in productive ways, the Ciulistet indicate how educational reform can proceed in fundamental ways. We believe that there is much conflict between community and school, mainstream or minority, in today's world. There is much conflict between community groups, between school and community, and between factions within schools. We believe that a slow, deliberate process of teachers becoming empowered by forming their own groups and by considering questions of teaching, learning, methodology, and school–community relationships becomes an excellent forum for beginning a process of school change and reform. The elder's notion of working together, keeping relationships harmonious, in fact, becomes a strong and productive vehicle for change. At least, in our circumstances, working together made for group solidarity, increased everybody's knowledge, and evolved creative approaches to teaching and learning. Other groups in other places may find different issues and concerns. Of course, others will find other ways of facing their issues. However, we believe that the processes outlined in this book and summarized earlier could be productively used in making long-term fundamental changes in education.

We end by highlighting what we believe represents the essence of our work and how these essentials can assist others in educational reform. The book initially raised a series of questions pertaining to what benefits could accrue from Yup'ik teachers working with Yup'ik children in Yup'ik communities. We believe that the data in this book makes a convincing case that because there were Yup'ik teachers who organized into a group, a whole host of possibilities arose, which in all probability would otherwise not have seen the light of day. Clearly, groups such as the Ciulistet provide a vehicle for connecting school and community in more productive ways, of transforming (slowly over time) a set of historically rooted relationships premised on dominant–subordinate relationships. Groups such as the Ciulistet also hold promise that their ways of being, the fundamental values of a particular cultural group, and ways of viewing and being in the world can have their rightful place within schooling.

Finally, we end this book optimistically, as progress is accelerating. We remain realistic about the fragile nature of this work, the threat to vernacular languages and cultures and to communities. Yet, indigenous teachers and elders continue to carry forward their struggle, persisting in the battle over ideology, language, culture, and schooling. As the transition between contact and modernism winds down, the Ciulistet and the associated elders have become even more determined to persist and prevail in the future.

Tua-ii ingruituq [This is not the end].

REFERENCES

Begay, S., Sells, D., Estell, D., Estell, J., McCarty, T., & Sells, A. (1995). Change from the inside out: A story of transformation in a Navajo Community School. *Bilingual Research Journal, 19*(1), 121–140.

Boggs, S. (1985). *Speaking, relating, and learning: A study of Hawaiian children at home and school.* Norwood, NJ: Ablex.

Carpenter, E. (1973). *Eskimo realities.* NY: Holt, Rinehart, & Winston.

Cummins, J. (1986). Empowering minority students: A framework for intervention. *Harvard Education Review, 56,* 18–36.

Deyhle, D., & Swisher, K. (1997). Research in American Indian and Alaska Native education: From assimilation to self-determination. In M. Apple (Ed.), *Review of research in education* (pp. 113–194). Washington, DC: American Educational Research Association.

Fienup-Riordan, A. (1994). *Boundaries and passages: Rule and ritual in Yup'ik Eskimo oral tradition.* Norman, OK: University of Oklahoma Press.

Fordham, S., & Ogbu, J. (1986). Blacks students' school success: Coping with the "burden of acting white." *The Urban Review, 18*(3), 176–205.

Harris, S. (1989). Teaching the space strand in Aboriginal schools. *Mathematics in Aboriginal schools project series.* Darwin, Australia: Northern Territory.

Harris, S. (1990). *Two-way Aboriginal schooling: Education and cultural survival.* Canberra, Australia: Aboriginal Studies Press.

Kawagley, O. (1995). *A Yupiaq worldview: A pathway to an ecology and spirit.* Prospect Heights, IL: Waveland.

Lipka, J. (1994). Language, power and pedagogy: Whose school is it anyway? *Peabody Journal of Education, 69*(2), 71–93.

Lipka, J., & Ilutsik, E. (1995). Negotiated change: Yup'ik perspective on indigenous schooling. *Bilingual Research Journal, 19*(1), 195–208.

Mohatt, G., & Erickson, F. (1981). Cultural differences in teaching styles in an Odawa school: A sociolinguistic approach. In H. Trueba, G. Guthrie, & K. Au (Eds.), *Culture and the bilingual classroom: Studies in classroom ethnography* (pp. 105–119). Rowley, MA: Newbury House.

Ogbu, J. (1987). Variability in minority school performance: A problem in search of an explanation. *Anthropology and Education Quarterly, 18*(4), 312–334.

Ogbu, J. (1992). Adaptation to minority status and impact on school success. *Theory Into Practice, 31*(4), 287–295.

Ogbu, J. (1995). Understanding cultural diversity and learning. In J. Banks & C. Banks (Eds.), *Handbook of research on multicultural education* (pp. 582–593). New York: Macmillan.

Ogbu, J., & Matute-Bianchi, M. (1986). Understanding sociocultural factors: Knowledge, identity, and school adjustment. In California State Department of Education, Bilingual Education office, *Beyond language: Social and cultural factors in schooling language minority students* (pp.73–142). Sacramento; California State University, Los Angeles, Evaluation, Dissemination, and Assessment Center.

Philips, S. (1972). *The invisible culture: Communication in a classroom and community on the Warm Springs Indian Reservation.* New York: Longman.

Sarason, S. (1996). *Revisiting "The culture of the school and the problem of change".* New York: Teachers College Press.

Stairs, A. (1988). Beyond cultural inclusion: An Inuit example of indigenous educational development. In J. Cummins & T. Skutnabb-Kangas (Eds.), *Minority education* (pp. 308–335). Clevedon, Avon, England: Multilingual Matters.

Watson-Gegeo, K. (1994). What's culture got to do with it?? Minority teachers teaching minority students. *Educational Foundations, 8*(2), 3–4.

Appendix:
Methodology

Jerry Lipka
University of Alaska, Fairbanks

This chapter provides an in-depth overview of our research methods through both personal narrative and a more formal presentation on research methodology. A series of interrelated relationships forms the core of our research procedures and the establishment of methodological procedures that match the context in which we worked. All the research reported herein arose from our efforts to increase the number of Yup'ik teachers in one region of southwest Alaska. To that end, issues of cultural and linguistic inclusion and adaptation to schooling became of primary importance as these first Yup'ik teachers both adapted to schooling and adapted schooling to them. We did not set out to do "objective" research but to document cultural knowledge and to analyze teaching practices of Yup'ik teachers. Epistemologically, we embraced a research paradigm that eschewed deficits, accepted cultural differences, and believed that these differences had a potential for enriching teaching and learning. Similarly, Deyhle and Swisher (1997) distinguished between research paradigms that are assimilative and those that are community-based models, viewing indigenous culture and language as assets. Here, we used and devised research methods that were not "objective and distant" but were more fitting for a group of insiders and long-term outsiders who had been engaged in joint work for more than 15 years, and where kin relations (including fictive kin) were critically important. In Smith's (1994) reflections on his biographical approach, he found that his microethnography and biography were, in fact, an epiphany for himself. Similarly, this experience was a turning point for us. Our research methods of classroom observations, individual and group interviewing, videotape analysis, biography, and cultural activity in and out of context were all framed within a paradigm of long-term community-based research.

This appendix situates our work within the evolving field of qualitative research. We show how the present work both contributes to the expanding conceptions of what constitutes qualitative research and raises long-term collaborative and community-based research as a paradigm that allows for a more inclusive and dynamic way of representing and legitimating knowledge. On a more practical level, the chapter highlights the process of entree into the setting, developing trust, and laying the groundwork for formal research. The chapter then describes our formal research methods in relation to the specific context and needs of the Ciulistet. Our methods and research questions continue to evolve. They are presented chronologically as the group responded to the changing circumstances of being Yup'ik teachers. Our first research question was, "What is Yup'ik about a Yup'ik teacher?" Our methodological approaches to this question included videotape analysis, discourse analysis, and group and individual interviews. Subsequently, we asked the question "how can we include the Yup'ik language in schooling?" This resulted in an action-research project. The methods involved included questionnaires, community interviews, group meetings, and classroom observations. During the time that we asked these questions, we also began to collect life histories—the teachers' experiences as students then as Yup'ik teachers. As we began to involve elders in our meetings, we became increasingly interested in epistemological questions concerning what constitutes legitimate school knowledge, for example, whose knowledge counts. We asked, "How can Yup'ik language and culture contribute to the education of today's children?" This phase of our work consisted of observation and participant observation, videotaping elders in meetings and as they taught us about a variety of topics. We translated and transcribed a portion of the elders' teachings, we interviewed elders in a group setting to clarify understandings, and we worked jointly to interpret and apply these learnings to schooling. Presently, we are beginning to ask "What support do teachers need to bring these learnings into the school?" Also, we are raising the question, "What changes within the school curricula and ways of evaluating students and teachers need to be made to accommodate Yup'ik knowledge and ways of conveying that knowledge?" Lastly, we have used a case study approach as we explore differences within and across teacher cases. We are able to compare novices and experienced teachers as teachers develop over time. We can also compare contextual differences in power relations and differences in the culture of schooling.

RESEARCH PARADIGM

Research methodologies are part of a larger social context, and as recent reviews of the field of qualitative research (Denzin & Lincoln, 1994; Guba & Lincoln, 1994) have indicated, the field has evolved from treating the "other" as an object—something to be studied—to more collaborative forms of research in which insiders and outsiders jointly formulate research questions, approaches, and interpretive frames. Guba and Lincoln (1994) viewed the stages of qualitative research as evolving through five distinct periods. By condensing their work, we have the traditional period of objective and colonizing accounts of the other, followed by a modern phase of rigorous qualitative studies that attempts to met validity and reliability criteria, followed by postmodern approaches where the researcher and the researched are interactive subjects, each with voice, thick description, and the crises of representation and authority. Postmodern approaches are more reflexive then previous genres, where the writing of ethnography and the field work itself become seen as one process—an interpretive and subjective one.

In this book, we require research methodologies that also reversed an historical long-term relationship of dominant–subordinate relations, emanating from the colonial past, to more egalitarian approaches in which insiders and outsiders each contributed. Studies concerned with the "lack" of performance in a language in which the student does not yet have linguistic competence are patently absurd. Yet, that is one legacy of colonialism; deficit-based research to fit the colonizer's vision. In this book, we provide some alternatives to deficit-based research.

Limitations

A few words on the limits of this book, our research, and its possible eventualities. Even in such a long-term collaborative and community-based venture such as ours, the teachers' cases cannot possibly represent so many years of a complex situation. Nor can the teachers represent the "group" because individuals differ across time and among themselves. We can provide generalized patterns and possibilities through our work. Our work has an ephemeral quality about it as its significance may only be in the "now" when the group met, where a zone of safety and proximal development occurred, and where relationships between insiders and outsiders developed into productive work; this research is neither about products, nor the number of teachers using "Yup'ik mathematics," but about a transformation of relationships, an inclusion of knowledge once considered outside of the bounds of the formal educational system. What may occur in the future may well be related to this work, but what actually occurs cannot be predicted.

Moving from deficit-based research to long-term collaborative and community-based research presents additional concerns beyond those reflected in the crisis of representation and authority. We worked in a meeting place of two cultures, the culture of the school and the community. This culture was and is very much negotiated and evolving, and as Narayan (1993) reflected, culture is a "continuing dialectic between creativity and tradition." This is all the more so in the dynamic relationship of two cultures as they evolve into a new one. We set out to document an "authentic" pedagogy representing Yup'ik teachers and elders, to systematically understand it, and apply it in the group and in the school. Each tradition validates and legitimates its own way, and for Yup'ik ways to be more systematically included in schooling, we needed to learn them. This is related directly to what Ilutsik so clearly stated in chapter 1. The process of documenting, understanding, analyzing, and interpreting from one cultural domain and context to another is problematic, all the more so when a oral language and culture becomes represented in another language and is "taught" in a distinctly different context. Further questions of legitimation or authenticity must be answered by the cultural bearers, in this case Yup'ik elders, and to a lesser degree, Yup'ik teachers. Systematically and intentionally building a body of knowledge and representing it within its own frames of reference and its own methodologies presents a challenge beyond those articulated by Denzin and Lincoln (1994). Without the legacy of colonialism, one would assume that such distinct indigenous groups as Yup'ik would continue to transmit and evolve a cohesive culture and would have their own researchers to document and interpret questions of importance to them. This is what the next phase of research ought to be.

The research in this book, although not at the level of being framed and conducted by insiders, responded to varying circumstances as insiders and outsiders worked together. Although we situate our work within both a critical theory and a constructivist framework, there are times and circumstances in which positivistic experimental designs would have been the appropriate approach for specific questions. Within each research framework, the ontology (form and nature of reality), epistemology (nature of the relationship between the knower and what can be known), and methodology (how the researcher goes about finding out) (Guba & Lincoln, 1994) differs substantially among the nexus of relationships between knowing and known, roles and relationships within a study, perspective on researcher/researched, and voice and authority. (See Table A.1 for a summary of the research methods, questions, roles, and relationships.)

To further contextualize the research conducted in this book, we placed it at the intersection of two distinct cultures, schooling and community, each evolving and dynamic, within a historical context. Because the culture of the school and the culture of the community, in indigenous contexts, partially constitute one another, our research focused on this dimension. Furthermore, the specific point of entree for the author was through a teacher training program that also intersected at the juncture of school and community. Within that space, the overarching goal of the group—students, professors, and community people of the X-CED program—was to increase the number of Yup'ik teachers in one Alaskan region. Stated differently, the first goal as a question was, "Who should teach Alaska Native children?" A second goal was the desire to contribute to their people. The teachers who helped to formulate these questions were the same persons presented in this book. Some of them as students experienced the humiliation of being punished for using their language in the same schools in which they presently teach. Since this was the experience of some of the coresearchers, it is not surprising that the formation of a

TABLE A.1

Summary of Research Goals and Methods

Phase	Years	Goals	Questions	Roles & Relationship (Epistemology)	Methods
Entree	1980–1986	To increase the number of Yup'ik teachers	How will this affect schooling?	Shaped by historical reality, by contemporary political realities including power and authority of the school district to hire and to determine the curriculum and the power and the authority of the university to confer degrees.	Through X-CED program and field-based courses, learning can occur in villages as well as on campus. Access to higher education. Observation of Yup'ik teachers-in-training in schools.
Sociolinguistics	1986–1990	To determine a basis for a Yup'ik pedagogy	How are Yup'ik teachers contributing to their community and schools?	Epistemologically, realities of teaching are considered relative, including ways of relating, organizing social space, and discourse. University researchers used their position and "authoritative voice," but work in egalitarian ways with the group, including the way we analyzed videotapes of classroom teaching. Teachers' reality based on a "up'ik frame of reference alters conceptions of "good" teaching.	Ciulistet formed; videotaping of classroom teaching group analysis, discourse analysis, group and individual interviews, and life histories collected.
Language of instruction	1990–1991	To reverse language loss	Should Yup'ik be the language of instruction in the village of Manokotak?	School is usually the "knower" and the community through its students come to school to know. Switching the language of instruction to Yup'ik affects the relationship between knowing and the known. Now the community and the Yup'ik teachers become the knower. Collaborative approach to responding to the "ought" question, What should be the language of instruction? Roles become equalized as school, community, and university have valid concerns, interests, and expertise. Relationship between school and university becomes strained as issues of authority, control, and legitimacy emerge.	School, community, and university participants hold meetings in the village school. Bilingual experts provide guidance and present research. Community survey conducted to determine language preferences of the community.
Everyday knowledge	1992–present	To construct curriculum and pedagogy based on Yup'ik knowledge and ways of teaching	How to construct authentic Yup'ik-based content and pedagogy for schooling?	Knowledge is situated and contextualized within a Yup'ik worldview and within subsistence practices. Elders become and have authoritative voice and determine legitimate knowledge. Teachers translate and adapt this knowledge for schooling. University consultants alter roles and become helpers in this process. Knowing and known become more complex as two systems of knowledge and ways of verifying the legitimacy of knowledge are both active.	Knowledge documented through participant observation, discussions, linguistic analysis, and the ethnographic record.

group of insiders was a prerequisite for establishing a zone of safety in which the larger social context could be related to how Yup'ik teachers teach today.

Of course, the typical role and relationship between researcher and researched was not applicable because research questions were formulated collaboratively between the group and the authors of this book. The initial research question of "how are we contributing to our people" resulted in videotaping and video analysis of classroom teaching. Although the university consultants were leaders and were instrumental in establishing some of the research procedures for conducting this type of research, the analysis was conducted as a group. This approach mitigated against the problems of representation and legitimation. The members themselves pinpointed key incidents in the tapes and discussed and analyzed sections of interest to them, as did the researchers. This approach began to differentiate interpretive frames of reference from the culture of the school and the culture of the teacher training profession to the local culture. In this manner, our earliest work in sociolinguistics began a larger inquiry into reconstructing, documenting, and understanding teaching within a modern-day Yup'ik cultural framework. Here we were no more or no less affected by problems of representation because the teachers' experiences were not ours and our portraying of those experiences was inevitably reinterpreted as we wrote. However, our joint work as described in the various chapters of this book showed, to some degree, the voice and the reality of the teacher. We tried to use to advantage our role as a powerful "other." When we contrasted our own teaching experience with that of the Yup'ik teachers, it was not to show "this is how" or "this is right," but to understand the cultural rules guiding behavior. The more we delved into videotape analysis and the more we observed the teachers, the clearer it became that a distinct pedagogy and epistemology existed.

As our knowledge grew and as we realized that we could discern distinct differences between cultural frames of reference and that teaching from a Yup'ik cultural framework involved substantially more than classroom management, including the transmission of knowledge, identity, frames of reference and validity, then we began to explore what a Yup'ik pedagogy might be. Because the teachers were subject to criticism from some insiders, teacher colleagues, and administrators, the group first operated as a zone of safety. Here the boundaries were drawn tight and the group become insulated. Within this stage, the source of legitimation and validity was the group itself. However, this boundedness and relationship to the school district was permeable: the teachers continued to teach in their respective schools and we only met as a group at most for 5 weekends and for one week per year. But this protected space, free from outside frames of reference and criticism, was critical to the emergence of the group. This space was fortifying. When we shared our growing knowledge with others, particularly other indigenous groups, and when we were criticized for being passive about the survival of the Yup'ik language, this catapulted us into action research. In a highly charged environment—public meetings with bilingual experts, school board members, district administrators, teachers, and university consultants—where the rules for decision making and frames of reference differed significantly from the group's, the result-ing tensions were predictable. Here the research question was, "What should be the language of instruction?"

Elders' knowledge, in particular, represented a rather large component of our research. Here the goals of research were to establish research procedures condu-cive to collecting data within a Yup'ik cultural group. Furthermore, this knowledge needed to be documented, recorded, and analyzed. Because elders' knowledge was no longer common knowledge, then procedures needed to be established to ensure that legitimate (traditional) knowledge was documented. Further complicating this was the fact that some of the knowledge was "told" and not experienced by the group. Other forms of knowledge and learning were experienced and discussed. All of the elders' knowledge was presented in Yup'ik and translated only occasion-ally for the benefit of non-Yup'ik speakers. In particular, we wanted to document as accurately as possible traditional Yup'ik knowledge related to subsistence living, traditional stories, and values. To facilitate elders' willingness to reveal knowledge required that we were a goal-oriented group who would productively use this knowledge in transmitting it to the next generation.

The elders preferred to work as a group, because no one person was responsible for "knowing." In a group, interactions and discourse spurred memories and reflections. Some knowledge was gendered, and on such occasions, the group split into male and female groups. We took the lead from elders and on many occasions never got to our "agenda." The joint work of the group seemed to be helping the next generation experience a different path, as Henry Alakayak (an elder and a leader) said a number of times. Furthermore, the elders realized that knowledge was no longer being transmitted from one generation to another with certainty. Working in a long–term collaborative group facilitated a process of documenting and learning legitimate knowledge. The elders themselves were learning and were interested in "getting it right" and making sure that we understood. Many hours were spent in discussing fine points. The group itself served as a check against erroneous information. Portions of meetings were transcribed and translated. Questions arising from one meeting would be revisited in another. Concepts that emerged in an earlier meeting would be revisited in a later meetings. Slowly, knowledge was accumulating. However, errors of interpretation, misunderstand-ings, incomplete understandings were all possible. This was particularly true in the situations where we were told as opposed to experiencing. Even when experiencing a subsistence activity or learning how to orient one's self, these activities differed substantially from living and being a subsistence hunter. The group itself changed the context for transmitting knowledge and even the knowledge itself. This was all the more so because this was a group of educators who were interested in re-pre-senting this knowledge to students in classrooms. Our "check" against such errors was to have teachers share either what they were planning to do or had done in schools that related to elders' knowledge. However, in practice, this only occurs sometimes. Also, elders did not typically criticize an individual even if the individual presented information erroneously. This made for a problematic situation. In effect, we had three cultural types; traditional Yup'ik knowledge and ways of learning; school-based Western knowledge and ways of learning; and an evolving third way that blended and adapted and evolved. It was under these circumstances that we developed various research methods for the various phases of our work.

In the next phase of our work, a more positivistic approach may be necessary. We will be interested in quantifying and finding out if teaching Yup'ik-based mathematics makes a difference. What kind of difference? What evidence do we have to support such claims or to deny them? We will be interested in documenting and describing a process of transference. Can we change a classroom and/or school environment so that problems formulated and solved in the context of everyday life can be incorporated sufficiently intact so that students, teachers, and elders who use such strategies in the community can use these in the school? Here we will need to pay particular attention to what constitutes a context. What features of everyday problem solving must be incorporated in schools so that these ways are still visible and part of the context? If the context of schooling can be transformed in some of these ways, what differences does it make? These are some of the research questions that will guide the next phase of our work. The next sections present the research procedures that we used in chronological order.

ENTREE TO THE SETTING

On one of my first trips to a village to tutor X-CED students, I arrived at the student's home, but no one was there. As I began entering the house, a 12-year-old girl told me, "there's food." She left and went next door. I sat down and waited for the student. She returned in another minute and said "there's food." She left again. I was still puzzled. Finally, she returned a third time and more directly escorted me next door to her grandparent's house and I sat down to dinner. This was my introduction to Yup'ik hospitality, indirectness, and kinship. I was invited to stay at this home during my many visits to the village, because, of course, there were no hotels in the village. In fact, in all of the years and times that I traveled to this village, I stayed in this home.

This student and I developed a special relationship, and we considered each other "*iluks*" [like close cousins]. He introduced me to the "society of steambaths" [*maqi*]; each extended family unit had a free-standing steambath. Each evening for 3 to 4 hours, the males and the females would steam separately. Here in the steambaths, politics, stories, teaching, joking, and steambath contests occurred. It was through my students' continuing introduction to and inclusion in the culture that they prepared me for our mutual work.

It was 5 or 6 years before the group and I began to discuss a research agenda. Our research emanated from shared experiences. During this phase of our work, we collaborated on a number of different action-oriented projects. We organized the Bristol Bay Curriculum Project, to develop locally relevant curriculum and annual youth conferences to discuss topical issues. The youth would meet with their elders and other community members in the regional center, discussing cultural, economic, political, and social issues. We connected the curriculum and the youth meetings with the ongoing processes of the region. Activities such as this brought me into contact with village and regional corporations and their officers, in addition to working with the schools and our X-CED students.

RELATEDNESS

It was the importance of being "related" that allowed a research agenda to evolve. The importance of relatedness in social and environmental concerns was demonstrated by Esther Ilutsik. Ilutsik, a founding member of the Ciulistet and my coworker in X-CED back in 1981, told a story of an elder who asked her in Yup'ik, "Who are you?" She answered, "I am Esther Ilutsik." He asked her again and she repeated her answer. The elder was getting annoyed. Finally, he conveyed more information and then she said her father's Yup'ik name, thus gaining recognition from the elder.

Without kinlike relations, an outsider has no standing with insiders, unless the outsider represents powerful social, political, or business interests. To gain entry, one had to become related. Becoming related entailed its own problems. When I became one student's *eluk* [like a cousin], I immediately inherited sets of relations with many others, some positive and some not. I received a Yup'ik name, as did my son and daughter. My daughter and Ilutsik's daughter received the name "Belina" after Nancy Sharp's (an X-CED student at that time) grandmother, making Sharp their "granddaughter."

However, my relationships with the students and theirs with me were also inevitably shaped by the colonial past. The prestige associated with being a "professor and a doctor," particularly at a time when I was known throughout the region as "the professor," were part of my role. My access to money and power through university grants and the X-CED program meant that we were not on equal footing. Our relationship was (and is) a microcosm of the larger postcolonial situation we shared.

The group's relatively quick acceptance of me was gained through the trust I earned by "seeing" their reality more and more often and our relative success in increasing the number of Yup'ik graduates. My support for the students and our shared work ethic of "doing what it takes"—in time and commitment—led to students sticking with the program and graduating. Yet even these first successes were caught in the larger politics of the day.

More and more, our work became "level," that is, leadership roles slowly became more equally distributed, depending on different situations and on the expertise required to fulfill those functions. Particularly when the Ciulistet was formed, who led and who followed changed depending on the circumstances.

School and Community

The relationship between school and community, its texture and form, became noticeable on my first trips to the Bristol Bay villages as I started to travel for the X-CED program to tutor and supervise students. When I first arrived in a village, it was obvious that the prefabricated teacher housing located in close proximity to the school and adjacent to one another created a boundary. The village stood off to the side of the school. The physical boundary between the two was immediately noticeable; less obvious boundaries slowly came into focus.

FORMAL RESEARCH:
THE FORMATION OF THE CIULISTET

In 1980 when I was being interviewed for the X-CED position in Dillingham, many of the individuals on that hiring committee were also the same individuals whose voices are expressed in this book. The possibility of their voices being expressed in this book is a direct result of our work in teacher education, slowly increasing the number of Yup'ik teachers in the region, leading to the formation of the Ciulistet. The Ciulistet clearly demarcates a time when the group was not only concerned with increasing the number of Yup'ik teachers but with the quality of that experience and the impact that the teachers had for their people. It was only after the establishment of the Ciulistet that we realized the naivete of transforming schooling by having more Yup'ik teachers. We slowly realized that it took more than changing *who* the teacher was; we had to change *what* and *how* they taught as well as the relationship of the school to the community. Our research advanced by asking the general question, "What are the educational possibilities when we increasingly change who the teacher is, from outsiders to insiders?" This led to our inquiring into what ways are the Yup'ik teachers contributing to their people. This was our first formal research question.

Because our group was composed of insiders (Yup'ik teachers), outsiders with high status made the group a microcosm of how asymmetrical power relations could be overcome and turned into a positive working force. Critical to this work was the mutual acceptance by outsiders and insiders. Facilitating this set of relationships was the common goal of increasing the number of Yup'ik teachers in the region. This process was a very public act. Community members and elders knew that their relations were attending the X-CED program and, during graduation ceremonies in the region, Gerald Mohatt (then dean of the College of Rural Alaska, University of Alaska Fairbanks) and I often made presentations or awarded the degree to the graduates. Participation in feasts, funerals, steambaths, and other community activities provided the public backdrop that identified these outsiders with insiders. Shared goals, kin and kinlike relationships, frequent gatherings, and hunting trips marked the ways in which relationships were built and trust earned. These commonalties, particularly those concerned with improving education by including

Yup'ik teachers, language, and culture in the equation were what formed the Ciulistet and the background to the work of the group.

INSIDERS AND OUTSIDERS: A THIRD WAY

The group itself became a "third way" of reconstructing and reforming schooling. First this occurred on the periphery of schooling within the confines of the group, however, this process and its curricular goals became adopted by a local school district. This third way included insiders and outsiders, Yup'ik perspectives and outside perspectives, and a desire to learn from each other. Elders characterized our work as "creating one mind" (Henry Alakayak often said this at and after our meetings, and other elders expressed the same sentiment).

In a very general way, our research moved ahead according to the anthropological dictum of "making the familiar strange" and "making the strange familiar." The insider–outsider dynamics were critical to this approach. As an outsider, I played the "dumb" role and asked questions that might have been obvious to an insider. This relieved insiders because of the inherent fear of being ridiculed for not knowing what they should and because of the role and relationship between elders and the younger generation. Also, Esther Ilutsik (1996) explained:

> We had hit an iceberg that had formed as a result of the domination of the Western cultural education system. Furthermore, the gates to the deeper cultural knowledge were closed. Being brought up in the Yup'ik culture … [we] were taught to respect our elders. We were taught not to ask questions of them, but observe and learn in that respect. With the introduction of schooling the descendants were no longer able to observe and learn. They were confined to the school grounds and much of the deeper cultural knowledge was lost. But they still continued with the proper cultural interaction with elders and their parents of being respectful and not asking questions of them…. There was a missing link, a cultural gap, that no one could readily identify as such…. Lipka's presence helped us to close that cultural gap and open up the gate. Through him the teachers had an excuse to ask questions indirectly to the parents and elders. I recall at some of our first meetings that Jerry was the voice for all. We would ask him questions and then he in turn would ask the elders and the elders would answer his questions. Gradually, the teachers started to ask them questions without being embarrassed. The elders began to understand and accept this procedure. (American Anthropological Association, 1996)

Elders increasingly changed their role in the group from "show and tell," (that is demonstrating traditional crafts, subsistence ways, and story telling) to coconstructing curriculum and pedagogy to taking a leadership role within our meetings and in meetings with other elders and teachers. The dynamics of the group reflected, to some degree, Yup'ik ways of organizing. Leadership shifted according to the task at hand. During times of videotape analysis, Lipka, Mohatt, and Nelson-Barber (a consultant to the group) played more of an active leadership role; whereas in disseminating our work, Yanez (an X-CED graduate and current bilingual coordinator for Southwest Region Schools) and Ilutsik played very active roles. Research, grant writing, and fund raising became the expertise of Lipka. Those with the expertise to demonstrate a particular skill or knowledge would take the lead. In these ways, this community of learners composed of teachers, elders, and university consultants voluntarily came together.

As noted earlier, the group was a "third way" for insiders and outsiders to work together, not Western or Yup'ik, but sometimes one, sometimes the other, and sometimes a coevolving of the two into something new. This created the possibility of transforming historical colonial relations into productive, more egalitarian relations. It is this story within a larger story where much of our work took place. Many of us involved in this work were changed by the experience. Alakayak, Ilutsik, Lipka, Sharp, and Yanez are most visibly changed by this experience, because each of them continues to spend a considerable part of their professional work developing the ideas discussed in this book. Alakayak, the elder, attends increasingly more meetings in a year both inside and outside of the region, becoming a more powerful leader. These considerations are at least as important as any of the "formal" research methods. Without these proper relations, no research would have been possible.

Transforming school–community relationships in a context of asymmetrical power relations requires strategies that alter these relationships. Ethnographic research in the 1970s and 1980s that documents cultural differences provides an insufficient base to transform schooling. Nonetheless, identifying differences may well be a first step in a long process of learning how another culture can alter the processes and content of schooling, and in time, can improve students' academic preparedness (Deyhle & Swisher, 1997). The framework of this book suggests that culturally based communication styles, locally based knowledge of the environment—social and ecological—and local values that indigenous and minority teachers bring to school can be important factors in transforming schooling. Furthermore, connecting community to school through local teachers is critical (Comer, 1986; Holm & Holm, 1990; Lightfoot, 1978; Lipka & McCarty, 1994; Sarason, 1996).

This action-oriented ethnographic approach to research, with its collaborative relationship between elders, Ciulistet, university consultants, and school personnel, is one way the context of schooling can be changed. Key elements, we believe, include a long-term relationship between all parties, trust earned through mutual work, and perseverance to see that work accomplished.

Although writing expresses linearity, the experiences of the authors and the Ciulistet are anything but linear. As always, planning and intentionality appear smoother in hindsight than during the action. In writing about our strategies, we have benefited from reflection and hindsight.

The Ciulistet and X-CED's attempt to transform their school setting occurred in multiple steps; (a) increasing the number of Yup'ik teachers, (b) officially forming the Ciulistet, (c) connecting Yup'ik language and culture to schooling, and (d) involving elders and community members in developing curriculum, pedagogy, and the politics of schooling.

From 1981 until 1986 or 1987, there were so few Yup'ik teachers in Bristol Bay that we were mainly concerned with simply increasing their numbers. It was not until the formation of the Ciulistet group that we engaged in emergent or formal research. Our methods developed slowly through the different phases of our work. For the purposes of this narrative, the methods are organized chronologically; the first phase had two major components—increasing the number of teachers and my entree into the setting. Both of these were precursors to the formation of Ciulistet; reaching a critical number of teachers so that a group could form and earning each others' trust so that we could effectively work together. The second phase concerned what happened to Yup'ik teachers when they reached the classroom, and it was driven by the question, "What is Yup'ik about a Yup'ik teacher?" The third phase initiated more action-oriented research concerned directly with school transformation. The first part of this work concerned what the language of instruction should be in Yup'ik speaking communities. Second, it concerned how the Yup'ik culture could be an important part of schooling. Finally, it concerned what role elders and community members could play in transforming schooling. The methods we used evolved according to the different time periods and concerns that we faced. All the research we engaged in was action research from within an ethnographic framework. We followed the work of Aronowitz and Giroux (1991) in developing our questions:

> [A] theory of border pedagogy needs to address the important question of how representations and practices that name, marginalize, and define differences as the devalued Other are actively learned, interiorized, challenged, or transformed. In addition, such a pedagogy needs to address how an understanding of these differences can be used in order to change the prevailing relations of power that sustain them. (p. 128)

Praxis

Praxis best describes the work reported in this book. Our approach to this research grew from my work as an educator in a teacher education program (X-CED) and the struggles of the then–undergraduate Yup'ik teacher education students. X-CED's primary goal was to increase the number of Alaska Native teachers. Even this goal, embraced by a mostly male Caucasian faculty, underscored neo-colonialism and the complex role the university undertook in the change process. We needed a methodology that not only transformed the more obvious external factors (such as the number of Native teachers) but also guided the more difficult transformations of psychological, social, and power relations between individuals, communities, schools, and the university. We needed a methodology that moved from the paternalistic stance of changing others to changing ourselves as well. Even more difficult, we needed a method that at least attempted to change the culture of school and the social and political context that surrounded schooling in these communities. To that end, Lather's (1986) and Freire's (1970) transformative approaches to working with oppressed groups and their emphasis on the dynamic interplay between insider and outsider, between minority and majority, and between those in power and those not have strongly influenced the course of our work.

WHAT IS YUP'IK ABOUT A YUP'IK TEACHER?

As the X-CED students became certified teachers, they faced a new set of obstacles and difficulties. These Yup'ik teachers were essentially without role models—being a teacher in Western society is, for most Yup'ik people, a very recent phenomena, particularly when one considers that schooling in one local community began only in the early 1950s.

At the time the Ciulistet was formed, there was severe criticism of Native teachers among other teachers and administrators, particularly concerning their management style. I was privy to this information in numerous discussions with teachers in the villages and at meetings. The few Yup'ik teachers at that time were isolated from one another. Each felt pressured to conform in order to be counted as a "genuine" teacher. Furthermore, other teachers and administrators responded to our concerns with "What Yup'ik culture?" They saw no difference between Yup'ik and outside teachers.

With this in mind, the group generated two critical questions: (a) How are Yup'ik teachers contributing to their people? and (b) In what ways are Yup'ik teachers Yup'ik? In response to the second question, one Yup'ik teacher asked me: "How can this program teach me to be a Yup'ik teacher?" He meant this at two levels: As a *kass'aq* [White person] how could I teach him to be a Yup'ik teacher, and more fundamentally, he felt the impossibility of being a Yup'ik and a teacher. For him, the term was an oxymoron. One can be a Yup'ik who is a teacher, but not a Yup'ik teacher.

The insider–outsider relationship allowed for a reflective process, in which Yup'ik teachers saw their own behaviors reflected back to them in novel ways, which made them increasingly conscious of their culturally based teaching. Typically, we viewed videotapes of each Ciulistet member in a group setting. We discussed points of interest, such as the relationship of the teacher to the students, particularly the teacher's intimate knowledge of some of the students. Insider–outsider reflections were very important during this phase of the research in that I, along with the consultants, noticed aspects of the teaching and the relationships between the teacher and the students that were, in a sense, too familiar for the Yup'ik teachers to notice. These perceptions led to further discussions. We audiotaped sections of video and transcribed them. We analyzed some of the teacher–student discourse, based on the culturally different ways insiders and outsiders viewed the tape. We noted after watching a number of tapes how different teachers began lessons and made transitions. We also paid attention to proxemics and prosody. Micro sections of tape were analyzed by the group, followed by an insider/outsider pair reviewing and analyzing collabora- tively. Outside consultants provided expertise in the use of space, voice, and movement, and an ethnomusicologist analyzed data by looking for differences in voice patterns between Yup'ik teachers and outside teachers. We also asked a few outside teachers, both experienced and inexperienced, to tape themselves teaching. These were also very instructive because differences between outside teachers, experienced or not, were obvious to the Ciulistet members who viewed them.

DATA SELECTION

The data presented in this book are but a part of a much larger corpus of data. For example, videotape of classroom teaching exceeds 50 hours of classroom footage. In selecting the videotape segments for analysis, we did not choose a process to simply obtain a representative sample. Instead, we were interested in answering the question "What is Yup'ik about a Yup'ik teacher?" Because our question called for a certain response, we viewed the tapes in a group setting for material that the group felt reflected their culture. We were looking for teaching exemplars, not normative cases. In addition, we paid attention to how teachers began lessons. We felt that lesson openings provided an excellent transition to see how Yup'ik teachers used talk, body movements, and established routines while making a transition from a recess or the beginning of the day to a lesson. These openings were instructive, because they highlighted many differences between insider and outsider teachers. Furthermore, we also analyzed videotape segments of teachers new to the region. These teachers consisted of both novice and expert teachers, newcomers and long-term teachers. Much of this data is beyond the present book. Some of it was reported in Lipka (1991).

VIDEOTAPE ANALYSIS

The first research topics generated by the group, as previously mentioned, con- cerned their contributions as Yup'ik teachers and the ways in which they were helping their people. The methodology we employed to respond to these questions was borrowed from sociolinguistics and from videotape analysis. The process of videotaping was straightforward. Video cameras were placed in classrooms, usually by the teacher, on a tripod and focused on as much of the classroom as possible. The camera tended to be focused on areas where the most student–teacher interac- tions occurred. Our methods borrowed heavily from Mohatt and Erickson (1981), as Gerald Mohatt was a consultant to our work. We engaged in a series of micro ethnographic studies, analyzing videotapes of Yup'ik classroom teachers. It became obvious to the Ciulistet and to consultants (such as Sharon Nelson-Barber, Malcolm Collier, and Fred Erickson) working with us that tape after tape showed similar teaching patterns in terms of pace, rhythm, proxemics, and prosody. These features were noted as similar to the Odawa tapes that Erickson and Mohatt (1982) previously analyzed, and according to Collier (personal communication, November, 1988), they were similar to Collier's (1979) analysis of Yup'ik teachers' ways of organizing classrooms.

While viewing the tapes with the Ciulistet teachers, we would sometimes play scenes with the sound turned off, with the sound on but the picture turned off, and, of course, with both sound and picture. We would play the tape in double time and in normal time. This way, different patterns would emerge having to do with the physical use of space and the use of talk. We could see patterns of interaction, synchronicity (Collier, 1979), when students and teachers expressed through their movements a flow and a pace that was in harmony between them. In other instances, physical dissonance between teacher and student became apparent. The use of verbal behavior contrasted sharply between insiders and outsiders.

After the group viewings of Yup'ik teachers' classroom videotapes, I would spend hours observing the tapes until I had them memorized, and I was aware of numerous differences between the Yup'ik teachers and myself. I noted some of these sections, and they were transcribed and analyzed. Later, I would watch the videotape with the teacher (this is reported in more detail in the Lipka and Yanez chapter) and we would stop the tape to discuss specific teaching behaviors and scenes, for example, why a teacher did or did not respond to a student in a particular instance. These interviews were extremely helpful in getting beyond Yup'ik teachers' individual behaviors and identifying the deeper cultural values underlying those behaviors.

In addition to group analysis, we gained additional data from cultural interviews (Trueba, 1989). In these cases, after becoming very familiar with the tape, I would interview the teacher and base some questions on the distinctly different ways I imagined I would have handled particular microclassroom events. Also the interviews concerned the teacher's life experiences and how those experiences may have influenced classroom decisions. This method was also effective in gaining a Yup'ik cultural understanding of the values and logic behind particular teacher behaviors.

DISCOURSE ANALYSIS

In two cases and in part of a third, we used discourse analysis somewhat differently to gain a more precise understanding not only of classroom interaction between teacher and student but between teacher, student, and the context of schooling. In the Parker and Mohatt case (chapter 3), teacher–student talk was viewed by producing a transcription of these classroom interactions, and by in-depth interviews concerning how and why Parker presented herself in the manner that she did. In the Yanez case (chapter 5), we took a more formal analysis of classroom talk following Sacks, Schegloff, and Jefferson's (1974) protocols, and this included pauses, emphasized words, overlapped speech, and other details of classroom discourse. However, in this case we also combined classroom discourse with in-depth teacher interviews to gain a fuller understanding of the context that surrounds teachers and affects how teachers decide to construct lessons.

In addition, within the Yanez case we used the discourse analysis somewhat akin to narrative analysis, a story with a beginning, middle, and end, and also because narrative classroom discourse has a structure and a function (see Coffey & Atkinson, 1996). By taking this approach, we could see how the form and structure of classroom narrative related to the context of schooling and to the context of community. For example, through discourse analysis, we gained insight into the structure of classroom discourse, how it differed from mainstream classroom discourse routines (Cazden, 1988), and how it was more like conversation. Through discourse analysis, interviews with Yanez about the lesson, and brief life history interviews with Yanez, we gained insights into how she constructed this lesson to weave Yup'ik values within a school context. More systematically, the transcription of the lesson was also analyzed into categories pertaining to items such as communication—turns at talk, who talks to whom (Philip, 1972) as well as uses of rewards and reprimands—and the use of cultural knowledge. Through this process, it was possible to identify Yup'ik cultural messages in the lesson.

Therefore, this approach opened the lesson to how it was structured, what topics were discussed, who spoke to whom, and who spoke how often. It also showed the underlying functional value of the lesson in terms of the Yup'ik moral imperatives that were brought to the students. The analysis assisted us in interpreting the lesson as a story about being a Yup'ik, how one becomes a Yup'ik, and how one is to act as a Yup'ik. Through this approach, we gained an appreciation of how lessons could be structured and could function as identity makers. In particular, the story line and values incorporated in the Yanez classroom segment showed how Yanez shaped the students to be Yup'ik. In addition, the story line of the lesson included ecology, categorizing fish, and seasonal changes as well as beginning and finishing a task; preparing, cleaning, and drying smelt.

INTERVIEWS AND LIFE HISTORIES

To deepen our understanding of the cultural basis of classroom teaching, we engaged in life history interviews, individual interviews, group interviews, and further analysis of videotaped lessons. Teachers' life histories established a deeper contextual understanding of the struggles, conflicts, and adaptations that they made as students and as novice and experienced teachers. Further, collecting brief life histories, particularly those concerned with being a student and a teacher, provided insight into Yup'ik ways of knowing, learning, and evaluating as well as into the "border context" of being a Yup'ik person within a school context. For example, Evelyn Yanez coined the term "teaching against my will" to represent some of her experiences as a Yup'ik teacher in her school. Sharp provided equally powerful imagery as she told how she felt married to a curriculum that excluded her cultural and linguistic strengths. These life histories were collected over a number of years (see chaps. 2 to 4).

Beyond the notions of struggle and the insights that brief life histories provided for understanding these struggles within the context of schooling, these interviews added to our growing understanding of how a Yup'ik teacher began to "Yup'ikize" schooling. When we connected our microethnography and sociolinguistic approaches with life history interviewing, we were then in a position to connect classroom behaviors to Yup'ik cultural values and to the pressures of teaching in a Western-oriented school. This enabled us to adapt an interpretive frame of reference that consisted of classroom narrative and actions in relation to historical and present-day relationships between school and community.

The approach of using videotape analysis, discourse analysis, life histories, and individual and group interviews provided a means to understand the meaning of lessons constructed by Yanez, Parker, Sharp, and Dull. We situated the meaning of these lessons within the nexus of the culture of the school and the culture of the community. Because this data included novice and experienced teachers, insiders and outsiders, we gained multiple perspectives on how different teachers along different stages of personal and professional development construct lessons. The process of doing this provided additional insights to the group about how being Yup'ik contributed to their teaching. What we did not expect was that they might be contributing beyond the confines of their classrooms to others.

EVERYDAY KNOWLEDGE AND PARTICIPANT OBSERVATION: ELDERS INSTRUCTING

In the second half of the book, we increasingly viewed Yup'ik knowledge as an asset that could contribute to schooling. In order for the group to learn, we invited elders as instructors and colleagues. This began a process of documenting their knowledge, understanding it, interpreting it for schooling, and sharing with the elders these school-based representations.

Participant observation combined with apprenticing refers specifically to the group's relationship with the elders as we engaged in discussions and activity related to subsistence living. We did not use participant observation as discussed in the more classical anthropological literature where "outsiders" participate in a yearly cycle of living. Of course, the insiders in this study all lived within the cultural cycle. However, as mentioned throughout this book, the cycle of knowledge passed on from generation to generation was no longer guaranteed. To increase the knowledge of the group, we engaged in a variety of activities with elders.

Sometimes elders eschew book knowledge for direct experience with the environment and in favor of traditional stories being passed down orally (Mathers, 1995). Elders' concern that the culture, language, and everyday knowledge may be lost and the opportunity to work with other elders seemed to be the catalysts that motivated the high level of elder participation in this phase of our work. Elders increasingly took a lead role. The approach to working with elders that appears to have made a positive difference was including at least five elders in each of our meetings and as many as 15. Because elders had other elders to talk to, topics that may have been only partially known by one person could be filled in by another person. This dynamic relieved elders of being on the spot and of being asked direct questions. More natural conversations could emerge and elders could feel more in control of the discussions and the agenda. Further, these meetings were held almost exclusively in Yup'ik, making elders feel comfortable. In sum, we created an environment in which elders not only felt comfortable but were and continue to be eager to assist. The predominate research method here was participant–observer. Taking this stance were both insiders and outsiders. We all learned together.

We held approximately three to four meetings a year. Most meetings were held in the local villages and occasionally meetings were held in Fairbanks and Anchorage. During these meetings, elders and the group chose particular topics, often topics related to the specific season and the subsistence cycle. Here elders instructed us through telling and through experience. For example, an important topic related to survival on the land was weather prediction. Elders took us "on field trips" to observe sunrises and sunsets and had us notice the color of the sky, wind direction, cloud formation, humidity, and other observable phenomenon. They related stories told them by their elders. Through a series of topics, the group increased its understandings.

Meetings were increasingly held in Yup'ik. Meetings were recorded, translated, and transcribed. We selected certain sections for transcriptions and indexed other sections for future transcriptions. As we were engaged in this phase of our work, it became obvious to all concerned that elders' empirical observations of the natural world provided a rich source of knowledge. The elders on their part became increasingly concerned that their knowledge would no longer be transmitted intact to the next generation. Yup'ik teachers became a very important audience for the elders' knowledge. Not only did the elders "show and tell," they became partners in knowledge production. As we translated elders' knowledge into school knowledge, the elders participated with us. They also, at times, experienced the creative ways in which the teachers adapted these lessons to school.

In hindsight, it is clear that we chose methods that provided insight into the processes that can reverse cultural and linguistic loss. Of the utmost importance was the inclusion of elders. Fortuitously, the interpretive approach to traditional knowledge is finally beginning to appeal to school districts. It is this phase of our work that holds the most promise for transforming a set of relationships between school and community—in the involvement of community members and elders, in the role that Yup'ik language and culture can play in curriculum and pedagogy, and in the choices that schools and communities can make as they openly perceive the possibilities that local cultures afford schooling.

Two broad categories of learning took place; discussion and situated activity. To contextualize the knowledge, we often engaged in situated activities in which elders could relate to the group as a community of apprentices. For example, in such activities as weather forecasting, we would go out at sunrise and sunset and observe the sky, wind, mountaintops, and humidity. One elder in particular led these events. These activities were typically organized by gender. We set up a temporary spring camp during the herring run as a way of engaging in traditional activities and storytelling relating to a particular place. We visited abandoned villages with elders who were raised in those places. This inevitably got the group talking about geographical place names and the stories associated with those places. We built fish drying racks, made traps, and discussed kayak building. We made headdresses, Yup'ik patterns for them and for *kuspuks* [dresses], grass baskets, and beadwork.

We participated in all of these activities and videotaped and/or audiotaped them. A smaller subset of these tapes was transcribed and most were indexed for retrieval purposes. The documentation and the "field experiences" allowed for both first-hand enculturation and for analysis of that process. Often the group spent considerable time discussing the root meaning of Yup'ik words to more clearly understand their more traditional meanings. Literal meanings such as those associated with numeration illustrate the body and its relationship to counting (see chapter 6).

ACTION-RESEARCH

Culture, Power, and Pedagogy

These research questions grew out of feelings of being marginalized and disrespected, and the frustration group members often felt were vented in the meetings. During this phase, we visited a variety of other schools in and out of Alaska. We also began to present our first research findings at national and international conferences, and reactions to our presentations became additional data. Ciulistet increasingly participated in a larger indigenous discourse. Our dialogue became influenced by issues of language and cultural survival, and we influenced others by our sociolinguistic and collaborative work. We visited bilingual programs in Anchorage where a Japanese immersion program in a public school clearly contrasted with what the group knew as *their* bilingual programs—mostly decontextualized English submersion programs. The group also visited Ottawa in order to present its work to the Mokakit conference, a First Nations indigenous research organization. The experience of being addressed first in French, then immediately in English if one didn't respond, greatly impressed the three attending Ciulistet members. Seeing bilingualism as a stable and normal part of life was a new experience. We also visited Chinese schools in San Francisco while we were collaborating with the Stanford University's Minority Consortium. Again, the group had a chance to see first hand a bilingual program that used the speakers' first language.

These experiences slowly accumulated to the point when we decided that we must take some action about language loss. Our work at that point became more involved in trying to change the school context.

As a step toward developing a Yup'ik immersion program, we invited outside experts in bilingual education to audioconference with school, community, and university participants in a project to decide if Yup'ik or English should be the first language of instruction. The community-based meetings were instrumental in opening these issues to the school district. Community surveys, interviews, and group discussions on the community's language preference were conducted. After the data was collected and analyzed, the group met again to discuss its implications. Overwhelmingly, the community voiced its support for a bilingual program, and for beginning with a Yup'ik immersion program. This project is briefly discussed in chapter 3 and in Lipka (1994). But this was not our only focus: We actively attempted to put into practice what we were learning in our group meetings in the classrooms. The group's deepest concern at that time was the survival of Yup'ik language and culture.

The collaborative action-research phase of our work included mobilizing community interest in achieving a Yup'ik immersion program, conducting community-wide interviews on the desire of the community to have a Yup'ik immersion program, and recording our meetings with the community, school, and university. An analysis of this action research points out important differences in perception about the role and function of Yup'ik language instruction. Further, this phase of our work resulted in difficult political questions about power and legitimacy. After the Yup'ik immersion program was constituted, our research agenda shifted toward the question, "What does Yup'ik everyday and subsistence knowledge have to do with schooling?"

The purpose of documentation and analysis was to bring the culture of the community and the voice of the community into formal schooling. Although this was problematic, this remains the strategy of the group. To that end, our action research impacted schooling in four distinct but related ways; language of instruction, pedagogical approaches to teaching, the use of Yup'ik knowledge for the teaching of mathematics and science, and recognition and inclusion of Yup'ik community members in matters affecting schooling.

Briefly, the language of instruction in the Manokotak school switched from English to Yup'ik for K–4 after the group, university, and school district engaged in a joint research project (Lipka, 1994; Sharp, 1994). Although the project created tensions between the university and the local school district, the school district mandated Yup'ik as the language of instruction. This change came about in part because of the degree of community representation and interest in this issue. The project was initiated by the university and the Ciulistet and accepted by the district and the school. Today, the teachers are beginning to use knowledge gleaned from our meetings in their teaching (see Mohatt & Sharp, chapter 2).

The very process of documenting Yup'ik teachers teaching Yup'ik children has led to a number of publications (Lipka, 1990, 1991; Lipka & Ilutsik, 1995) and has reinforced these ways of teaching as legitimate. The inclusion of key school district personnel in our meetings has also led to a recognition of cultural differences in teaching as an acceptable alternative.

The development of pedagogical and content approaches emerging from Yup'ik knowledge (Lipka & McCarty, 1994 and chapter 6 in this book) has impacted schooling. Today, the local school district is including this knowledge as part of its district's goals and objectives. The inclusion of Yup'ik teachers and elders demonstrating this knowledge to others is a sign of this change.

The comments by elders across many meetings that knowledge that was hidden is now revealed speaks directly to the changing role that they have in relationship to schooling. Although the elders meet with the group in a setting that is marginally connected to schooling the impact of these meetings has tied the elders more centrally to schooling. Now their knowledge is not only being revealed, it is valued.

CASE ANALYSIS

Cross-Case Analysis

The summation of the individual life histories, videotape analysis of classroom teaching among novices and experts, classroom videotape analysis of insiders and outsiders, and contextual differences in schooling, between state-controlled schools with a local and regional school board and a local Indian controlled school all provided data for a comparative analysis. Throughout all the cases, we saw that all the life histories we collected demonstrate the recurring theme of struggle, or as Nancy Sharp said "mountains and valleys." We found this in the narratives of experienced and inexperienced teachers and those in band-controlled schools and those in state-controlled schools. The combined effect of having multiple cases across a number of important variables strengthens each life history. This information then strengthens efforts at reversing the conditions that caused these struggles in the first place.

The microanalysis of videotaped classroom teaching became connected to macroissues because of the life history interviewing. The relationship between microevents in the classroom and these larger issues was made visible by this research methodology. The teaching cases of this book illustrate this point.

The microanalysis of videotaped classroom scenes and insider and outsider collaborative analysis also yielded insights into the way that these novice to expert teachers constructed classroom discourse. Through our set of data it became clear that it was not an isolated phenomena that this individual teacher taught in a way that differed from mainstream norms of nomination, elicitation, response, and evaluation. We analyzed the five teaching cases and contrasted the nomination, elicitation, response, and evaluation approach to the more conversational manner of conducting classroom discourse. We were able to do this within cases and across cases. We were able to compare distribution of talk between teachers and students, the length of student talk, and the nature of the talk. We were able to document the quality of classroom discourse by examining talk and variables associated with that talk across cases. For example, a few of the cases showed the effect of nominating and "spotlighting" students.

These cases began to shed light on the effects of who is the teacher, what is considered legitimate knowledge, how that knowledge is constructed, and the language of instruction. These cases then began to provide insights into the question that the Ciulistet teachers raised: How are we contributing to our people? What is Yup'ik about a Yup'ik teacher?

Within Cases: Negative Cases

Our long-term collaborative research in two contexts, a Yup'ik and an Odawa one, provides an opportunity to make contrasts within and across teaching cases. For example, in one case, a teacher changed her discourse style and general manner of relating to the students to provide Mohatt with a "reading lesson." This failed lesson became the object of Mohatt's work in the present volume. Here we have a negative case, when the teacher performed in a manner distinctly different from her own norms. This case, reported on by Mohatt, showed how the students in the class were sensitive to the discourse routines established by the teacher. In the Mohatt and Parker case, they explored another failed lesson. In this lesson, Parker attempted to use the canonical form of classroom discourse, nomination, elicitation, response, and evaluation. By doing this, the students responded in monosyllables, if at all. Parker contrasts this way of interacting in the classroom with the way the community interacted. In contrast to the Parker case, the Yanez case shows that a Yup'ik teacher can create a classroom environment in which the discourse routines of school resemble those at home. Here, students shared in the discussion and took the initiative in turns at talk as well as in topics of talk.

Summary of Cases

In summary, the life histories, discourse analysis, videotape analysis, and group and individual interviews combine to build a case for how Yup'ik teachers construct classroom space, school content, and values in a manner that reflects the culture of the school as well as the culture of the community. Some of this adaptive teaching is uniquely Yup'ik, other teachings reflect a unique blend of Yup'ik and Western, and other teachings reflect a Western style of teaching and learning. These cases provide data that begins to show the importance and impact of who the teacher is, what the content is, and how it is taught. The combination of who, what, and how is critical to the identity formation of both teachers and students. However, it is not simply a case of adding up discourse styles and effects to pronounce a judgment or prescription about classroom teaching in indigenous contexts. As Parker recalls in her case, although students did not respond well to the alien style of relating, she now feels this is a style that the students should learn. Questions of "should" ought to be negotiated at the school and community.

This sociolinguistic research was also politically charged, in that we reached a point when these differences in teaching were no longer seen as mere happenstance but as part of Yup'ik culture. At the same time, it also became obvious to the group that being a Yup'ik teacher in school meant that one was severely constrained in the use of Yup'ik language and culture in the classrooms and schools of this region. The group's research agenda inevitably became more political, and new research questions evolved: (1) Whose school is it? (2) Whose language, culture, knowledge, and values ought to be represented in schooling? and (3) Who decides these questions?

A QUESTION OF CHANGE AND TRANSFERENCE: MOVING FROM THE ZONE OF PROXIMAL DEVELOPMENT TO CLASSROOM EFFECTIVENESS

The last research question the group generated has to do with the question of transfer. What barriers exist between the innovations and developments experienced in the Ciulistet group with elders and the process of transferring this knowledge to classrooms and schools? During the past 3 years, we have been working with the elders innovating such novel content and pedagogical approaches as teaching base 20 subbase 5 through Yup'ik dance, but only some of the teachers are implementing these innovations into their daily teaching routines. This last question is beyond the scope of this book. However, it is a question that will increasingly guide our work into the next few years. It is becoming increasingly clear that having a zone of proximal development, in which teachers, elders, and university consultants work together to produce knowledge and ways of teaching that knowledge is insufficient to transferring this knowledge from one context to another. This is not to say that no innovations have taken place beyond the group. Quite the contrary. Ilutsik continues to work with teachers in the Dillingham City Schools, implementing and piloting units on Yup'ik patterns. Yanez continues to develop interdisciplinary approaches to bilingual aides and teachers. Yet, it is our informal assessment that more transference can occur between the group and the classroom.

SUMMARY

Although we have engaged in traditional research methodologies in order to conduct sociolinguistic research and microethnographic work, employing methods from ethnomusicology to conversation analysis, the most critical elements in our work were the formation of the Ciulistet, the perseverance of the teachers and the authors, the trust and working relationship, and the steady support and knowledge of the elders. Yup'ik elders often said to the group, "we have to be of one mind, then we can do anything." At times, the group functioned in this capacity, and to whatever extent we have accomplished anything, the value of everyone working together has been instrumental.

Presently, we have raised an additional research question, while still responding to the more politically charged issues: In what ways are science and mathematics embedded in everyday experiences at fish camp, and in other subsistence activities? In responding, the Ciulistet has been joined by elders from seven villages and experienced Yup'ik bilingual aides from an adjacent region.

Our work has become a combination of a teacher study and research group, collaboratively conducted, and a politically concerned group interested in and working toward a long-term evolving school culture, one that reflects the community by creating an atmosphere in which issues of critical importance to it—cultural and linguistic survival, and the future of their children—are discussed openly.

The Group: A Zone of Safety

Equally important to the group's sociolinguistic analysis of videotapes and work on obtaining a Yup'ik immersion program was the "safe zone" the group created. Because the Ciulistet was a formal and voluntary association of Yup'ik teachers and aides, predominantly from one school district, it allowed like-minded individuals to work on common problems. Although the school district provided funds and sanctioned meetings, the group was independent from it. The University of Alaska Fairbanks assisted by providing funds through grants for Ciulistet activities. The cultural boundaries created a zone in which the Ciulistet were able to explore multiple issues—cultural, educational, and political—without risking ridicule or observation by unsympathetic others. Within it, the group freely discussed their thoughts and dreams concerning schooling. Also, the group was able to acknowledge gaps in their own knowledge and to learn from the elders without feeling threatened or denigrated.

Occasionally these meetings provided a place and time where members vented their emotions; they identified different ways in which they felt singled out, uncomfortable, restricted, or wounded by prejudice. These sessions created and strengthened bonds between them, and many members felt supported in their work for the first time.

It was at such times that, informally at first, different teachers gave "testimony" to the struggles of being a Yup'ik teacher. More formally, years later, we conducted interviews with different teachers, expanding on the themes of personal struggle and on being a Yup'ik teacher in a Western school. These formal interviews were typically audiotaped at times when Mohatt, Nelson-Barber, Ferdinand and Nancy Sharp, Parker, Ilutsik, Yanez, and myself met privately. The interviews focused on life histories and important cultural learnings that appeared to affect the attitudes Ciulistet members held toward schooling and how these affected their ways of teaching. We attempted to draw connections between behaviors observed in class-rooms and their underlying Yup'ik or personal values, and possibly to where and how these values were learned. All cases reported in this book reflect the results of life history interviews as well as more structured interviews concerning particular classroom events.

After the struggles of obtaining a Yup'ik immersion program, the group needed a respite from highly charged political issues. The following section reports on methods and questions guiding our latest work.

Culturally Negotiated Pedagogy

In the last few years, our work is still concerned with language and cultural survival; however, we have approached it from a different perspective. The group has generated a new research question: How is Yup'ik language, culture, and everyday experience related to school mathematics and science? In addressing this query, we decided to videotape work groups at fish camp; chapter 9 details this work. In some ways, this phase of our research is most important because it involves elders and community members directly in the work of the Ciulistet. Elders share their knowledge and instruct teachers about traditional culture, and in the process, they open the group to the larger Yup'ik community. The elders' recognition that their culture might not be passed on to the next generation particularly motivated them to share their knowledge of the land, traditional stories, and crafts—subjects of interest not only to the Ciulistet but to other teachers, community members, and the school district.

The elders' instruction clearly demonstrated how Yup'ik culture and language connect to mathematics and to science. For example, the group spent a great deal of time reviewing the Yup'ik numeration system with the elders, who demon-strated counting in Yup'ik by using their fingers and bodies. As we inquired into the meaning of Yup'ik words, it became obvious that the numeration system was connected to the body with words such as *talliman* [five, or literally translated "one arm"]. Also, apparently the body can be used as an axis—somewhat like coordinate geometry. Through demonstrations, questions and interviews with elders, and linguistic analysis of the meaning behind the words studied, we entered a new phase of our work.

Because the Ciulistet believes that elders from different communities have different knowledge, this also led to further increasing the number of community people who interacted with the Ciulistet. The school district became increasingly aware of the possibility of using the Yup'ik culture to teach core subjects—math and science—and took a renewed interest in the work of the Ciulistet.

This phase of our work continues today. Elders, teachers, and consultants worked side by side, constructing curriculum and pedagogy based on Yup'ik culture and language. The elders are not only being asked to "tell their stories" but to actively construct curriculum and pedagogy. The elders are learning from the teachers and the consultants how we interpret and adapt their knowledge to schooling. The elders are asked to be "students" and experience their knowledge being taught to them in ways appropriate for schooling. These meetings take place in different Yup'ik communities, increasing the number of communities and individuals involved in the project. During meetings, we demonstrate to elders the science involved in their traditional knowledge about the ecosystem. The interest from outsiders in their work and the interest from the Yup'ik teachers appears to be motivating the elders.

The group received an additional boost from attending national conferences and presenting with other indigenous educators. This cross fertilization and support increasingly produced an understanding that the experiences of Yup'ik teachers in southwest Alaska were similar to many others. The X-CED program encouraged such opportunities, hosting meetings with Canadian indigenous teacher education programs. During the past years, we were able to obtain funding for teacher exchanges with Yakutsk (an autonomous province in the Russian Far North). Yakutia is embarking on a program of culturally based education. Having educators from Yakutsk visit Yup'ik villages and share their ways of incorporating their culture in mathematics was particularly impressive. Simultaneously, when these meetings were held in villages, community members would want to know why such a project as this was not in motion here. These meetings productively raised numerous issues.

Today, the group is still learning from elders, learning from work groups, and learning from each other. We have spent time analyzing these tapes not only with the group but with elders. This has been extremely helpful. Elders not only discussed the tapes, but they began instructing the group in a variety of cultural topics. Other indigenous researchers such as Claudette Bradley, Oscar Kawagley, and Walkie Charles joined the group as specialists in culturally based mathematics, science, and literacy, respectively. We worked collectively, and again insiders and outsiders informed each other. We have established ourselves as an inquiring community as we learn both about Yup'ik culture and about the processes of schooling. We are presently applying this knowledge to schooling through workshops with schools and communities as we share our growing understanding of how Yup'ik culture and language can have a place within formal Western schooling.

REFERENCES

Aronowitz, S., & Giroux, H. (1991). *Postmodern education: Politics, culture, and social criticism.* Minneapolis, MN: University of Minnesota Press.

Cazden, C. (1988). *Classroom discourse.* Portsmouth, NH: Heinemann.

Coffey, A., & Atkinson, P. (1996). *Making sense of qualitative data.* Thousand Oaks, CA: Sage.

Collier, M. (1979). *A film study of classrooms in western Alaska.* Fairbanks, AK: University of Alaska Fairbanks Center for Cross-Cultural Studies.

Comer, J. (1986, June). Parent participation in the schools. *Phi Delta Kappan,* 695–696.

Deyhle, D., & Swisher, K. (1997). Research in American Indian and Alaska Native education: From assimilation to self-determination. In M. Apple (Ed.), *Review of research in education* (pp. 113–194). Washington, DC: American Educational Research Association.

Denzin, N., & Lincoln, Y. (1994). Introduction: Entering the field of qualitative research. In N. Denzin & Y. Lincoln (Eds.), *Handbook of qualitative research* (pp.1–18). Thousand Oaks, CA: Sage.

Erickson, F., & Mohatt, G. (1982). Cultural organization of participation structures in two classrooms of Indian students. In D. G. Spindler (Ed.), *Doing the ethnography of schooling* (pp. 132–174). New York: Holt, Rinehart, & Winston.

Freiere, P. (1970). *Pedagogy of the oppressed.* New York: Herder and Herder.

Guba, E., & Lincoln, Y. (1994). Competing paradigms in qualitative research. In N. Denzin & Y. Lincoln (Eds.), *Handbook of qualitative research* (pp. 105–117). Thousand Oaks, CA: Sage.

Holm, A., & Holm, W. (1990). Rock Point, a Navajo way to go to school: A valediction. In C. B. Cazden & C. E. Snow (Eds.), English Plus: Issues in bilingual education (pp. 170–184). Newbury Park, CA: Sage.

Ilutsik, E. (1996). *Long-term collaboration between the Ciulistet teacher leaders and university colleagues.* Paper presented at the American Anthropological Association 1996 Annual Meeting, San Francisco.

Lather, P. (1986). Research as praxis. *Harvard Education Review, 56*(3), 257–277.

Lightfoot, S. (1978). *Worlds apart: Relationships between families and schools.* New York: Basic Books.

Lipka, J. (1990). Integrating cultural form and content in one Yup'ik Eskimo class. *Canadian Journal of Native Education, 17*(2), 18–32.

Lipka, J. (1991). Toward a culturally based pedagogy: A case study of one Yup'ik Eskimo teacher. *Anthropology and Education Quarterly, 22*(3), 203–223.

Lipka, J. (1994). Language, power, and pedagogy: Whose school is it anyway? *Peabody Journal of Education, 69*(2), 71–93.

Lipka, J., & Ilutsik, E. (1995). Negotiated change: Yup'ik perspectives on indigenous schooling. *Bilingual Research Journal, 19,* 195–207.

Lipka, J., & McCarty, T. (1994). Changing the culture of schooling: Navajo and Yup'ik cases. *Anthropology and Education Quarterly, 25*(3), 266–284.

Mathers, E. (1995). With a vision beyond our immediate needs: Oral traditions in an age of literacy. In P. Morrow & S. Schneider (Eds.), *When our words return* (pp. 13–26). Utah: Utah State University Press.

Mohatt, G., & Erickson, F. (1981). Cultural differences in teaching styles in an Odawa school. In H. Trueba, G. Gutherie, & K. Au (Eds.), *Culture and the bilingual classroom: Studies in classroom ethnography* (pp. 105–119). Cambridge, MA: Newbury House.

Narayan, K. (1993). On nose cutters, gurus, and storytellers. In S. Lavie, K. Narayan, & R. Rosaldo (Eds.), *Creativity/anthropology* (pp. 30–53). Ithaca, NY: Cornell University Press.

Philips, S. (1972). Participant structures and communicative competence: Warm Springs Indian children in community and classroom. In C. Cazden, V. John, & D. Hymes (Eds.), *Functions of language in the classroom* (pp. 370–394). New York: Teachers College Press.

Sacks, H., Schegloff, E., & Jefferson, G. (1974). A simplest systematics for the organization of turn-taking for conversation. *Language, 50,* 696–735.

Sarason, S. (1996). *Revisiting "The culture of the school and the problem of change."* New York: Teachers College Press.

Sharp, N. (1994). Caknernarqutet. *Peabody Journal of Education , 69*(2), 6–11.

Smith, L. (1994). Biographical method. In N. K. Denzin & Y. S. Lincoln (Eds.), *Handbook of qualitative research* (pp. 286–305). Thousand Oaks, CA: Sage.

Trueba, H. (1989). *Raising silent voices: Educating the linguistic minorities for the 21st century.* New York: Newbury House.

Epilogue

Jerry Lipka and Gerald V. Mohatt
University of Alaska, Fairbanks

Transforming the culture of schools through collaborative work humbled each of us. Naively, we thought that increasing the number of Yup'ik teachers would, in and of itself, transform schooling. However, the group learned very rapidly that was not the case. The teachers wondered if they made a difference and what difference they could make to their people. Implicit in this question is the importance of personal and familial relationships. Meaningful acts of teaching emanate from kin relationships and improving life for the next generation. The research process we engaged in, we hoped, mirrored this ethos. It was, and is, relational, long term, and primarily focused on developing a cadre of teachers who could use their local knowledge as one way to transform schooling. Increasing the potential of local schools occurs, of course, within a nexus of interactions at multiple levels. The people who make up this interactive ever-changing constellation move in and out and become situated in new roles. School change and reform is a dynamic, and, to some degree, an unpredictable phenomena. The dynamic nature of school reform and change becomes even more profound in a context where the culture of schooling includes a high rate of teacher and principal turnover, and rapid cultural, linguistic, and social change. Furthermore, the Yup'ik teachers' stories reported in this book speak of a time when they were virtually the first Yup'ik teachers in their communities. Today, many of these teachers are approaching 20 years of teaching as a licensed teacher, as well as 10 years of teaching as a teacher's aide. The possibilities for reforming school have changed because of the growing expertise of these local teachers and the rapidly changing context in which schooling takes place. Here, we briefly describe some of these recent contextual changes, the complexity of school and community reform, and present some concluding thoughts about our research methodology.

THE ROLE OF THE UNIVERSITY

Sometimes it is not possible to know the importance of a person or an institution until they are no longer present. Unfortunately, the University of Alaska, Fairbanks, once an instrumental and vocal supporter for Native and rural programs in the state of Alaska has moved far from its commitment and mission. This has been paritally caused by fiscal shortfalls in the state, political changes, and changes in the educational leadership at the university. The Cross-Cultural Educational Development Program [X-CED], a vital part of the educational changes taking place in rural parts of the state for the past 27 years, has succumbed to these changes. Today, this program has been discontinued at the secondary level and, for all practical purposes, at the elementary level as well. The same institution that once was a seamless and influential part of the process of increasing and changing the nature of schooling in rural Alaska is no longer part of the context. These are not easy words to write as a former faculty member in this program and as a former dean of the College of Rural Alaska. Once a thriving program with more than 10 faculty, in eight regions of the state, and with a budget in excess of 1 million dollars, today it has three full-time faculty, almost no support staff, and a substantially reduced travel budget. A change in the leadership of the University of Alaska, Fairbanks, criticism of the X-CED program in some quarters, and major decreases in state funding for higher education have all contributed to its demise. What does this mean? This means access to the teacher profession has been substantially limited for Alaska Native people, particularly those who need to live and work in their home village. The university is in the process of establishing a new program. However, this program to date has no faculty nor is it a degree-granting program.

Ironically at the very time the University of Alaska, Fairbanks has retrenched, individual faculty have been very successful in bringing in outside funding. Today, a few large grants from the National Science Foundation and the Annenberg Foundation infuse new resources into the quest for developing culturally authentic curriculum and pedagogy. In contrast to the university, local school systems that were once resistant to innovation are becoming proactive. These school systems that once suppressed, denied, and resisted Alaska Native language and culture as a central part of school have actively instituted language immersion programs in the vernacular language, support Alaska Native teacher groups, and are integrating Alaska Native culture and language into their core academic school programs. Leadership in education has shifted out of the university.

YUP'IK LANGUAGE, INSTITUTIONS, AND COMMUNITY

A perennial question has been "What should be the language of instruction, Yup'ik or English?" For decades, teachers' aides and the few Yup'ik teachers used Yup'ik to explain concepts and to assist students in their learning. This was done "behind closed doors," as aides and bilingual teachers understood that English was the language of instruction. Bilingual aides found clever ways to increase the amount of Yup'ik used in classroom in the 1980s. In the late 1980s, with the assistance of the university, one school initiated a Yup'ik immersion program that continues to operate today. However, the program has not developed to its potential. To meet this potential requires an understanding of the role of culture and language in learning. One does not simply teach the same content in another language. Unfortunately, the University of Alaska, Fairbanks' retrenchment has marginalized those doing this type of research. To develop this approach to schooling requires school, univeristy, and community partnership, as each brings its own expertise to schooling. To get all parties to work together has proven far more difficult than one would ever imagine. Yet, the influx of grants, groups such as the Ciulistet, and an increased willingness on the part of local school systems has recently opened new pathways to this development. Again, elders have played an instrumental role as they continue to share more and more knowledge.

Langauge shift continues to complicate this work. The Yup'ik language carries more than the language, it shapes and organizes the rich knowledge that it carries. In Bristol Bay (southwest Alaska), the village of Manokotak remains the only one (out of approximately 26) in which children still come to school speaking Yup'ik. As elders pass on and as the next generation reaches childbearing age they are increasingly choosing English as the language of home. Elders who once only spoke Yup'ik to Jerry Lipka (translated into English), now speak directly in English. What does this mean for the process of transforming the culture of schools? It appears that a significant need exists for collaborative work between community, school, and university. The forces at work in generating innovation at the policy and practice level are multiple. Institutions of higher education influence these forces by how they prepare school leaders, teachers, and also through their research. Individuals in each context shape the questions of importance and how the social context changes determines sustainability of programs, as well as how questions are asked and answered—particularly those related to language teaching and the viability of indigenous language. Answers to questions are never really final; they shift and change as the context changes. To be responsive and productive, one has to have long-term relationships of a collaborative nature, sustained both by individual efforts in the context of an institutional commitment. Our sense is that since we began this book, important changes in community ethos and institutional leadership have changed. Possibilities remain for continuing the process of school transformation, but the ever-changing nexus of institutional relations changes the direction of change. Certainly, external funding, such as grants from the National Science Foundation and the Annenberg Foundation, help stimulate innovation, but sustainability demands continuity of commitment. In fact, what we have experienced is intermittent support from the university and schools, as well as barriers within each of the institutions. Despite these obstacles, individuals and groups like the Ciulistet continue to persist and innovate. Long-term relationships, partially shaped by the university, serve as a foundation for resistance to the vagaries of changes in institutional policy and leadership.

LOCAL TEACHERS:
ADAPTING AND CHANGING SCHOOLING

The promise of programs such as X-CED is to change the ethnic composition of who is a teacher, the curricular promise to change what constitutes legitimate school knowledge, and the pedagogical promise to change ways of teaching that knowledge continue to develop. The groups of Alaska Native teachers graduating from X-CED in 1980s have had close to two decades to adapt and accommodate to schooling and simultaneously have influenced and, in effect, have had schools adapt to having local teachers. This very dynamic process continues, as does the dynamic process of cultural, linguistic, and contextual change. Margie Hastings, one of the graduates of both a campus-based teacher education program and X-CED, recently stated

> Jerry, 12 years ago, when I first started teaching, I taught the way I was told to teach, the Madeline Hunter method. Right now, I teach from my heart and my mind. I use my Native ways of feeling and not being fake. When I taught the Madeline Hunter method, good for some people, I felt really fake. It was not me. We have superintendent support, staff that has been there for awhile. Even though we have a new principal, his approach is one of blending. That really helped. I am doing it my way. I think it is a better way. I felt comfortable. I did it my way because it works. (Hastings, personal communication, November, 1997)

Time (more than a decade in some cases), struggle, experience, and support from groups like Ciulistet and local principals and educational leaders is required for teachers to develop their way of teaching so that they no longer feel "fake." Nancy Sharp, a contributor to a chapter in this book, also continues to evolve as an educator. For example, in Nancy Sharp's class you will hear more Yup'ik spoken than a decade ago, although the students may be less fluent in Yup'ik than previously. Because Nancy is able to use the Yup'ik language freely in her instruction she does not need to worry that "someone is watching her." Furthermore, cultural artifacts, cultural knowledge, and knowledge of the community continue to grow and evolve in these classrooms. Beyond the typical curriculum, students may engage in such culturally based activities as making a black fish trap, setting it, and harvesting the catch. Students in another class "storyknife" with their teacher. Evelyn Yanez, now the bilingual coordinator for a local school district, infuses Yup'ik cultural content into both the bilingual program and the core academic program. None of this was to be seen during the 1980s and early 1990s, nor was the commitment of elders to encourage these changes. Today these "culturally relevant" activities emphasize the teaching of math and science through a culturally embedded knowledge base. In individual classrooms through-out the region, there are signs of change and models of what is possible.

RESEARCH

We began a process of engaging with the elders, at first clumsily, through an "outsiders" voice (Lipka's, as described by Ilutsik in the previous chapter), but today it has become almost commonplace for elders and Yup'ik teachers to talk directly, seek information, and fill in cultural knowledge. Slowly, this process of insiders speaking directly to insiders is changing the role and relationship of "outsiders" and what we mean by collaborative research. Leadership in this process that was once highly concentrated in a few a people, has spread out among many Yup'ik teachers in a variety of ways. Teachers are taking on leadership roles in their school, community, and in documenting cultural knowledge and transforming that knowledge into curriculum and pedagogy. Who leads the collaborative research has changed as well among insiders. Elders who first joined the Ciulistet in the early 1990s, are now finding leadership roles within the region and beyond it. All of this is positive. However, change is not without cost. Role uncertainty, an evolving context, influx of money and opportunity, and changes in persons and personnel make this second wave of collaborative research an exciting and scary time. There are no models or examples to follow. This requires research methods to evolve into, and be in consort with this rapidly changing context. It appears that insiders may well lead the next phase of collaborative research with the assistance, if necessary, of outsiders. Also, as the descriptive and documentation phases of research conclude and new ways of teaching "old" knowledge evolve, there may well be a need for other research paradigms beyond thick description. As conflict between school and community inevitably winds down, if the number of local teachers continue to increase, a shift in research questions and methodology should also occur. Questions of, "How am I helping my people?" may now be answered in a variety of ways beyond the descriptive ethnographies. These classroom ethnographies have laid the groundwork for other research lenses that may investigate the effects of using local knowledge by teachers who are free to teach in ways more commensurate with their communities.

The nature of relational research by definition is conservative, following the lead of elders and traditional knowledge. Yet, it is also subject to rapid change because it is very much like interpersonal and familial relations. Individual leaders in schools can have a profound affect on policy and practice, provided they learn how to share power, shift their roles to more horizontal and relationally based problem solving, embrace multiple solutions rather than unitary ones, and be willing to maximize and support the expertise of their colleagues. This is the model of leadership that has guided the work in this book. The guidance and leadership came from elders as they moved along their pathways. We, elders, teachers, and university-based researchers, continue to struggle to find ways to bring this knowledge to schooling and adapt schooling to this knowledge while maintaining authentic practice. This remains our challenge and our struggle.

Author Index

Subject Index